P9-CKL-620

THE QUICK

INTERVIEW

AND SALARY

NEGOTIATION

BOOK

by J. Michael Farr

jist the job search people

Riverside Community College
Library
'98 4800 Magnolia Avenue
FEB Riverside, California 92506

HF 5549.5 .I6 F37 1995

Farr, J. Michael.

The quick interview and
  salary negotiation book

...b search and career topics have collectively sold more than one and a half million copies collectively. Here are some of those you are most likely to find in a bookstore or library:

- *The Very Quick Job Search — Get a Good Job in Less Time*
- *The Quick Resume and Cover Letter Book*
- *America's 50 Fastest Growing Jobs*
- *America's Top Jobs for College Graduates*
- *America's Top Office, Management and Sales Jobs*
- *Job Strategies for Professionals*
- *Getting the Job You Really Want*

See the last pages of this book for an order form that includes these books by Mike Farr and other books of interest from JIST.

Errors and Omissions: We have been careful to provide accurate information throughout this book but it is possible that errors and omissions have been introduced. Please consider this in making any career plans or other important decisions. Trust your own judgment above all else and in all things.

JIST Works, Inc.

720 North Park Avenue

Indianapolis, IN 46202-3431

(317) 264-3720 or FAX (317) 264-3709

© Copyright 1995, by JIST Works, Inc. All rights reserved. No part of this book may be reproduced in any form or by any means, or stored in a database or retrieval system, without prior written permission of the publisher except in case of brief quotations embodied in articles or reviews.

Library of Congress Cataloging-in-Publication Data

Farr, J. Michael.
    The quick interview and salary negotiation book : dramatically improve your interviewing skills and pay in a matter of hours / by J. Michael Farr.
        p. cm.
        ISBN 1-56370-162-6
        1.   Employment interviewing.   2. Wages.   I. Title.
        HF5549.5.I6F37   1995
        650.14—dc20
                                                94-49076
                                                    CIP

ISBN 1-56370-162-6

HOW TO USE THIS BOOK

Don't be intimidated by the size of this book—I've put all the essential informa-tion in section 1. It provides you with a "mini book" of techniques I have refined over 20 years and that have been proven to cut your job search time in half.

Since you obviously want to do well in an interview, I assume that you are also looking for a job—or are thinking about doing so. That being the case, here is what I suggest as the best way to use this book:

1. **Review the Table of Contents.** This will give you an overview of the book and its chapters.

2. **Read the Chapters in Section 1.** These chapters will quickly help you improve your interviewing skills—enough for an interview later today or tomorrow. They provide a short but thorough interviewing course and will teach you far more than most of your competition knows about interviewing.

3. **Go Out and Get Interviews.** You have to *get* interviews before you can do well in them. So, as soon as you learn to improve your interviewing skills, your next task is to get lots of interview. I've provided a quick review of the most effective methods I know to get more and better interviews. Read chapter 6 and then use the techniques you learn there to get more interviews. If all goes well, this may be all you need to know.

4. **Customize Your Learning.** Once you learn to do better in interviews (from Section 1) and are out *getting* interviews (chapter 6), you can decide what you most need next. For example, chapter 7 provides information on writing a resume, should you need one. Section 3 does a thorough job of helping you identify your skills, accomplishments, job objective, and other matters that should be very important to you. More interviewing details and additional salary negotiation techniques are provided in Section 4. Average wages for hundreds of jobs are given in Section 5. There is no need to read these materials sequentially, just spend time where you think the biggest payoff is for you.

There you are. While this may seem like a big book, it is really quite easy to use. And, true to its title, I hope you find the essential information quick to find and read.

QUICK CONTENTS

SECTION ONE:
ALL THE INFORMATION AND TECHNIQUES
THAT MOST PEOPLE NEED TO DO WELL IN INTERVIEWS

Chapter 1:	The seven steps for getting the job you want	5
Chapter 2:	Know more before you go—Do some background research on yourself, the job, the industry, and the employer	11
Chapter 3:	The 60 minute drill—essential tips on traditional and nontraditional interviews	27
Chapter 4:	The seven phases of an interview	41
Chapter 5:	Answers to 10 key interview questions—and a technique to answer hundreds more	67

SECTION TWO:
JOB SEEKING SKILLS—YOU HAVE TO GET INTERVIEWS
BEFORE YOU CAN DO WELL IN THEM

Chapter 6:	How to get a good job in less time	101
Chapter 7:	Quick resume tips and samples	123

SECTION THREE:
MORE THOROUGH PREPARATION FOR THE INTERVIEW

Chapter 8:	Develop your skills language	153
Chapter 9:	The skills and characteristics employers want	161
Chapter 10:	Document your experience	173
Chapter 11:	Be clear about your job objective	189
Chapter 12:	Research before the interview—print and computer sources	215
Chapter 13:	Dress and grooming tips and other last-minute preparations that win the interview	239

SECTION FOUR:
HOW TO ANSWER TOUGH INTERVIEW QUESTIONS
AND HANDLE UNUSUAL INTERVIEW SITUATIONS

Chapter 14:	How to answer problem interview questions—A review	251
Chapter 15:	Answers to specific problem questions	263
Chapter 16:	Nontraditional interview Approaches	301
Chapter 17:	Pre-employment testing	335

SECTION FIVE:
SALARY NEGOTIATIONS—HOW TO MAKE
A FEW THOUSAND DOLLARS A MINUTE

Chapter 18:	Salary negotiations—the one who speaks first loses	347
Chapter 19:	Researching what others earn in similar positions—plus average earnings for hundreds of jobs	367

C O N T E N T S

HOW TO USE THIS BOOK...**III**

FOREWORD..**X**

SECTION ONE: ALL THE INFORMATION AND TECHNIQUES THAT MOST PEOPLE NEED TO DO WELL IN INTERVIEWS

You should be able to read the chapters in this section in a few hours. They will give you enough information to improve your interviewing skills for an interview tomorrow.

CHAPTER 1: THE SEVEN STEPS FOR GETTING THE JOB YOU WANT **5**

■ Not just any job will do—nor any job search
■ An overview of the seven steps to getting the job you want

CHAPTER 2: KNOW MORE BEFORE YOU GO—DO SOME BACKGROUND RESEARCH ON YOURSELF, THE JOB, THE INDUSTRY, AND THE EMPLOYER **11**

■ Have good information about yourself
■ The three types of skills—the skills triad

CHAPTER 3: THE 60 MINUTE DRILL—ESSENTIAL TIPS ON TRADITIONAL AND NONTRADITIONAL INTERVIEWS...**27**

■ Five things to do to have a successful interview
■ The three types of interviews

CHAPTER 4: THE SEVEN PHASES OF AN INTERVIEW..............**41**

■ The seven phases of an interview
■ Phase 1: Before you go in
■ Phase 2: Opening moves
■ Phase 3: The interview itself
■ Phase 4: Closing the interview
■ Phase 5: Following up
■ Phase 6: Negotiating
■ Phase 7: Making a final decision

V

CHAPTER 5: ANSWERS TO 10 KEY INTERVIEW QUESTIONS— AND A TECHNIQUE TO ANSWER HUNDREDS MORE..**67**

- The 10 most frequently asked interview questions
- Remember the three-step process to answering interview questions
- Answers to the top 10 problem interview questions
- Handling obvious and not-so-obvious "problems"
- Some topics that should not be an issue—but sometimes are
- Some final interview tips

• •

SECTION TWO: JOB SEEKING SKILLS—YOU HAVE TO GET INTERVIEWS BEFORE YOU CAN DO WELL IN THEM

Chapter 6 will give you a quick review of the job search methods I have developed that have proven their ability to cut your job search time in half. And, since most people assume that a resume is an essential job search tool, I've included a chapter on them.

CHAPTER 6: HOW TO GET A GOOD JOB IN LESS TIME **101**

- Changing jobs and careers is often healthy
- A review of the seven steps for getting the job you want— emphasizing job seeking skills
- The quick job search review

CHAPTER 7: QUICK RESUME TIPS AND SAMPLES **123**

- Quick resume writing tips
- Writing a simple chronological resume
- Tips for writing a chronological resume
- Tips for writing an improved chronological resume
- Writing a skills or combination resume
- Instant resume worksheet
- Sample resumes

• •

SECTION THREE: MORE THOROUGH PREPARATION FOR THE INTERVIEW

The chapters in this section provide a thorough review of a range of topics related to the job search. Chapter 8 is particularly important because knowing your skills and presenting them effectively in an interview is a most important issue in the job search.

CHAPTER 8:   DEVELOP YOUR SKILLS "LANGUAGE" **153**
- The skills triad
- Identifying your skills
- Identifying your job-related skills

CHAPTER 9:   THE SKILLS AND CHARACTERISTICS
EMPLOYERS WANT **161**
- The skills employers want—the results of a survey of employers
- Some tips on creating a positive impression
- Key evaluation factors for selecting managers and executives
- What employers don't want under any circumstances
- The last word

CHAPTER 10:   DOCUMENT YOUR EXPERIENCE **173**
- Education and training worksheet
- Work and volunteer history worksheet
- Key accomplishments and skills to tell an employer

CHAPTER 11:   BE CLEAR ABOUT YOUR JOB OBJECTIVE...........................**189**
- Consider jobs within clusters of related occupations
- Values, preferences, and other matters to consider in defining your job objective
- Write a clear job objective statement—just as you need to do on a resume
- Job objective worksheet

CHAPTER 12:   RESEARCH BEFORE THE INTERVIEW—
PRINT AND COMPUTER SOURCES.......................................**215**
- The basics: information about the occupation, the industry, and the organization
- Information about the occupation
- Information about the interviewer
- Computer online services

CHAPTER 13:   DRESS AND GROOMING TIPS AND OTHER
LAST-MINUTE PREPARATIONS THAT WIN
THE INTERVIEW **239**
- Pack your briefcase like a professional
- Dress professionally
- One final dress and grooming tip

SECTION FOUR: HOW TO ANSWER TOUGH INTERVIEW QUESTIONS AND HANDLE UNUSUAL INTERVIEW SITUATIONS

Much of this section provides detailed information that you may want to refer to as needed.

CHAPTER 14: HOW TO ANSWER PROBLEM INTERVIEW QUESTIONS—A REVIEW **251**
- To be considered, you must meet an employer's expectations
- The ten most frequently asked problem questions
- A quick review of the three-step process
- Legal and illegal questions
- And now, a word on behalf of our employers

CHAPTER 15: ANSWERS TO SPECIFIC PROBLEM QUESTIONS **263**
- Typical problem areas
- Answering questions in an unorganized interview
- Sensitive questions having to do with your personal situation or status
- 90 more practice questions
- Practice, practice, practice

CHAPTER 16: NONTRADITIONAL INTERVIEW APPROACHES **301**
- Nontraditional techniques for getting interviews
- How to shine in unusual interview situations
- Interview techniques employers use to psych you out
- Conquer interview fear through practice

CHAPTER 17: PRE-EMPLOYMENT TESTING **335**
- Types of tests

• •

SECTION FIVE: SALARY NEGOTIATIONS—HOW TO MAKE A FEW THOUSAND DOLLARS A MINUTE

While I covered basic salary negotiations strategies in Section 1, there are additional details here, including a listing of average pay for the most popular jobs in the workforce.

CHAPTER 18: SALARY NEGOTIATIONS—THE ONE WHO SPEAKS FIRST LOSES 347

- ■ The art of negotiation
- ■ The key question: "what sort of pay do you expect to receive?"
- ■ Some additional negotiation tips from experts
- ■ What to say when it's time to get serious
- ■ They offer, you want it —now it's time to negotiate!

CHAPTER 19: RESEARCHING WHAT OTHERS EARN IN SIMILAR POSITIONS—PLUS AVERAGE EARNINGS FOR HUNDREDS OF JOBS 367

- ■ The top excuse for avoiding research
- ■ Sources of information on salary and wages

• •

FOREWORD

With all the increases in sophisticated technology, most people still get hired—or screened out—based on a personal interview. This low-tech interaction is thousands of years old and it remains the most important part of getting a job offer.

Of course, you do need job-related skills to be considered for a job. An accountant, for example, will need to understand accounting and not just be "good with numbers" in order to get a professional position. But someone who can do well in an interview often will get a job offer over someone else with better credentials because the employer had a better "feeling" for the first person.

So, assuming that you do have the credentials to at least be considered for the job you seek, is it possible to improve your interviewing skills? And, if you can, will it help you get a better job than you might otherwise? The answer is "Yes!" And that is what this book is about.

You can learn techniques to present yourself more effectively in an interview. Most people can dramatically improve their interviewing skills in a short time. My experience in teaching thousands of people is that just a few hours of learning and practice is often enough to make a big difference. You will probably notice this as you read through this book.

You will learn more than just how to interview. While improving your interviewing skills is certainly important, this book is about more than that. First, the interview only makes sense in the context of a successful job search, so I will teach you ways to get interviews *and* do well in them. But even more importantly, I will help you put your job search in the context of what is important to do with your life. I will encourage you to define your ideal job and then to seek a job that approximates it. I will encourage you to develop a deeper sense of yourself and what you are good at — and to use this new skills "language" in your interviews. The quick improvements in your interviewing skills can be exciting, and the related understanding can even have a profound effect on your career and your life.

Unlike some interviewing experts, I believe that you should tell the truth in an interview. I don't believe it is either necessary or good to manipulate a prospective employer into hiring you based on phony interviewing skills. While many of the techniques I present in this book could be used that way, I suggest that doing so will harm you. Instead, I encourage you to identify the skills you have and where you want to use them. Then, if you present those skills to the right people (who need them), you will get the right job for the right reasons. If you are persistent. If you are honest. If you are willing to compromise. If you believe in yourself.

By misrepresenting yourself, you are immediately establishing a dishonest and manipulative relationship. Employers can often tell the difference and so will you.

The interviewing techniques are based on common sense and research. You will notice throughout this book that I have included a variety of research on interviewing and related topics. While I certainly have my opinions, many of the methods I suggest have a solid basis in research and have been field tested over many years by me or by others. There is, however, no substitute for common sense and many of the things I suggest will simply make good sense to you. Part of the reason for this is that I am not a theorist, academic, personnel manager, or researcher. Instead, I am someone who has learned from working with job seekers. My interest has always been to find more effective ways to help people get good jobs in less time. Often, research just seems to back up what makes sense.

It all comes down to just a few simple things:

- Know what you are good at—and look for a job that is a good match.
- Get more interviews.
- Present yourself well in your interviews.
- Work hard, do good, and do well.

I wish you good fortune in your interviews and your life.

Mike Farr

P.S. Please send me stories about how you got your jobs. I'd like to collect them for use in a future book.

ALL THE INFORMATION AND TECHNIQUES THAT MOST PEOPLE NEED TO DO WELL IN INTERVIEWS

Introduction

Most people don't do much to prepare for interviews. In an odd way, this can work in your favor because, if you present yourself well, you can easily impress an interviewer more than those who have better credentials, but who don't present themselves as well as you do in an interview.

The chapters in this section cover interviewing techniques that I believe are most important for you to know. My objective is to give you specific tips to improve your interviewing skills as quickly as possible. This means that if you have an important interview tomorrow, this section will help you do far better in it than you otherwise would. And it just might be enough to help you get the job you want; getting lots of interviews is clearly to your advantage. But you should also consider going on to the other sections in this book. Section 2, for example, provides important information on job seeking. Other sections in the book cover career decision making, skills identification, salary negotiations, and problem questions asked in interviews in much greater detail than this first section. I encourage you to learn as much as you can.

Chapters in This Section

Chapter 1: The Seven Steps for Getting the Job You Want

An overview of how the interview is one element of a successful job search.

Chapter 2: Know More Before You Go—Do Some Background Research on Yourself, the Job, the Industry, and the Employer

Tips to identify your key skills, define the ideal job, and get more information on the industry, job, and employer.

Chapter 3: The 60 Minute Drill—Essential Tips on Traditional and Nontraditional Interviews

A new way to define an interview, plus lots of techniques to improve your interview results.

Chapter 4: The Seven Phases of an Interview

Breaks the interview into easily understood segments, with tips for handling each.

Chapter 5: Answers to 10 Key Interview Questions—and a Technique to Answer Hundreds More

Knowing how to answer these key questions will prepare you to answer most others as well.

C H A P T E R

1

THE SEVEN STEPS FOR GETTING THE JOB YOU WANT

Quick Tip

While the interview is a most important part of the job search, you do need to put it into its proper context—you are looking for the best job you can get, in as little time as possible. This chapter will give you an overview of the career planning and job search process and will show you how the interview best "fits" into an effective job search campaign.

NOT JUST ANY JOB WILL DO— NOR ANY JOB SEARCH

Doing well in a job interview only has value in the context of looking for a job. To put the interview into its proper context, I think it is important for you to see how the interview fits into what I consider to be the essential steps needed for a successful job search.

The Seven Steps of a Quick and Successful Job Search

▲ **1.** Know your skills.

▲ **2.** Have a clear job objective.

▲ **3.** Know where and how to look.

▲ **4.** Spend at least 25 hours a week looking.

▲ **5.** Get two interviews a day.

▲ **6.** Do well in interviews.

▲ **7.** Follow up on all contacts.

If you can master each of these seven steps, you are much more likely, in my experience, to get a better and more satisfying job—and you will likely do it in less time than is otherwise possible. With an obvious emphasis on the job interview, much of the rest of this book will help you master each of the seven steps. Following is a brief introduction to each one.

● ●

AN OVERVIEW OF THE SEVEN STEPS TO GETTING THE JOB YOU WANT

STEP 1: KNOW YOUR SKILLS

An effective career plan requires that you know your skills. A survey of employers found that 80 percent of the people they interviewed did not do an effective job in presenting the skills they had for the jobs they wanted. They could not provide a good answer to the question, "Why should I hire you?"

The consequence of not being able to answer that question, as you might guess, is that your chances of getting a job offer are greatly reduced. Knowing your skills, therefore, offers you a distinct advantage in the job search. It will help you better identify appropriate job targets, present yourself more effectively in interviews, write better resumes, and land a better, more satisfying job.

Several of the chapters in this book will help you identify your skills by using skills lists and other activities. I strongly suggest that you review that material before you go on with your search for a job.

STEP 2: HAVE A CLEAR JOB OBJECTIVE

Having a good job objective is not just an issue for finding job leads and handling the interview. While I realize how difficult it can be to figure out just what sort of job you want, it is essential that you do so before you begin your search for a job. Even if you don't know exactly what you want to do long term, you at least have to decide what you want to do next.

It is not easy to fake your way through an interview for a job that you don't know much about or are not sure you want. It is unlikely that you will know the skills you need to do well in that job and just as likely that you don't have them. So, even if you do well enough in an interview to get that job, your chances of liking it and doing well in it are greatly diminished.

Chapter 11 reviews the basics for researching a job objective and it is most important that you do so. Other chapters will help you identify sources of those jobs and help you write a job objective for your resume and other tasks. If, after completing chapter 11, you are still not sure about what sort of job you want, you should at least settle on something that is reasonably acceptable to you—and that you can convince someone else you are able to do. Later, you should spend more time making a good decision regarding your long-term career plans.

❝*One survey found that 85 percent of all employers don't advertise job openings at all.***❞**

STEP 3: KNOW WHERE AND HOW TO LOOK

One survey found that 85 percent of all employers don't advertise their job openings at all. They hire people they already know, people who find out about the job through word of mouth, or people who simply happen to be at the right place at the right time. This is sometimes just luck, but this book will teach you ways to increase your "luck" in finding job openings.

Chapter 6 will provide you with tips on how the labor market works, how to find job leads in the hidden job market, how to organize your time to get results, and other job search basics. While that is a short chapter, it summarizes my many years of research and experience with techniques that result in getting better jobs in less time.

There are no guarantees, of course, but the techniques I present in chapter 6 have proven their effectiveness with many, many people and they do work. While luck does play a part in the job search process, I have found that the harder you work—and the more you know—the more likely you are to become lucky.

STEP 4: SPEND AT LEAST 25 HOURS A WEEK LOOKING

About 85 percent of all job seekers spend 15 hours a week or fewer actually looking for a job. They are also unemployed an average of three or more months! People who follow my advice spend much more time than average on their job search each week. They also get jobs in less than half the average time.

Knowing how to find job leads that are hidden from most who use traditional job search methods is one of the keys to finding better jobs in less time. Another key is time management. Chapter 6 provides additional details on how to develop a job search schedule and which activities work most effectively.

STEP 5: GET TWO INTERVIEWS A DAY

The average job seeker gets about 5 interviews a month—fewer than 2 interviews a week. Yet many job seekers using the job search techniques I suggest find it easy to get 2 interviews a day—about 40 interviews a month. This is a much higher level of activity than most job seekers are able to accomplish. To do this, you must redefine what an interview is.

I'll provide more information on various types of interviews in chapter 3, but, just to get you thinking, here is my new definition of an interview:

> ## A New Definition of an Interview
>
> ▲ An interview is any face-to-face contact with someone who has the authority to hire or supervise a person with your skills. This person may or may not have a job opening at the time you interview with them.

Once you understand how to use my new definition of an interview, it is *much* easier to get them. You can now interview with all kinds of potential employers, not just those who have a job opening. Many job seekers use the *Yellow Pages* to get 2 interviews after just an hour of calling by using the telephone contact script that I review in chapter 6. Others simply drop in on potential employers and ask for an unscheduled interview—and they get them. Not always, of course, but often enough.

Getting 2 interviews a day equals 10 a week—over 40 a month. That's 800 percent more interviews than the average job seeker gets. Who do you think will get a job offer sooner?

STEP 6: YOU MUST DO WELL IN THE INTERVIEW

No matter how you get an interview, once you are there, you will have to create a good impression.

Even if you have the best of credentials.

Even if your resume is one of the ten best ever written.

Even if you *really* want the job.

While the job search consists of *getting* interviews, you must do well in them in order to get a job offer. There are very few exceptions to this and there is absolutely no doubt that you must do well in the interview in order to be considered for the job.

Many of the chapters in this book will help you understand the interview process and to take control of it in a positive way. I dare say that if you read this book carefully and complete the activities thoroughly, you will know more about the interview process than most of the interviewers you will meet. And that will give you a definite advantage over other applicants.

Quick Reminder

STEP 7: FOLLOW UP ON ALL CONTACTS

People who follow up with potential employers and others in their network get jobs faster than those who do not. It is as simple as that.

There are a variety of chapters in this book that will teach you more about follow-up techniques. Various chapters on the interview process will help you learn how to close an interview by setting a time to follow up. Chapter 6 will show you how to use three-by-five-inch cards to organize your follow-up contacts by date. You will also learn about sending thank-you notes in chapter 6, an important but often overlooked job search technique.

While there is much more to learn, these seven steps form the basis for a successful job search. The rest of this book elaborates on this framework.

2

KNOW MORE BEFORE YOU GO— DO SOME BACKGROUND RESEARCH ON YOURSELF, THE JOB, THE INDUSTRY, AND THE EMPLOYER

Quick Tip

This chapter will present some of the basic techniques for preparing for an interview before you get there. It will help you to know more about yourself, the occupation, the industry, and the employer. All of these things are essential for you to master in order to do a good job in an interview. Each of these topics is also covered in more detail in other chapters of this book, although this chapter will give you enough to get a quick start.

Most people do not present themselves well in an interview because they do not prepare well in advance. For example, what are you good at? What skills do you have that are needed in this job? Can you give examples to support those skills? What do you know about this industry and trends in this occupation that could be helpful to the employer? Why, indeed, should you be hired? While most of the topics presented in this chapter are covered more thoroughly in Section 2, there is enough here to help you start preparing for your next interview.

HAVE GOOD INFORMATION ABOUT YOURSELF

It should seem obvious that you need to know a lot about yourself in order to present yourself well in an interview. But I have found that most people are not good at explaining something as basic as what they are good at doing. Employers also find this to be a major problem, with one survey of employers finding that more than 80 percent of those interviewed did not do a good job presenting the skills they had. So, let's begin with a quick review of skills.

● ●

KNOW YOUR KEY SKILLS

Write down the three things about yourself that you think make you a good worker. Don't struggle with this and don't be analytical, just write down in the spaces below whatever occurs to you:

THREE THINGS ABOUT YOU THAT MAKE YOU A GOOD WORKER

1. _____

_____

2. _____

_____

3. _____

_____

I have asked this same question to thousands of people. In most cases, people will write down things like:

I am reliable.

I work hard.

I am loyal.

I am honest.

Most people would not consider those things skills at all and most would not bother to mention or emphasize them in an interview. And that would be a big mistake.

You see, interviewers want to know more than just your credentials—they want to know that you have a good character. Employers want to know that, yes, they can depend on you to work hard and to do your best. In an interview, those who learn to present these types of personal characteristics often get job offers over applicants with better credentials.

"When asked, few can quickly tell me what they are good at."

Most people are not good at expressing the skills they have. (I can tell you this based on many years of working with groups of job seekers.) When asked, few can quickly tell me what they are good at and fewer yet can quickly present the specific skills they have that are needed to succeed in the job they want.

A variety of research studies have concluded that the inability to communicate well in the interview will hurt you greatly. It is problem number one in the interview process and this has been documented in a variety of employer surveys.

THE THREE TYPES OF SKILLS—THE SKILLS TRIAD

There is more to know about your own skills than you might realize. Very often, we are not at all good at explaining to others what we are good at. Our culture calls this "bragging" and few learn how to do it well. Yet, in an interview, no one else will do it for you. It is essential that you know what you are good at and how to present these skills.

Quick Reminder

In examining your skills, it is best to see them in three distinct groupings.

Adaptive Skills: These skills are more like personality traits. They allow you to adapt and get along in new situations. They include things such as working hard, being reliable, and accepting responsibility. Most people don't think of them as skills and, in a way, they aren't. But employers are interested in them and you certainly need to know how to accentuate your own.

Transferable Skills: These are skills and abilities that are not specific to one job and can be transferred from one to another. Examples include strong verbal communication, the ability to organize events, supervisory skills, effective written communications, and many others.

Job-Related Skills: These are skills, knowledge, or abilities that are specific to a given job and are necessary to perform that job. For example, an accountant would need to know how to balance a general ledger, use a computer spreadsheet program, prepare financial statements, and perform related tasks.

While I will cover each of these skill types in more detail later in this book, I have included a few things for each skill type to allow you to quickly identify your key skills so that you can emphasize these skills in your next interview.

IDENTIFYING YOUR SKILLS

Because it is so important to know your skills, I have included several checklists to help you identify the skills that will be most important to present in an interview. More thorough versions of these lists are found in chapter 8.

ADAPTIVE SKILLS

You have already written down the three things about yourself that you believe make you a good worker. One or more of these are likely to have been adaptive skills. They may be among the most important things that an employer will want to know about you.

Quick Tip

Review chapter 8 for more details on skills. That chapter provides longer skills lists, a more thorough explanation of different types of skills, and additional information on skills. Knowing your skills and developing a "skills language" are essential to doing well in an interview and I strongly recommend that you know as much about this as possible.

Key Adaptive Skills Checklist

Following is a list of adaptive skills that most employers consider essential. Typically, they will not hire someone who has problems in these areas. Check those that are a particular strength for you, and be sure to emphasize them in your interview.

- ☐ Have good attendance
- ☐ Be honest
- ☐ Arrive on time
- ☐ Follow instructions
- ☐ Meet deadlines

- ☐ Get along with supervisor
- ☐ Get along with co-workers
- ☐ Work hard
- ☐ Work productively

Add any adaptive skills you have that are not listed but that you think are important to include. These should include any "good worker traits" you listed earlier in this chapter.

_____   _____

_____   _____

_____   _____

TRANSFERABLE SKILLS

If you are changing jobs or even careers, you can often use skills that you have used in the past to help you in a new job. Some of these skills you may have developed in work, school, family, or leisure activities.

Key Transferable Skills Checklist

Look at the list of skills that follows and check those that you feel you have and that you enjoy using.

☐ Meeting deadlines
☐ Planning
☐ Speaking in public
☐ Controlling budgets
☐ Supervising others
☐ Increasing sales or effiecncy

☐ Accepting responsibility
☐ Instructing others
☐ Solving problems
☐ Managing money or budgets
☐ Managing people
☐ Meeting the public

☐ Negotiating
☐ Organizing or managing projects
☐ Communicating in writing

Add any additional skills that are not listed above. Emphasize those that you most want to use in your next job or that you feel are most important to emphasize in an interview.

_____   _____

_____   _____

_____   _____

_____   _____

_____   _____

_____   _____

JOB-RELATED SKILLS

Most jobs require some skills that are specific to that job. Obviously, employers will want to know about these skills before they will make a hiring decision. In most cases, you will not even be considered unless you have the minimally acceptable job-related skills required for the job.

Quick Tip

The Transferable Skills Checklist in chapter 8 includes skills in a variety of groupings including:

- *Using your hands and dealing with things*

- *Dealing with data*

- *Working with people*

- *Using words and ideas*

- *Leading others*

- *Using creative and artistic skills*

I encourage you to complete that checklist since it is most helpful in preparing for interviews.

The "Review Your Accomplishments" section of this chapter will help you identify some of the job-related skills you have and will also help you identify key accomplishments. Chapter 8 will help you identify your job-related skills in a thorough way. It will help you review your past experiences in work, education, training, leisure activities, and other areas. This process will help you identify the key skills you have to support the job you want—and will give you many examples to support those skills during an interview.

IT IS ESSENTIAL TO COMMUNICATE YOUR SKILLS

It is essential to know your skills in order to do well in an interview. Many employers will hire a person who does not have the best credentials (job-related skills) because they do a superior job in presenting their adaptive and transferable skills during an interview.

Because there is almost always someone who has better credentials than you do, how you present yourself in an interview can make a big difference. For example, if you present a convincing case that you are a hard worker and fast learner (both adaptive skills) and can use these and your other skills to quickly master the specifics of a new job, you just might get a job offer over more qualified applicants who did not do as well in presenting their "other" skills.

Quick Tip

Chapter 10 provides a series of worksheets that collect similar information in much greater detail than is provided here. Doing that extra "homework" can pay dividends in an interview.

REVIEW YOUR ACCOMPLISHMENTS

Saying that you are good at something is important. However, in an interview situation, that may not be convincing unless you can support that skill with specific examples of where you have used it in the past.

The worksheet that follows is designed to help you identify key things in your background that you can use in an interview to support your ability to do the job.

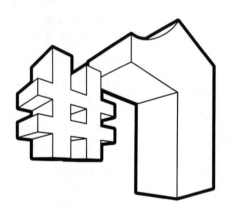

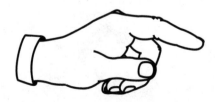

ACCOMPLISHMENTS WORKSHEET

···

EDUCATION/TRAINING

Include only highlights and the more important information that you might want to present in an interview. Emphasize any accomplishments, activities, or skills that would tend to support your job objective. Emphasize any transferable skills that could be used in a new job.

School/attended years: _____

Courses, subjects, or specific things you learned that might relate to the desired position: _____

_____

_____

_____

Any special accomplishments, extracurricular activities, things you did well: _____

_____

_____

_____

School/attended years: _____

Courses, subjects, or specific things you learned that might relate to the desired position: _____

_____

_____

_____

Any special accomplishments, extracurricular activities, things you did well: _____

_____

_____

_____

WORK

Include details on previous jobs, including military or significant volunteer work. When possible, include numbers such as people supervised, units sold, dollars saved, or other measures. Emphasize skills and accomplishments that would support your ability to do the job you want. You can handle any major promotions as a separate job.

Job title/years worked: _____

Skills used to relate to the job you want now: _____

_____

_____

_____

Accomplishments and results: _____

_____

_____

_____

Job title/years worked: _____

Skills used to relate to the job you want now: _____

_____

_____

_____

Accomplishments and results: _____

_____

_____

_____

Job title/years worked: _____

Skills used to relate to the job you want now: _____

_____

_____

_____

Accomplishments and results: _____

_____

_____

_____

Job title/years worked: _____

Skills used to relate to the job you want now: _____

_____

_____

_____

Accomplishments and results: _____

_____

_____

_____

Job title/years worked: _____

Skills used to relate to the job you want now: _____

_____

_____

_____

Accomplishments and results: _____

_____

_____

_____

OTHER ACTIVITIES

Consider skills and accomplishments that you gained in other areas of your life. Emphasize those that best support your ability to do the job you want.

Hobbies and leisure activities: _____

_____

_____

_____

Family responsibilities: _____

_____

_____

_____

Volunteer work not covered elsewhere: _____

_____

_____

_____

Any other activities or interests: _____

_____

_____

_____

HAVE THOROUGH INFORMATION ABOUT THE OCCUPATION

Most people are not all that well informed about the jobs that they say they want. In many cases, their experience in that occupation is limited because they are relatively new to the field. Even more experienced workers have typically gained their experience with just a few employers and don't know much about other work settings.

During your search for a new job, it is likely that you will also interview for jobs that are somewhat different from those with which you are most familiar. Knowing more about what that job requires will enable you to emphasize the skills you have that most closely match the job requirements.

While chapter 12 provides much more information on gathering details about a particular job, the following are a few essential things to be done.

THE OCCUPATIONAL OUTLOOK HANDBOOK (OOH)

This is a book that is revised every two years to include the latest information on the 250 or so most popular jobs. About 85 percent of us work in one of these jobs, so it is likely that you will find something very close to what you are looking for in this book.

The *OOH* is published by the U.S. Department of Labor and is widely available in libraries and other career resource centers and can be ordered from most bookstores. Each job is described in a few pages that are packed with information on the nature of work, working conditions, skills required, education and training needed, growth projections, average salaries paid, and more.

It is a good idea to read each and every job description you have held in the past to help you identify transferable skills you can use in your new job. In addition, it is most helpful for identifying jobs you may want to consider in the future. You should consider the *OOH* required reading before an interview for a particular job. Doing so will tell you just what skills to emphasize during the interview and it will surely help you present yourself more effectively.

Quick Reference

OTHER SOURCES OF OCCUPATIONAL INFORMATION

As mentioned earlier, chapter 12 provides additional sources of information on jobs. Several of these sources allow you to quickly access detailed information on the more than 12,000 job titles tracked by the Labor Department. Since you can access clusters of related jobs by interests, skills, and other criteria, these resources can be particularly helpful for identifying more specific job targets within a more specialized area.

Quick Reminder

HAVE GOOD INFORMATION ABOUT THE INDUSTRY

Let's say that you are interested in a job (or have an interview tomorrow) in a hospital. Even if you hope to work in a nonmedical area such as accounting, in this example, you will do better in the interview if you know something about the health care industry.

Once again, chapter 12 elaborates upon resources that provide industry-specific information in more detail, but the following is one particularly helpful source of information.

Quick Reference

THE CAREER GUIDE TO AMERICA'S TOP INDUSTRIES

This is another book published by the U.S. Department of Labor that is of particular value to job seekers. It provides helpful descriptions for 40 major industries—about 75 percent of all jobs. Like the *OOH*, the *Career Guide* is easy to read and provides information that can help you present yourself well in an interview.

Each description includes an overview of the industry, types of jobs it offers, employment projections, earnings possible, training required, working conditions, advancement opportunities, industry trends, sources of additional information, and more.

THE U.S. INDUSTRIAL OUTLOOK

This book provides descriptions of the 350 major industries. Published by the U.S. Department of Commerce, it provides details on industry trends and the effects of foreign competition, among others. While it is not specifically written for a job seeker, it provides valuable information that will be useful in preparing for an interview in an industry that is not familiar to you.

You should be able to find the *Occupational Outlook Handbook,* the *Career Guide to America's Top Industries,* and the *U.S. Industrial Outlook* in most good libraries or bookstores. They can also be ordered directly from JIST and are included in an order form at the back of this book.

Quick Reminder

KNOW ABOUT THE SPECIFIC EMPLOYER AND JOB

It is important for you to evaluate employers just as carefully as they might evaluate you. This is even more true if you plan on interviewing with an organization that particularly interests you.

The best information to have about an employer is that which is provided by someone who works (or used to work) there. That person can often provide you with inside information that can be invaluable in an interview. But let's say that you don't know someone who works there—what can you do? One thing is to go to the source. Often, a receptionist can get you product catalogs, brochures, reports, or other literature that explains the purpose, products, or services of the organization. Study them and you will have more knowledge of the organization than other applicants.

You can also go to the library and ask the librarian to help you locate any local or national information about the organization. You can often look up recent newspaper articles and, particularly for larger organizations, information in various industrial and other directories.

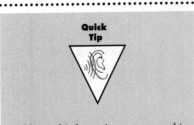

Quick Tip

Additional information on researching a particular employer is included in chapter 12.

The more you know about the job, the industry, and the employer, the more likely you are to present yourself well in the interview. More importantly, you will be better able to evaluate whether a particular job is "right" for you.

3

THE 60 MINUTE DRILL— ESSENTIAL TIPS ON TRADITIONAL AND NONTRADITIONAL INTERVIEWS

Quick Tip

All interviews are not equal. This chapter presents the basic types of interviews and suggests that the traditional interviews are not the only ones you should look for. It also provides a variety of suggestions for handling this critical 60 minutes in the job search process.

The interview is the most important 60 minutes in the job search. It requires a certain sort of communication skill that most people just don't have. There is good research indicating that interviews are not a valid way to select good employees. Most employers would agree. But while it is not always the best method, the fact is that how you do in an interview is very important in whether or not you will be considered for a job. Doing well in an interview is, more or less, a requirement for getting a job offer and this chapter will consider just what an interview is—and how to handle the process.

Five Things to Do to Have a Successful Interview

In order to have a successful interview you must do five things:

▲ **1.** Make a positive impression
▲ **2.** Communicate your skills
▲ **3.** Answer problem questions
▲ **4.** Help the employer know why he or she should hire you
▲ **5.** Follow up after the interview.

These are interview essentials, and if you do them well, you can dramatically increase your chances of getting a job offer.

Quick Reference

TIPS TO OVERCOME YOUR FEAR OF INTERVIEWS

An interview is intimidating and stressful to most people. We aren't often evaluated as intensely as we are in an interview and the stakes are high. I believe one of the reasons so many people withdraw from an active job search is because of their fear of rejection, which is unavoidable in most traditional interviews. If you don't get a job offer, does it mean that you are not a worthy person? While the answer is often no, it is hard not to internalize the stress of hoping to be selected and the disappointment of not getting the job. But there are some things you can do to reduce the stress of interviews.

REJECT REJECTION

The word "interview" has two parts: "inter," which means "between" and "view," which surely means "look at." I do not claim to be an expert on root words, but it does seem that "interview" means, roughly, "two people looking at each other." In a job interview, that is precisely what should be going on. More often, however, there is the one-sided feeling that the all-powerful employer is giving the job seeker a thorough looking over. The job seeker conducting a conventional job search is likely to get rejected, which does not feel good.

YOU HAVE TO GET REJECTED BEFORE YOU CAN GET ACCEPTED

One way to look at the interview is as a series of rejections, like this:

No No No No No No No No No No No No No No No No No No No
No No No No No No No No No No No No No No No No No No No
No No No No No No No No No No No No No No No No No No No
No No No No No No No No No No No No No No No No No No No
No No No Yes

Finally, you meet someone who makes you a job offer. If you accept, that's a "yes." Along the way, however, the rejection doesn't have to be one-sided. An interview should be, after all, a two-way communication. Employers are not the only ones who can say no.

Quick Reference

UNDERSTAND "INTUITION" AND USE IT TO YOUR ADVANTAGE

Many employers claim they get a "feel" for a person during an interview. I have often heard interviewers say they did or did not hire someone based on a "gut reaction." This can be a very unnerving thought until you understand that what they feel can often be predicted. And if you know what might cause a negative reaction, you can try to change your behavior accordingly.

Most gut reactions are really responses to nonverbal cues. Many of your most powerful signals can be nonverbal. As evidence of this, think about how a lie detector works. Your body gives off electro-chemical signals that can be measured. Even if you try, you can't keep this from happening—and the machine can read your "real" reaction. Your voice, facial expressions, posture, and other subtle signals give you away too.

Obviously, the only way to avoid this problem in a job interview is to be honest. If you overstate your abilities, you often unconsciously communicate that you are hiding something, which many interviewers will notice.

Often, you may be completely unaware of how your nonverbal signals are creating a negative impression. Perhaps your grooming is inappropriate or out-of-date; maybe you play with your hair or slouch in your chair; or you may have a hard time expressing yourself without moving your hands too much.

Quick Case Study

Some time ago, I worked with a college graduate who had been chronically unemployed or underemployed for more than ten years. His credentials were great—a prestigious school, good grades, a desirable degree in business. Yet, I immediately knew why he had such a hard time getting a decent job—his handshake was limp, he slouched terribly, his hair looked oily, and he looked like he had slept under a bridge. While many of his problems were personality-related, his job search was bound to be unsuccessful based simply on his appearance. Any employer would react negatively to him.

The good news is that you can change many of your undesirable mannerisms. Ask an objective person or friend to role-play interviews with you and provide constructive feedback on your nonverbal image. By becoming aware of negative signals, and by practicing to eliminate or change them, you can make an employer's "intuition" work for you.

> **"***It is helpful to remind yourself that most bosses started out as job seekers.***"**

INTERVIEWERS ARE PEOPLE, TOO

If you tend to think of an interviewer as the enemy, you should reconsider. It is helpful to remind yourself that most bosses started out as job seekers and will very likely take on that role again. You should also realize that most interviewers have reasons of their own to be nervous:

✔ **They probably have no training in interviewing.** Just as most job seekers don't know how to find jobs, interviewers often don't know how to interview. How would they have learned? It is not at all unusual for a well-trained job seeker to be a better interviewer than the interviewer. (Really!) I often hear job seekers say, "They didn't even ask me any hard questions! I had to tell them what I was good at because they never asked."

✔ **If they hire you, and you don't work out, they lose.** If they make a mistake, their boss will know. Since it costs lots of money to train new staff, their decision is literally worth thousands of dollars. In small organizations or departments, if one person does not work out, everyone else feels the extra workload. The person who hired you could lose credibility (and maybe even his or her job).

✔ **Everyone likes to be liked.** I've known employers who hate to interview because they don't like to turn people down. They are not comfortable in screening people out. You don't have to feel sorry for them, but it is something to think about.

So, you see, interviewers are not to be feared at all. Employers are just like us because they *are* us. Their roles are just a little different at the moment.

Quick Fact

THE THREE TYPES OF INTERVIEWS

Too many people think of a job interview too narrowly. One of the big tasks in a successful job search is to get more interviews. But if you define an interview in a narrow and traditional way, you will miss out on meeting many perspective employers who in many cases are willing to talk to you even before a job opening exists.

Consequently, how you define an interview is a critical part of a successful job search. To open yourself up to a more creative and effective job search, consider that there are many types of interviews. For our purposes, the major ones are:

1. The traditional job search interview

2. The information interview

3. The JIST job search interview

Quick Fact

Much of this book works on the assumption that an interview can include something more than the "traditional" interview. All three types of interviews share some characteristics, but there are significant differences too. If you know how to conduct yourself in each type of interview, you will have a distinct advantage over most job seekers. Let's take a closer look at each type.

Quick Reference

THE FIRST INTERVIEW TYPE: THE TRADITIONAL JOB INTERVIEW

The following is what job seekers usually think of when the word "interview" is used.

A TRADITIONAL INTERVIEW IS...

> *a meeting with a person who has a job opening for which you might qualify, who is actively looking for someone to fill it, and who has the authority to hire you.*

While this is certainly an interview, it does have a few problems. For one thing, most jobs get filled before a traditional interview is needed. Employers often hire people they came to know before the job became available. An important lesson to learn is that if you wait until the opening, the job is likely to be filled.

This is not to say that traditional job interviews are not important. They are. But it would be irresponsible not to tell you that more than half of all jobs are filled in a different way. If you believe in your heart that an interview can happen only if you get a "Yes" to your question, "Do you have any job openings for me?", you will miss some of the very best opportunities.

☑ MANIPULATION AND COUNTER-MANIPULATION

In the traditional interview, your task is to present yourself well. The task of the interviewer is to find out what's wrong with you so you can be eliminated from consideration. This is not the friendliest of social situations. If the interviewer has any training on how to interview, you will face techniques intentionally designed to reveal your flaws. In a book considered by many to be required reading for interviewers, *The Evaluation Interview*, Richard Fear wrote, "Since most applicants approach the interview with the objective of putting their best foot forward, the interviewer must be motivated from the very beginning to search for unfavorable information."

In a traditional interview, any good interviewer will encourage you to be yourself and let your guard down. In an article by John and Merna Galassien titled "Preparing Individuals for Job Interviews: Suggestions From More Than 60 Years of Research" they conclude that the primary role of interviewers is to weed out the "undesirables." Their goal is to manipulate you to reveal negative information, if at all possible.

A job seeker's reaction to all this manipulation is natural enough: you try to hide your faults and emphasize your strengths. Your objective, in these traditional interviews, is to get a second interview. If you leave the interview and that decision has not been made, go after a second interview in your follow-up efforts. I'll tell you more about following up later in the chapter.

☑ THE MAJOR TYPES OF TRADITIONAL INTERVIEWS

In addition to much manipulation, you are likely to encounter different interviewing styles. So that you will not be taken by surprise, let's take a look at some of the more common methods used in traditional interviews.

ONE-ON-ONE

This is by far the most common preliminary interview, where you meet with a person whose role is to screen applicants and arrange follow-up interviews with the person who has the authority to hire. Other times, you may meet directly with the hiring authority. These one-on-one interviews are the focus of the techniques presented later in this chapter.

GROUP/PANEL

While still not as common as the one-on-one interview, group interviews are gaining popularity. It's possible you could be asked to interview with two or more people involved in the selection process. I've even known of situations where a group of interviewers met with a group of applicants—all at the same time. Many of the techniques used in this book will work well in these settings too.

NONDIRECTIVE

Some interviewers will ask few direct questions and, instead, encourage you to tell them whatever you want. For example, instead of asking "How did you do in your math classes?", they might ask, "What did you like best about school?" If you are not prepared for such open-ended questions, you could quickly put your foot in your mouth.

STRESS

Some interviewers intentionally try to get you upset. They want to see how you handle stress, whether you can accept criticism, or how you react to a tense situation. They hope to see how you are likely to act in a high-pressure job.

For example, they might try to get you angry by not accepting something you say as true. "I find it difficult to believe," they might say, "that you were responsible for as large a program as you claim here on your resume. Why don't you just tell me what you really did?"

Another approach is to quickly fire questions at you but not give you time to completely answer or to interrupt you midsentence with other questions. Not nice.

But now you've been warned. I hope you don't run into this sort of interviewer but if so, be yourself and have a few laughs. The odds are the interview could turn out fine if you don't take the bait and throw things around the room. If you do get a job offer following such an interview, you might want to ask yourself whether you would want to work for such a person or organization. (It might be fun not to accept the job and then tell them what you think of their interviewing technique.)

STRUCTURED

In light of current legislation overseeing hiring practices, a structured interview is becoming more common, particularly in larger organizations. The interviewer may have a list of things to ask all applicants and a form

Quick Reference

to fill out. Your experience and skills may be compared to specific job tasks or criteria. Even if highly structured, there is usually the opportunity for you to present what you feel is essential information.

REALITY TYPE

Many Fortune 1000 companies, including Radisson Hotels International, Hershey's, and S.C. Johnson & Co., have switched to an interviewing method known most often as "reality interviewing." These companies believe that the more traditional way of rating candidates' answers to questions only encourages the interviewers to pick new employees who are just like themselves.

According to Arthur H. Bell, author of *Extraviewing*, there are three simple steps to the reality interview:

1. *Ask applicants to describe their realities—what they did do or are doing—rather than their impressions, attitudes, or ideals.* The idea here is to sidestep canned answers. So instead of being asked "What do you believe is the best way to handle conflict?" the question will be phrased, "Tell me about a time you experienced conflict with another worker. How did you handle it?"

2. *Probe the applicant's past and present realities in direct relation to his or her future responsibilities with the company.* Simply stated, the past is dead and buried as far as the interviewer is concerned. In the reality interview, the person on the other side of the desk wants to know which parts of your past will be useful for the specific job you now want with his or her company. In this situation, do not expect any questions that require you to judge or give value to anything—that is the interviewer's task. As Bell reports one interviewer's explanation, "I want an applicant to tell me about what he ate, not how he liked it. I want the meal, not the burp." Questions here will be posed as, "What were the events that led to the incident?" "Who was involved?" "What exactly did you do and say?" "What was the outcome?"

3. *Pose situational questions in addition to past experience questions.* Again, the situational questions are specific, which prevents you

from answering vaguely. For example: "As a seafood buyer, you are responsible for the availability of halibut to 30 supermarkets in our chain. You manage to lock in a large purchase of halibut at an attractive price from suppliers. Based on this purchase, management decides to feature halibut prominently at rock-bottom prices in its double-page newspaper ads. The ads work too well: Within hours of ad publication, customers have cleaned out the supermarkets of their halibut stock. Managers from most of the stores are calling you for more halibut. What would you do?" Notice this does not invite an "I-think-buying-should-always-be-done-within-budget" answer!

Nor is it a good idea to blurt out, "I'd just buy more halibut as fast as I could and get it out to the stores," Bell said. Your answer must keep the company's situation firmly in mind, as well as save your own rear end.

Although the reality interview demands more than the surface research we all wish we could get by on, it definitely can stack the cards in your favor. The *Wall Street Journal* reported that S.C. Johnson & Co. interviewed a woman for a sales position using this situational method. Her background was in theater—not exactly an area that excited interviewers. Furthermore, she was up against several experienced salesmen and the interviewers had never hired a woman for such a position. However, the reality interview gave her a chance to score higher than the other applicants and get the job offer. She eventually broke sales records in the company.

Similarly, L'Oreal has used this interview method since 1988. From 1988 to 1990, the number of employees hired through this method was lower (33 versus 41), but of those 33, only five were separated from the company compared to 17 people who were let go after passing the more traditional interview. Furthermore, two reality interview graduates were promoted to management, whereas none from the other interview styles were so honored.

If you do run into a reality interview format, depending on the field, you might anticipate situational questions like these:

▲ **Real Estate:** Describe a sales experience in which you received two or more offers for the piece of property at the same time. How did you handle the situation?

▲ **Law Enforcement:** You have just completed your training as a police officer and have been given your regular assignment on foot patrol. As you walk your beat, you see two young men approximately 17 or 18 years of age hanging around. On your second day on the beat, as you pass them for the third time, one says, "Does your father work for a living?" The other replies, "No, he's a cop." What would you do?

▲ **Case Worker:** When given a form to complete, a client hesitates, tells you he cannot fill out forms too well and is afraid he will do a poor job. He asks you to do it for him. You are quite sure, however, that he is able to do it himself. What do you tell him?

DISORGANIZED

Let's face it, you will come across many interviewers who will not know how to interview you. They may talk about themselves too much or neglect to ask you any meaningful questions. Many people are competent managers but poor interviewers. The best way to help such lost souls learn about the true you is by providing some answers to questions they may not have asked.

Quick Fact

THE SECOND INTERVIEW TYPE: THE INFORMATION INTERVIEW

This is an interview that has become widely used (and often abused) since the mid-1970s, when Richard Bolles popularized it in his book *What Color Is Your Parachute?* It is supposed to be used by job seekers who have not yet decided what they want to do—or where.

To correctly use the technique, you must first define your ideal job in terms of skills required, size and type of organization, salary level, interests, what sort of co-workers, and other preferences.

The next step is to gather information on just where a job of this sort might exist and what it might be called.

**Quick
Reminder**

If you are interested in defining your ideal job, if you do your homework before using this method, and if you are truly honest and sincere about seeking information but not a job, then the information interview technique is both effective and fun.

Unfortunately, this technique has often been misused. People who really want to get a job have used the technique as a trick to get in to see someone. ("I'm not looking for a job but I am conducting a survey ...") Well, that is dishonest and most employers resent the misrepresentation. Many employers are now wary about anyone, even the sincere ones, asking to see them for any reason. Many who support the use of information interviews lament this and point out that some career counselors and others who should know better have encouraged this dishonesty. Proponents do point out, however, that the technique is still useful, particularly outside larger cities and with smaller organizations.

**Quick
Fact**

"PROFIT" INTERVIEWS

Years before information interviewing, Bernard Haldane developed a technique for those seeking managerial and professional positions. He explained his approach in a book that I consider to be a classic, titled *How to Make a Habit of Success*, originally published in 1960. In it, you identify an employer that is of particular interest. That organization meets most of the criteria set by the job seeker *and* the job seeker clearly sees how that organization could benefit from employing him or her.

Once that happens, the job seeker carefully puts together a written business proposal to be presented to the person (or persons) within that organization who makes decisions. The plan would address what you propose to do; how it would be done; how much money (or other benefits) the project or activity will generate; how much it will cost (including your salary and benefits); and why you are the one person uniquely qualified to successfully fill the position.

The key word in all this is "profit," since if you propose other benefits, but not more profit, your case is surely weakened. If all goes well, you have a job created for you where none existed before. It *does* happen! In fact, Haldane and Associates, the career counseling firm founded by Bernard Haldane, provides data indicating that almost two-thirds of the people they work with have jobs created just for them by using this technique.

THE THIRD INTERVIEW TYPE: THE JIST JOB SEARCH INTERVIEW

Almost everyone thinks in terms of this type of interview being equal to the traditional interview. The job search consists, in that framework, of getting in to talk to employers about jobs that are now open. But I believe that using the traditional definition of an interview—and a job search—results in many people being out of work longer than they need to be.

I propose that you consider defining the interview in a new way. While this is a simple definition, it has enormous implications in how you go about your job search. My definition of an interview is quite nontraditional:

A JIST JOB SEARCH INTERVIEW IS...

any face-to-face contact with someone who hires or supervises people with your skills—whether or not they have a job opening now.

This interview type refers to a variety of situations where a job opening may or may not exist, but where it still makes sense to go in and speak with someone about the possibility of present or future employment.

For example, if you seek an interview for a job that is now open (a traditional job opening), you would ask an employer "Do you have any job openings?" And very often, the answer would be "no" and that would be the end of that. If, on the other hand, you had said "I would like to speak with the person in charge of (this or that)," you would probably get to talk to them. That would be an interview, in the way I define it, even if there is no job opening yet.

Quick Fact

THE CRITERIA FOR A SUCCESSFUL JIST JOB SEARCH INTERVIEW

Because there are far more employers who don't have a formal job opening at any one time, it should be obvious that this new definition of an interview will allow you to talk to more employers than restricting your search to specific openings. But not every conversation with an employer is an interview. To get the most from this type of interview, here is what you need to know or do:

Three Things You Need to Know or Do for a JIST Job Search Interview

▲ **1.** You must know what sort of job you want, and

▲ **2.** You must be able to communicate clearly why someone should hire you for that job, and

▲ **3.** The interviewer must know something about the sort of job you are looking for or, at the very least, know other people who may know.

Quick Tip

Nontraditional job search methods are covered in more detail in chapter 16. I strongly suggest that you read that chapter since, in order to do well in interviews, you first have to get them ...

The JIST Job Search Interview provides a tremendous advantage to you. Now you can interview with employers before they have a job opening and often completely avoid the competition from other job seekers. And, because the employer won't be trying to eliminate you from the pool of applicants (as is done in the traditional interview), the interview can be much more relaxed.

Keep the new definition of an interview in mind as you continue reading this book. It is an important definition that can make a very big difference in how effective you are in finding job openings.

4

THE SEVEN PHASES OF AN INTERVIEW

Quick Tip

An interview is a complex human interaction. There is more going on than can be explained or understood easily, which is why there is no "one way" to handle an interview. But I believe that an interview can be divided into distinct elements or phases. This chapter divides the interview process into seven such phases, and it provides additional details on each one. This format allows you to understand what goes on in each phase of an interview and to learn what you can do to present yourself well in each one.

I n a traditional interview, the objective is to get a job offer. It is that simple. But in situations where there may not be a job opening just yet, the objective may be to make a good impression and get referrals to other people. The topic of getting interviews is covered in chapter 6 and an effective job search requires you to get as many traditional and nontraditional interviews as you can.

A certain amount of judgment is required for you to know how to act in various sorts of interviews. If there is a job opening and you want it, you would behave differently than in an interview where no opening existed. But just what *do* you do during the interview?

Fortunately, there has been much research on the interview process. That research indicates that some things are clearly very important to an employer in deciding on one person over another. For example, it should be obvious that your dress and grooming can create a positive or negative first impression. But just how *should* you dress and groom for an interview?

What else do employers find important—and what can you do about it? The answers to these and other questions fill this book, but I think you will find the following review of the interview process will give you enough information for most situations.

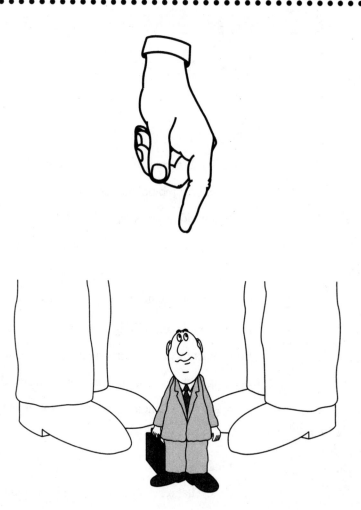

THE SEVEN PHASES OF AN INTERVIEW

As mentioned earlier, an interview is a complex interaction that is best understood when broken down into more easily examined segments. I have broken the interview into seven distinct phases. You could argue that an interview has more or fewer phases, but I happen to think that seven is just right.

The Seven Phases

▲ **Phase 1: Before You Go In.** Before you even meet the interviewer, you will create an impression. If it's bad, nothing good can come of it.

▲ **Phase 2: Opening Moves.** An interview isn't a game, exactly, but how you begin it will often affect whether you win or lose.

▲ **Phase 3: The Interview Itself.** This is the longest and most complex part of an interview. It's here that you are asked problem questions and have the opportunity to present your skills. The impression you make here is highly dependent on your self-understanding regarding what you have to offer and your ability to communicate it.

▲ **Phase 4: Closing the Interview.** There is more to ending an interview than simply saying good-bye. This phase can allow you to wrap up the interview in a positive way and can be a prelude to the next phase.

▲ **Phase 5: Following Up.** An interview is not over until you send a thank-you note and schedule follow-up contact of some sort. People who follow up get jobs over those who do not. It's that simple.

▲ **Phase 6: Negotiating.** Discussing money in an initial interview can quickly get you screened out. Knowing what to do, and how, can be worth many, many dollars.

▲ **Phase 7: Making a Final Decision.** Once you get a job offer, you have to decide whether to accept or reject it—or negotiate for something "better." The stakes are high here and you may have to live with a bad decision for some time. Provided in this chapter are some tips to help you evaluate an important life decision on its own merits. Now let's get started with some specific techniques to help you present yourself well in each of the seven phases of an interview.

PHASE I: BEFORE YOU GO IN

While often overlooked, what transpires before the interview is very, very important. Before you actually meet the prospective employer, you often have indirect contact with those who know the interviewer. You might even contact the interviewer directly, through correspondence or a phone call. This contact creates an impression. Let's take a look at the issues here and see what you can do to prepare yourself.

PRELIMINARY CONTACTS

There are three ways an interviewer may form an impression of you before meeting you face-to-face:

Quick Fact

1. The Interviewer Already Knows You

There are many situations where an interviewer may know you from previous contacts or from someone else's description of you. When this is so, your best approach is to acknowledge that relationship, but to treat the interview in all other respects as a business meeting. Even if you are the best of friends, remember that a decision to hire you involves hard cash. It will not be done lightly.

2. Through Previous Phone Contacts

The phone is an important job search tool. How you handle yourself on the phone will create an impression, even though the contacts are brief. If you set up an interview with the employer, you have already created an impression.

Secretaries and other staff you have contact with may also mention their observations to the interviewer, so be professional and friendly in all encounters with staff.

You should consider calling the day before the interview to verify the time. Say something like: "Hi, I want to make sure our interview for two o'clock tomorrow is still on." Get any directions you need. This is just another way of demonstrating your attention to detail and helps communicate the sense of importance you are giving this interview.

3. Through Previous Paperwork

Prior to most interviews, you will provide the employer with some sort of paperwork that will create an impression. Sending a note or letter beforehand often creates the impression that you are well organized. Copies of applications, resumes, and JIST Cards sent in advance help the interviewer know more about you. If they are well done (as they must be) they will help create a positive impression. For these reasons, all paperwork you present to an employer must be as professional and well-done as possible.

Quick
Tip

The JIST Card is a type of mini-resume that presents key information about yourself on a three-by-five-inch card. It is covered in more detail in chapter 6, but here is an example of one, just so that you know what it looks like:

GETTING TO AND WAITING FOR THE INTERVIEW

There are several details to consider before the interview itself.

☑ GET THERE ON TIME

Try to schedule several interviews within the same area of town and time frame to avoid wasted time in excessive travel. If you are driving, get directions from the receptionist and be sure you know how to get there and how long it takes. Allow plenty of time for parking and plan on arriving for the interview 5 to 10 minutes early. If you are using public transportation, make sure you know what to do to get there on time.

Jonathan Michael

Home: (614) 788-2434
Message: (614) 355-0068

Objective: Management

More than 7 years of management experience plus a B.S. degree in business. Managed budgets as large as $10 million. Experienced in cost control and reduction, cutting over 20% of overhead while business increased over 30%. Good organizer and problem solver. Excellent communication skills.

Prefer responsible position in a medium to large organzation

Cope well with deadline pressure, seek challenge, flexible

☑ FINAL GROOMING

Arrive early enough to slip into a restroom and correct any grooming problems your travel may have caused (wind-blown hair, etc.).

☑ THE RECEPTIONIST

Many organizations have a receptionist and this person is important to you. Assume that everything you say or do will get back to the interviewer. (It typically will.) A friendly chat with the receptionist can also be a productive way to find out more about the organization. For example, if it seems appropriate, ask the person what it is like to work there, what he or she does in the job, or even what sort of a person the boss is. They are often happy to share these things with you in a helpful way. A thank-you note to him or her following your interview will surely create a positive impression. Treat all support personnel with respect and they will help you by saying nice things about you to the boss; mistreat them and you will probably not get a job there.

Quick Case Study

I once worked in a busy office that had a public waiting room that was often crowded. When I was interviewing people, the receptionists often interacted with applicants as they waited for me. If the person being interviewed acted strangely or did not treat those staff members with respect, they would give me a covert thumbs down sign. Those interviews were very short. I figured that if the applicant did not treat my staff well before the interview, they would only show the same lack of interpersonal skills on the job. The moral: Receptionists are real people and their opinions of you do count.

☑ WAITING ROOM BEHAVIOR

It is important to relax and to look relaxed. Occupy yourself with something businesslike. For example, this could be a good time to review your notes on questions you might like to ask in the interview, key skills you want to present, or other interview details. Bring a work-related magazine to read or pick one up in the reception area. They may also have publications from the organization itself that you may not have seen yet. During the entire interviewing process, I advise you not to smoke since a nonsmoker is often seen as a more desirable worker. You may have other mannerisms that create negative impressions, too. Don't slouch in your seat. Don't create a mess by spreading out your coat and papers across the next seat.

☑ IF THE INTERVIEWER IS LATE

Hope that it happens. If you arrive promptly but had to wait past the appointed time, that puts the interviewer in a "Gee, I'm sorry, I owe you one" frame of mind. If the interviewer is 15 minutes late, approach the receptionist and say something like: "I

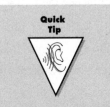

Quick Tip

Here is a helpful way to evaluate your waiting room behavior—if your mom would comment negatively on what you do there, you probably shouldn't do it.

have an appointment to keep yet today. Do you think it will be much longer before (insert interviewer's name) will be free?"

Be nice, but don't act like you can sit around all day either. If you have to wait more than 25 minutes beyond the scheduled time, ask to reschedule at a better time. Say it is no problem for you and you understand things do come up. Besides, you say, you want to be sure Mr. or Ms. So-and-So doesn't feel rushed when they see you. Set up the new time, accept any apology with a smile, and be on your way. When you do come back for your interview, the odds are that the interviewer will apologize—and treat you very well indeed.

"*I cannot stress enough the importance of appearance in the job search.***"**

PHASE 2: OPENING MOVES

You've gotten to the right office, on time, and the interviewer now walks into the room. What is the first thing that will happen? While this may seem obvious, the first thing that will happen is that he or she will see and react to you.

☑ APPEARANCE COUNTS

In a monumental and thorough work entitled *Job Search, A Review of the Literature,* Steven Magnum found that "Appearance, communication skills, and attitudes dominate the research. Attire and physical attractiveness visibly influence the hiring process."

I cannot stress enough the importance of your appearance in the job search. It is a major factor in the interview process and in getting a job offer—or getting eliminated from consideration.

Quick Case Study

▲ The importance of appearance is highlighted by the results of a study that evaluated the effect of nonverbal communication style on employers. Two actors—one male and one female—were videotaped while role-playing an interview. Two tapes were made of each, using precisely the same responses to the same questions. In one tape they made good eye contact while speaking, spoke clearly, presented good posture. In the other, they did not. They dressed the same for each and, I emphasize, used the same words in responding to the same questions.

▲ These tapes were then randomly shown to 52 professional interviewers who were asked to score the interviews in various categories. No interviewer saw the same actor in both roles. What do you suppose happened? It would be no surprise to guess which job seeker role was rated more positively. Naturally, the "good" interview was chosen over the "bad" one. What was astonishing was that, of all the interviewers, not one would have invited back the person who had poor nonverbal skills. The same people using the same responses (but who displayed good nonverbal communication skills) would have been invited back by 88 percent of the interviewers. The results of this study show that your various personality traits (adaptive skills) are observed by interviewers.

Let's look at some of the other appearance-related issues employers use to define your personality and make hiring decisions.

☑ DRESS AND GROOMING

How you dress and groom can create a big negative or positive impression even during the first few seconds of an interview. With so many options in styles, colors, and other factors, the "correct" approach can get quite complex. Entire books have been written on the subject and there are many differences of opinion on just what is right for various occasions. To avoid the complexity, I present this simple rule for you to follow:

MIKE FARR'S INTERVIEW DRESS AND GROOMING RULE

> *Dress and groom like the interviewer is likely to be dressed—but neater.*

Quick Reference

My rule means that a bank teller would dress, when going to an interview, like his or her boss would dress. An auto mechanic, on the other hand, would look inappropriate going to an interview dressed like the manager of a bank. If there is any doubt about just how to dress or groom, guess conservative. Pay attention to details. Do your shoes look presentable? Are your clothes clean and pressed? Is your hair neat? Are you absolutely clean? Have you looked closely at yourself in the mirror?

It is best to get someone else's opinion on the impression you make. A better clothing store can help you select a coordinated job-search outfit. Plan to invest some money in at least one set of good quality interviewing clothes. Notice, when you are all spruced up, how good you feel. That can affect your whole performance in the interview.

Quick Tip

Additional tips on dress and grooming are provided in chapters 9 and 13.

☑ A FIRM HANDSHAKE AND GOOD EYE CONTACT

Shaking hands is a common custom and, while it seems a small detail, do learn to execute this formality properly. If the employer offers his or her hand, give them a firm-but-not-too-firm handshake as you smile. As ridiculous as it sounds, a little practice helps. Avoid staring but do look at the interviewer when either of you is speaking.

It will help you concentrate on what is being said as well as indicate to the employer that you are listening closely and have good social skills.

☑ POSTURE AND MORE

The very best way to see yourself as others see you is to role-play an interview while it is videotaped. Looking at and listening to the video playback is sometimes shocking to people. If this equipment is not available to you, all is not lost. Pay close attention to your own posture, mannerisms, and other body language. Ask yourself how an employer might evaluate you if they saw that behavior. Look at other people and copy the posture and behavior of ones you think would look good in an interview situation. Let's look at some problem areas to watch for and improve.

Act interested. When you are sitting, lean slightly forward in your chair and keep your head up, looking directly at the interviewer. This helps you look interested and alert.

Eliminate annoying behaviors. Try to eliminate any distracting movements or mannerisms. A woman in one of my workshops saw herself in a videotape constantly playing with her hair. It was only then that she realized she did it at all, and how distracting it was. Listen to yourself and you may notice that you say "aaahhh" every 10 seconds, or say "you know what I mean?" over and over, or use other repetitive words or phrases. You may hardly be aware of doing this, but do watch for it. Seek out and eliminate similar behavior from the interview.

Pay attention to your voice. If you are naturally soft-spoken, work on increasing your volume slightly. Listen to news announcers and other professional speakers who are good models for volume, speed, and voice tone. I, for example, have a fairly deep voice. I have learned to raise it up and down while doing presentations, so everyone doesn't go to sleep. Your voice and delivery will improve as you gain experience and conduct more interviews.

"Play the chit-chat game for awhile."

ESTABLISHING THE RELATIONSHIP

Open the interview with an approach intended to establish a relaxed, social tone. Here are some ideas of what to say in the first few minutes.

Use the interviewer's name as often as possible, particularly in the early part of the interview and again when you are ending it. Be formal, using "Mr. Jones" or "Ms. Smith," unless they suggest otherwise.

Play the chit-chat game for awhile. The interviewer will often comment on the weather, ask if you had trouble getting there, or some other common opening. Be friendly and make a few appropriate comments. Do not push your way into the business of your visit too early because these informal openings are standard measures of your socialization skills. Smile. It's nonverbal and people will respond more favorably to you if you smile at them.

Comment on something personal in the interviewer's office, like "I love your office! Did you decorate it yourself?" or "I noticed the sailboat. Do you sail?" or "Is that a Phantom II computer I noticed downstairs? How do you like it?" or "Your receptionist is great! How long has he been here?" The idea here is to express interest in something that interests the employer and encourage her or him to speak about it. It is a compliment if your enthusiasm shows. This tactic can also provide you the opportunity to share something you have in common, so try to pick a topic you know something about.

SOME RELATIONSHIP-BUILDING TIPS
FROM A VARIETY OF EXPERTS

Use this informal discussion time to pick up on a few clues about the interviewer's personality and what will appeal to him or her. It's a strategy salesman Michael J. Fogel has built his career on at CNA Insurance Corp. "If there's a plaque on the wall dating back to 1968, you know the person likes praise," he advises.

If the person appears forceful, impatient, or even rude, he or she has an exceedingly fast processing speed, so cut to the chase—it will score points in your favor. Likewise, if the person is very soft spoken and pronounces

Quick
Reference

words very clearly and at a slow pace, mirror that in both your verbal and nonverbal language. "Make no mistake about it: Any two people who possess different personalities will be in conflict," says Sal Divita, George Washington University professor of marketing. "Most of us fail to recognize that the breakdown was caused by our inability to speak the other person's nonverbal language. It is possible to speak anybody's nonverbal language; it simply requires being attentive to the other person's pace." Your biggest cue comes the moment you shake hands, since a person's handshake often reflects his or her pace. And, as Fogel recommends, don't stop at copying only the conversation style. If the interviewer takes off his or her jacket, do the same. "If the person seems to be in a bad mood, I'll tell him he looks busy and maybe we should reschedule," the salesman adds. There's no reason why this advice wouldn't work in your favor during job interviews, too.

Quick
Alert

UNDERSTAND PERSONALITY TYPES

Here's a list of personality types and how to spot them, from *The Perfect Interview*, by John Drake, a licensed psychologist and the founder and former CEO of Drake Beam Morin—a career counseling firm.

ACTIVATORS

These people have a "do-it-now" mentality. They are concerned with end results and what is practical and tangible. Activators are often attracted to jobs in production, professional athletics, or fast-paced work environments.

Ways to Identify an Activator: Desk is cluttered and disorderly. Likely to be filled with piles of papers. Possibly two phones. Wall hangings are strictly business (picture of the company's product) or highly action-oriented. Questions are brief, to the point, and focus on results you've accomplished. Don't ramble—emphasize your ability to get things done.

FEELERS

Feelers rely on gut reactions. They are perceptive to the needs of others, often sensing the right thing to say or do. Feelers are often attracted to jobs in areas such as sales, human resources, and customer service.

Ways to Identify a Feeler: Office is filled with personal memorabilia such as family photographs, mementos from previous jobs, diplomas, and famous quotes. This person will spend significant time in small talk. Will probably ask questions about your relationships with others, such as your boss, your subordinates, even family. Adopt the informal approach and share a common family or community interest, if possible.

ANALYZERS

Analyzers are logical, systematic, orderly, and structured. They are fact oriented. They are often attracted to jobs in accounting, engineering, and data processing.

Ways to Identify an Analyzer: Space is neat and orderly. Sometimes almost bare, except for calculator or computer. Charts and graphs are important giveaways. Will ask for many facts and figures such as your grade point average and your contributions to profits. Avoid digressions and excessive expressions of emotion.

CONCEPTUALIZERS

Conceptualizers are concerned about future events, not the here and now. They think by intuitively linking ideas rather than by processing them logically and deductively. Conceptualizers are often attracted to jobs in strategic planning, academia, and advertising.

Ways to Identify a Conceptualizer: Work area is piled with books. Often two piles of reports, side by side, being studied for trends. Bookcase is filled with technical literature and the room may include intellectual toys (three-dimensional tic-tac-toe). Questions will center around your ideas and concepts. Expect this person to go off on tangents, and follow along.

Quick Reference

ASK SOME OPENING QUESTIONS

As soon as you have both completed the necessary pleasant chit-chat, be prepared to ask a few light questions to get the interview off in a useful direction. This can happen within a minute of your first greeting, but is more likely to take up to five minutes. Some of the transitional questions that follow could be used in a traditional interview setting, while others assume that you are interviewing before a job is actually open.

Some Questions to Ask Early in an Interview

▲ "How did you get started in this type of career (or business, or whatever)?"

"I'd like to know more about what your organization does. Would you mind telling me?"

"I have a background in _____ and am interested in how I might fit into an organization such as yours."

"I have three years' experience plus two years' of training in the field of _____. I am actively looking for a job and, although I know you probably do not have openings now, I would be interested in future openings. Perhaps if I told you a few things about myself, you could give me an idea of whether you would be interested in me."

▲ Some questions are more assertive than others, but a busy employer will prefer this over a "Gee, I'm not really sure why I'm here" approach. Whatever questions you ask, the objective is to make a smooth transition from the opening moments to the heart of the interview where you present your skills and are evaluated as a person.

PHASE 3: THE INTERVIEW ITSELF

If you have created a reasonably positive image of yourself so far, an interviewer will now be interested in the specifics of why they should consider hiring you. This back-and-forth conversation usually lasts from 15 to 45 minutes and many consider it to be the most important—and most difficult—task in the entire job search.

Fortunately, by reading this book, you will have several advantages over the average job seeker:

1. You know what sort of job you want.

2. You know what skills are required to do well in that job.

3. You have those very skills.

The only thing that remains to be done is to communicate these three things. This is best done by directly and completely answering the questions an employer will ask you.

"Employers will try to uncover problems or limitations you might bring to their job.**"**

HANDLING PROBLEM INTERVIEW QUESTIONS

According to employers in the Northwestern University's Endicott Survey, about 80 percent of all job seekers cannot provide a good answer to one or more problem interview questions.

All employers will try to uncover problems or limitations you might bring to their job. Everyone has a problem of some sort and the employer will try to find yours. Expect it. Let's say, for example, that you have been out of work for three months. That could be seen as a problem, unless you can provide a good reason for it.

MEET AN EMPLOYER'S EXPECTATIONS

Your task in the interview is to understand what an employer is looking for. Research indicates that most employers will react to three issues during the interview. If any of these "employer's expectations" are not met, it is unlikely that you will get a job offer. They are:

The Three Major Employer Expectations

▲ **1. Appearance**—Do you look like the type of person who will succeed on the job?

▲ **2. Dependability**—Can you be depended upon to be reliable and to do a good job for a reasonable length of time?

▲ **3. Credentials**—Do you have the necessary training, experience, skills, and credentials to do the job well?

Quick Fact

Most problem questions have to do with either the second or third expectations.

View every interview question as an opportunity to support your ability to do the job. Your interview will be short, so you must make the most of it. Each question provides a chance to present the skills you have that are needed by the employer. Remember that the interviewer is a person just like you. You must be honest and be able to support, with proof, anything you say about yourself. If you have carefully selected your job objective and know your own skills, you will find it easy to present reasons why the employer should hire you.

You should also be prepared to ask some questions early on. Some interviewers are happy to discuss details of the position you seek. If possible, find out as much as you can about the position early in the interview. Ask about the type of person they are looking for to fill this position, what sort of people have done well in those jobs before, or what sorts of responsibilities the job requires. Once you know more about what the interviewer is looking for, you can "fit" your later responses to what you now know the company wants.

Let's say you've found out that the position requires someone who is good at meeting people and who is organized. Assuming you have those skills, you could later emphasize how good you are at meeting people. The examples you use to support this skill could also provide evidence of how organized you are.

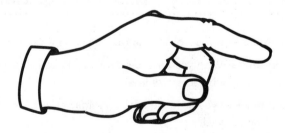

Quick Tip

The Three-Step Process is used in the next chapter to develop answers to 10 frequently asked interview questions. Knowing how to answer these ten key questions will allow you to handle most interviews well—and will teach you how to apply the technique to most other questions. Guidance for answering more specific problem interview questions—such as those related to age and experience—is provided in chapter 15. As you practice using the Three-Step Process, it becomes easier to provide a good response to almost any interview question that is asked.

THE THREE STEPS TO ANSWERING PROBLEM QUESTIONS

There are thousands of questions that could be asked of you in an interview. There is no way you can memorize a "correct" response for each possible question. Interviews just aren't like that. They are often conversational and informal. The unexpected often happens. For these reasons, it is far more important to develop an *approach* to answering an interview question rather than memorizing a "correct" response for each.

I have developed a technique that you can use to fashion an effective answer to most interview questions. To make it easy, I have given the technique a name—The Three-Step Process for Answering Interview Questions.

The Three-Step Process for Answering Interview Questions

▲ **Step #1: Understand What Is Really Being Asked**

Most questions relate to Employer Expectation #2 regarding your adaptive skills and personality. This includes such questions as: Can we depend on you? Are you easy to get along with? Are you a good worker? The question may also relate to Employer Expectation #3, namely, do you have the experience and training to do the job if we hire you?

▲ **Step #2: Answer the Question Briefly, in a Nondamaging Way**

A good response to a question should acknowledge the facts and present them as an advantage, not a disadvantage.

▲ **Step #3: Answer the Real Question by Presenting Your Related Skills**

Once you understand the employer's real concern, you can answer the often hidden question by presenting the skills you have that relate to the job.

AN EXAMPLE OF AN ANSWER USING THE THREE-STEP PROCESS

EXAMPLE PROBLEM QUESTION

> *"We were looking for someone with more experience in this field. Why should we consider you over others with better credentials?"*

Here's how one person might construct an answer to this question, using the Three-Step Process.

Quick Reference

STEP 1: UNDERSTAND WHAT IS REALLY BEING ASKED

The question above is often asked in a less direct way, but it is a frequent concern of employers. To answer it, you must remember that employers often hire people who present themselves well in an interview over those with better credentials. Your best shot is to emphasize whatever personal strengths you have that could offer an advantage to an employer. The person wants to know whether you have anything going for you that can help you overcome a more experienced worker.

Well, **do** you? Are you a hard worker? Do you learn fast? Have you had intensive training or hands-on experience? Do you have skills from other activities that can transfer to this job? Knowing in advance what skills you have to offer is essential to answering this question.

Quick Tip

Lots of people have problems coming up with reasons why someone should consider them over someone else. That is one reason why I have included so many self-exploration activities in Section 2 of this book. While you may be tempted to avoid that section, the payoff comes in your ability to respond more effectively in an interview. You should also gain insight into just what sorts of things you would most enjoy doing.

STEP 2: ANSWER THE QUESTION BRIEFLY, IN A NONDAMAGING WAY

Here is an example of how one person might answer the question without damage:

"I'm sure there are people who have more years of experience or better credentials. I do, however, have four years of combined training and hands-on experience using the latest methods and techniques. Because my training is recent, I am open to new ideas and have gotten used to working hard and learning quickly."

STEP 3: ANSWER THE REAL QUESTION BY PRESENTING YOUR RELATED SKILLS

While the above response answers the question in an appropriate—and brief—way, it might continue with additional details that emphasize key skills needed for the job:

"As you know, I held down a full-time job and family responsibilities while going to school. During those two years, I had an excellent attendance record both at work and school, missing only one day in two years. I also received two merit increases in salary and my grades were in the top 25 percent of my class. In order to do all this, I had to learn to organize my time and set priorities. I worked hard to prepare myself in this new career area and am willing to keep working to establish myself. The position you have available is what I am prepared to do. I am willing to work harder than the next person because I have the desire to keep learning and to do a good job. With my education complete, I can now turn my full attention to this job."

This response presents the skills necessary to do well in any job. This job seeker sounds dependable, which meets Employer Expectation #2. And he gave examples of situations where he had used the required skills in other settings, thus meeting Employer Expectation #3. It was a good response.

Just to remind you, here are the three major employers' expectations presented earlier in this chapter:

1. **Appearance**—Do you look like the type of person who will succeed on the job?

2. **Dependability**—Can you be depended on to be reliable and to do a good job for a reasonable length of time?

3. **Credentials**—Do you have the necessary training, experience, skills, and credentials to indicate that you are able to do the job well?

QUESTIONS YOU MIGHT ASK THE INTERVIEWER

Even if you don't ask any questions during an interview, many employers will ask you if you have any. How you respond will affect their evaluation of you. So be prepared to ask insightful questions about the organization.

Good topics to touch on include:

✔ the competitive environment in which the organization operates

✔ executive management styles

✔ what obstacles the organization anticipates in meeting its goals

✔ how the organization's goals have changed over the past three to five years

Generally, it is most unwise to ask about pay or benefits or other similar areas. The reason is that it tends to make you seem more interested in what the organization can do for you. It is also not a good idea to simply have no questions at all. Doing so makes you appear passive rather than curious and interested.

PHASE 4: CLOSING THE INTERVIEW

There are a few things to remember as the interview is coming to an end. Let's review them briefly.

Quick Tip

From "America Online's Career Center," hosted by Jim Gonyea,

Q: I've been on several interviews lately, and invariably the interviewer invites me to ask questions about the position or the company. What kinds of questions would be most appropriate to show genuine interest? I know what not to ask, e.g. "How much am I gonna make at this place?" Still, I think it is possible that I have done less than my best in this regard.

A: I would ask the following questions:

1. *What are the main objectives and responsibilities of the position?*

2. *How does the company expect these objectives to be met?*

3. *What obstacles are commonly encountered in reaching these objectives?*

4. *What is the desired time frame for reaching the objectives?*

5. *What resources are available from the company and what must be found elsewhere to reach the objectives?*

Don't let the interview last too long. Most interviews last 30 to 60 minutes. Unless the employer asks otherwise, plan on staying no longer than an hour. Watch for hints from the interviewer, such as looking at a watch or rustling papers, that indicate he or she is ready to end the interview. Exceptions to the 1-hour rule should be made only at the interviewer's request.

Summarize the key points of the interview. Use your judgment here and keep it short! Review the major issues that came up in the interview. This is an optional step and can be skipped if time is short.

If a problem came up, repeat your resolution of it. Whatever you think that particular interviewer may see as a reason not to hire you, bring it up again and present your reasons why you don't see it as a problem. If you are not sure, be direct and ask, "Is there anything about me that concerns you or might keep you from hiring me?" Whatever comes up, do as well as you can in responding to it.

Review your strengths for this job. This is another chance for you to present the skills you possess that relate to this particular job. Emphasize your key strengths only, and keep it brief.

Use the "Call-Back Close." This is an approach that is quite strong. You may not be comfortable with it at first but role-play and practice in your early interviews will help you get more comfortable. The Call-Back Close does work, and it works as follows:

The Call-Back Close

▲ **1. Thank the interviewer by name.** While shaking hands, say: "Thank-you (Mr. or Mrs. or Ms.) _____ for your time today."

▲ **2. Express Interest.** Depending on the situation, express your interest in the job, organization, service, product, person ...

"I'm very interested in the ideas we went over today."

"I'm very interested in your organization. It seems to be an exciting place to work."

"I enjoyed the visit with you and am impressed by all you have accomplished."

or, if a job opening exists and you want it, definitely say,

"I am definitely interested in this position."

▲ **3. Mention your busy schedule.** Say "I'm busy for the next week, but..."

▲ **4. Arrange a reason and a time to call back.** Your objective is to leave a reason for you to get back in touch and to arrange for a specific day and time to do so. For example, say "I'm sure I'll have questions. When would be the best time for me to get back in touch with you?"

Notice that I said "When can I...?" rather than "Is it OK to...?" The first way does not easily allow a "no" response. Get a specific day ("Monday") and a best time to call ("between 9:00 and 10:00 A.M.").

▲ **5. Say "thank-you" and "goodbye."**

PHASE 5: FOLLOWING UP

The interview has ended, you made it home, and now it's all over, right? Not right. You need to follow up. As I've said throughout this book, following up can make the difference between being unemployed and getting a good job fast. Here is what you should do when you get home.

Make notes on the interview. While it is fresh in your mind, jot down key points. A week later, you may not remember something essential.

Schedule your follow up. If you agreed to call back next Monday between 9:00 and 10:00 A.M., you are likely to forget unless you put it on your schedule.

Tips for developing a system for following up will be covered in chapter 6. More details on thank-you notes are also found in that chapter.

Send your thank-you note. Send the note the very same day if possible.

Call when you said you would! If you call when you said you would, you will create the impression of being organized and wanting the job. If you do have a specific question, ask it. If a job opening exists and you do want it, say that you want it and why. If no job opening exists, just say you enjoyed the visit and would like to stay in touch during your job search. This would also be a good time to ask, if you had not done it before, for the names of anyone else with whom you might speak about a position for a person with your skills and experience.

Schedule more follow up. The last thing to do is to schedule the next time you want to follow up with this person.

PHASE 6: NEGOTIATING

Sending thank-you notes and following up are very important steps, though they are often overlooked in the job search literature. Do send thank-you notes. They are covered in chapter 6 and they are very important. Additional follow-up techniques are also covered in that chapter as well as in other sections of this book.

Once a job offer is made, negotiations can be as simple as saying "When can I start?" However, there is far more you should know about negotiating a job offer. Additional details on negotiating salary are provided in chapter 5 and other details in chapters 18 and 19. Here are a few essential tips to remember.

1. **The time to negotiate is after you've been offered the job.** Do not discuss your preferred salary or an other negotiable subject in an interview until after a job offer has clearly been made. Many, many job seekers have been eliminated from consideration over this very issue.

2. **Don't say "no" too quickly.** NEVER, EVER turn down a job offer in an interview! Even if you are certain that you won't accept the job because, say, it pays too little, always ask to consider it overnight. You can always say no tomorrow. If your decision to refuse the job as offered remains firm, you can always suggest (tomorrow) that you appreciate the offer but ask that they consider you for other opportunities, give you higher wages, or whatever. This is no time to be playing games, but many people have turned down one job only to be offered a better one later simply because the employer had time to think about things.

3. **Don't say "yes" too quickly either.** As with saying "no" too quickly, take time to think about accepting a job too. If you do want it, do not jeopardize obtaining it with unreasonable demands. Ask for 24 hours to consider your decision and, when calling back, consider negotiating for something reasonable. A bit more money, perhaps—or the promise of a salary review after 90 days. But make it clear that you do want the job in any case and don't be difficult. If you want the job, say so—and don't quibble over things that are not important to you.

PHASE 7: MAKING A FINAL DECISION

Quick Fact

It is rare to find the perfect job. There are usually compromises to be made. But, too often, a job is accepted without thorough knowledge of just what it would be like to actually work there. At the time, it seems to be a good idea. Unfortunately, what seemed good at first doesn't always turn out that way later. The major problem is that many people never make a careful decision at all. They don't take the time to weigh the pros and the cons of their decision. One job leads to another and careers develop by accident. There is an alternative.

In a book entitled *Decision Making*, Irving Janis and Leon Mann present research and theory on the process—and consequences—of making important decisions. They found that various groups who used this process were more likely to stick to their decision and have fewer regrets afterwards then those who did not. To make any important decision they suggest that you consider the alternatives in a systematic way.

You can easily adapt their decision-making process for use in making career decisions. Let's say that you are considering a job offer, but it requires you to move—something you would rather not do. They suggest that you create a simple form with four boxes, like this:

	Pros	Cons
For Me		
For Others		

Simply writing in the pros and cons for yourself and for others (if this is an issue for you) will help you make a good decision. It's that simple.

5

ANSWERS TO 10 KEY INTERVIEW QUESTIONS—AND A TECHNIQUE TO ANSWER HUNDREDS MORE

Quick Tip

In the previous chapter you learned how to handle each of the seven phases of an interview. This chapter builds upon that knowledge by providing specific techniques and examples for answering problem interview questions. This is a very important issue since, according to one survey of employers, 80 percent of the job seekers they interviewed were unable to adequately answer at least one interview question. And it is clear that if you leave the interviewer with a negative or uncertain impression of your ability or interest in doing the job, you won't get a job offer.

THE 10 MOST FREQUENTLY ASKED INTERVIEW QUESTIONS

Knowing and practicing answers to a relatively small but important cluster of difficult questions will prepare you to answer many others. Some questions are asked more than others. Others are seldom asked directly but are the *basis* for other questions. For example, a conversational question about your family relationships may really be an attempt to discover whether or not you will be a reliable worker.

From the thousands of questions that *could* be asked, I have constructed 10 questions that represent the types of issues that concern most employers. The following list of questions is partly based on questions employers actually ask, and partly on my sense of which questions provide the best patterns for teaching you the principles of constructing good overall responses.

The 10 Most Frequently Asked Interview Questions

▲ **1.** Why don't you tell me about yourself?

▲ **2.** Why should I hire you?

▲ **3.** What are your major strengths?

▲ **4.** What are your major weaknesses?

▲ **5.** What sort of pay do you expect to receive?

▲ **6.** How does your previous experience relate to the jobs we have here?

▲ **7.** What are your plans for the future?

▲ **8.** What will your former employers (or teachers, if you are a recent student) say about you?

▲ **9.** Why are you looking for this sort of position and why here?

▲ **10.** Why don't you tell me about your personal situation?

"It is important to learn a strategy for answering an interview question."

REMEMBER THE THREE-STEP PROCESS TO ANSWERING INTERVIEW QUESTIONS

Recall that in the last chapter, I discussed the Three-Step Process for answering interview questions. Because each of you is different—and each interview is different—there can be no one correct way to answer an interview question. For this reason, it is important for you to learn a *strategy* for answering any interview question. One important strategy presented in the previous chapter is the Three-Step Process reviewed below.

Review of The Three-Step Process for Answering Interview Questions

▲ **Step #1: Understand What Is Really Being Asked.**

It usually relates to Employer Expectation #2, regarding your adaptive skills and personality: Can we depend on you? Are you easy to get along with? Are you a good worker?

▲ **Step #2: Answer the Question Briefly, in a Nondamaging Way.**

Acknowledge the facts, and present them as an advantage, not a disadvantage.

▲ **Step #3: Answer the Real Question by Presenting Your Related Skills.**

Once you understand the employer's real concern, you can get around to answering the often hidden question by presenting your skills and experiences related to the job.

Quick Reference

The Three-Step Process is important for understanding that the interview question being asked often is looking for underlying information. The technique that follows will help you provide that information in an effective way.

THE "PROVE IT" TECHNIQUE

In the third step of the Three-Step Process you are to provide an answer to the real question being asked. In doing so I have found it important to structure your response to include the following elements:

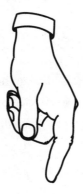

THE "PROVE IT" TECHNIQUE

1. **Present a Concrete Example:** People relate to and remember stories. Saying you have a skill is not nearly as powerful as describing a situation where you used that skill. The story should include enough details to make sense of the who, what, where, when, and why.

2. **Quantify:** Whenever possible, numbers should be used to provide a basis for what was done. For example, give the number of customers served or the amount of cash handled.

3. **Emphasize Results:** It is important to provide some data regarding the positive results you obtained. For example, sales increased by 3 percent over the previous year or profits went up 50 percent. Use numbers to quantify your results.

4. **Link It Up:** While the connection between your story and doing the job well may seem obvious to you, make sure it is clear to the employer. A simple statement is often enough to accomplish this.

   If you do a thorough job in completing the activities in Section 2 of this book, it should be fairly easy to provide proof to support the skills you discuss in an interview. This technique is the basic interview strategy to use. I will refer to it in sections that follow and it is most important that you remember the basic steps.

ANSWERS TO THE TOP 10 PROBLEM INTERVIEW QUESTIONS

In this section, I will use the Three-Step Process and "Prove It" techniques to create sample answers to the 10 problem questions listed earlier in this chapter. For each question, I will provide an analysis of what the question is really asking followed by a strategy for answering it. I will also provide one or more sample responses. In each case I will use the Three-Step Process, including the "Prove It" approach for constructing a response.

While your answers will differ from the sample answers provided, you will learn how to use the basic techniques and apply them to your own situation.

QUESTION 1:	■ "Why don't you tell me about yourself?"

ANALYSIS:

This is an open-ended question. You could start anywhere, but telling your life's history in two hours or less is *not* what is really being asked. Instead, such a question is a test of your ability to select what is important and communicate it clearly and quickly. Obviously, the questioner expects you to relate your background to the position being considered.

STRATEGY:

There are several basic approaches that could be used. One would be to go ahead and provide a brief response to the question as it is asked and the other is to request a clarification of the question before answering it. In both cases, you would quickly turn your response to focus on your skills, experience, and training that prepared you for the sort of job you now want.

EXAMPLE 1:

If you answered the question as it was asked you might say something like this:

"I grew up in the Southwest and have one brother and one sister. My parents both worked and I had a happy childhood. I always did well in school and by the time I graduated from high school I had taken a year's worth of business courses. I knew then that I wanted to work in a business setting and had several part-time office jobs while still in high school. After high school I worked in a variety of business settings and learned a great deal about how various businesses run. For example, I was given complete responsibility for the daily operations of a wholesale

distribution company that grossed over two million dollars a year. That was only three years after I graduated from high school. There I learned to supervise other people and solve problems under pressure. I also got more interested in the financial end of running a business and decided, after three years and three promotions, to go after a position where I could have more involvement in key strategies and long-term management decisions."

COMMENTS:

Notice how this job seeker provided a few bits of personal history, then quickly turned the interviewer's attention to skills and experiences directly related to the job now sought.

You could ask the interviewer to help you narrow down things he or she really wants to know with a response such as this:

EXAMPLE 2:

"There's so much to tell! Would you like me to emphasize my personal history, the special training and education I have that prepared me for this sort of position, or the skills and job-related experiences I have to support my objective?"

COMMENTS:

If you do this well, most employers will tell you what sorts of things they are most interested in and you can then concentrate on giving them what they want.

Quick Tip

Honesty is always the best policy, but that old adage doesn't rule out marketing yourself in the best light during an interview. As James Huntington-Meath, owner of Career Directions, a private guidance agency in Chapel Hill, N.C., puts it, "I am always going to counsel individuals to be positive about themselves. I don't think it's unethical to coach people in that direction, either." So stay away from taking credit for something you don't deserve, claiming to have experience you don't have, or bragging about a poor performance. But feel free to talk up your achievements, awards, and promotions with no fear of misrepresenting yourself.

| QUESTION 2: | ■ "Why should I hire you?" |

ANALYSIS:

This is a direct and fair question. Though it is rarely asked this clearly, it is *the* question behind any other question that will be asked. It has no hidden meaning.

STRATEGY:

A direct question deserves a direct response. Why *should* they hire you? The best response provides advantages to them, not to you. This often involves providing proof that you can help them make more money by improving efficiency, reducing costs, increasing sales, or solving problems (by coming to work on time, improving customer services, organizing one or more operations, or a variety of other things).

EXAMPLE:

Here is an example of a response from a person with considerable prior experience:

"You should hire me because I don't need to be trained and have a proven track record. I have over 15 years of education and experience related to this position. Over 6 of those years have been in management positions similar to the one available here. In my last position, I was promoted three times in the 6 years I was there. I most recently had responsibility for supervising a staff of 15 and a warehousing operation that processed over 30 million dollars worth of materials a year. In the last 2 years, I managed a 40 percent increase in volume processed with only a 6 percent increase in expenses. I am hard-working and have earned a reputation as a dependable and creative problem solver. The opportunities here excite me. My substantial experience will help me know how to approach the similar situations here. I am also willing to ask questions and accept advice from others. This will be an important factor in taking advantage of what has already been accomplished here."

COMMENTS:
....

This job seeker's response emphasized the "Prove It" technique. While she presented her skills and experience in a direct and confident way, she avoided a know-it-all attitude by being open to others' suggestions.

Quick Tip

Completing this brief activity might be quite a challenge unless you have first completed the activities in Section 2 of this book. If you do find it difficult to clearly identify why someone should hire you, you'll need to consult Section 2.

The Reasons Why Someone Should Hire You

In the spaces below, list the major advantages you offer an employer in hiring you over someone else. Emphasize your strengths. These could be personality traits, transferable skills, special training, prior experience, or anything else you think is important. These are the things to emphasize in your interview.

1. _____

   _____

   _____

2. _____

   _____

   _____

3. _____

   _____

   _____

QUESTION 3:	■ "What are your major strengths?"

ANALYSIS:

Like the previous question, this one is quite direct and has little hidden meaning.

STRATEGY:

Your response should first emphasize your adaptive or self-management skills. The decision to hire you is very much based on these skills and you can deal with the details of your specific job-related skills later. Remember that here, as elsewhere, your response must be brief.

Quick Tip

Chapter 6 provides details on the JIST Card. Once you have done a JIST Card of your own, it lists the key skills to emphasize in your response to this question.

EXAMPLE :

Here is a response from a person who has little prior work experience related to the job he now seeks:

"One of my major strengths is my ability to work hard towards a goal. Once I decide to do something, it will probably get done. For example, I graduated from high school four years ago. Many of my friends started working and others went on to school. At the time I didn't know what I wanted to do, so furthering my education at that point did not make sense. The jobs I could get at the time didn't excite me either, so I looked into joining the Navy. I took the test and discovered a few things about myself that surprised me. For one thing, I was much better at understanding complex problems than my grades in high school would suggest. I signed up for a three-year hitch that included intensive training in electronics. I worked hard and graduated in the top 20 percent of my class. I was then assigned to monitor, diagnose, and repair an advanced

electronics system that was worth about 20 million dollars. I was promoted several times to the position of Petty Officer and received an honorable discharge after my tour of duty. I now know what I want to do and am prepared to spend extra time learning whatever is needed to do well here."

COMMENTS:

Once you begin speaking about one of your strengths, the rest of your response often falls into place naturally. Remember to provide some proof of your skills, as this response did. It makes a difference.

QUESTION 4:

■ **"What Are Your Major Weaknesses?"**

ANALYSIS:

This is a trick question. If you answer the question as it is asked, you could easily damage your chances of getting the job. By trying to throw you off guard, the employer can see how you might react in similar tough situations on the job. I have often asked this question to groups of job seekers and usually get one of two types of responses. The first goes like this:

"I really don't have any major weaknesses."

That response is obviously untrue and evasive. The other type of response I usually get is an honest one like this:

"Well, I am really disorganized. I suppose I should do better at that, but my life has just been too hectic, what with the bankruptcy and embezzlement charges and all."

While this type of response might get an "A" for honesty, it gets an "F" for interview technique.

STRATEGY:

What's needed here is an honest, undamaging response followed by a brief, positive presentation to counter the negative.

EXAMPLE 1:

"Well, I have been accused by co-workers of being too involved in my work. I usually come in a little early to organize my day and stay late to get a project done on time."

EXAMPLE 2:

"I need to learn to be more patient. I often do things myself just because I know I can do them faster and better than someone else. This trait has not let me be as good at delegating tasks as I want to be. But I am working on it. I'm now spending more time showing others how to do the things I want done and that has helped. They often do better than I expected if I am clear enough about explaining what I want done—and how."

COMMENTS:

These responses could both be expanded with some "Prove It" content but they successfully use the three basic steps in answering a problem question as outlined earlier in this chapter.

QUESTION 5:

■ **"What sort of pay do you expect to receive?"**

ANALYSIS:

If you are unprepared for this question, it is highly probable that any response will damage your ability to get a job offer. The employer wants you to name a number which can then be compared to a figure the company has in mind. For example, suppose that the employer is looking to pay someone $25,000 a year. If you say you were hoping for $30,000, you will probably be eliminated from consideration. They will be afraid that, if you took the job, you may not stay. If you say you would take $20,000 one of two things could happen:

ANALYSIS:

1. You could get hired at $20,000 a year, making that response the most expensive two seconds in your entire life or,

2. The employer may keep looking for someone else, since you must only be worth $20,000 and they were looking for someone, well, worth more.

This question is designed to help the employer either eliminate you from consideration or save money at your expense. You could get lucky and name the salary the company had in mind but the stakes are too high to recommend that approach. Which brings me to the most important salary negotiation rule …

FARR'S SALARY NEGOTIATION RULE 1

Never talk money until after they decide they want you.

STRATEGY:

Your objective in an initial interview is to create a positive impression. It is unlikely you will get a firm job offer in a first interview. If salary comes up, avoid getting nailed down. Here are some things you could say:

EXAMPLE:

"Are you making me a job offer?" (A bit corny, yes, but you just might be surprised at the result) or,

"What salary range do you pay for positions with similar requirements?" or,

"I'm very interested in the position and my salary would be negotiable" or,

"Tell me what you have in mind for the salary range."

Quick Tip

"Employers are anxious to know how your joining the organization will impact their bottom line, and they'll try to get to the subject as soon as possible," says Doug Matthews, managing director of Right Associates' Cincinnati office—an executive outplacement firm.

Salary issues are the main reasons candidates are knocked out of the running during screening interviews and informational meetings, according to outplacement industry surveys. In fact, responding appropriately to salary questions can get you past screening interviewers, who rarely have authority to negotiate salaries, and in front of decision-makers with whom the real negotiations take place.

So, always be coy and defer the question as many times as you have to until you are sure it's the real thing and not just part of a screening process. Then, when the timing is right, maneuver the interviewer into naming the starting point. Remember the most important rule: He who speaks first loses.

ANALYSIS:

In most situations, these responses will either get the employer to name a salary range, or put the subject to rest until the proper time. But let's suppose you run into a clever, demanding interviewer who insists you disclose your salary expectations before telling you what he or she is willing to pay. Here is what I suggest:

FARR'S SALARY NEGOTIATION RULE 2

Know, in advance, the probable salary range for similar jobs in similar organizations.

STRATEGY:

To find out comparable salary ranges, phone around and ask questions. Those in the business will know what similar jobs in your area are paying. The trick here is to think in terms of a *wide range* in salary.

Quick Tip

I have developed a list of about 250 jobs and the salary ranges you can expect for each. Look for it in chapter 19 of this book. These jobs cover about 85 percent of the workforce and the list will give you a good place to start in finding out what pay to expect for various jobs.

EXAMPLE:

Let's say that in the previous example you figure the employer's range to be somewhere between $22,000 and $27,000. That is a wide range, but you could then say: "I was looking for a salary in the mid to upper twenties."

That covers a lot of territory! It would include from $22,000 to $29,000 a year or so. You can use the same strategy for any salary bracket you may be considering. For example, if you wanted $28,000 a year and their range might be $25,000 to $33,000, you could say "A salary in the mid-twenties to low-thirties." This technique is called "bracketing" and is the third salary negotiation rule:

FARR'S SALARY NEGOTIATION RULE 3

Always bracket your stated salary range to begin within their probable salary range and end a bit above what you expect to settle for.

If you are offered the job, you are likely to get offered more than they (or you) may have originally been willing to consider. Which brings me to the last rule:

FARR'S SALARY NEGOTIATION RULE 4

Never say no to a job (or salary) offer either before it is made or within 24 hours afterwards.

ANALYSIS:

Perhaps you think it impossible to say no before an offer is made but I have seen it done many times. In a first interview, let's say that salary does come up. If you were hoping to get a minimum salary of $25,000 a year and the interviewer mentions that he is hoping to pay $23,000, you just might show some disappointment. You might even say something like, "Oh no, I couldn't consider that!" and if you did, that would be the end. Before you were even offered the job, you turned it down.

But suppose that particular job turned out to be (if you had only hung around to find out more) the perfect job for you in all respects except the salary. You may have been delighted to take it. Suppose also that the employer (if only it had gotten to know the delightful person you are) found you to be the kind of person to hire even if it took a few extra dollars—say $2,000—to get you. In either case, you would strike a bargain.

For this reason, NEVER give a hint that the salary mentioned is not acceptable to you. You might say, instead,

> *"That is somewhat lower than I had hoped but this*
> *position does sound very interesting. If I were to*
> *consider this, what sorts of things could I do to*
> *quickly become more valuable to this organization?"*

STRATEGY:

Remember that a discussion of salary is not necessarily a job offer. Do not let an employer eliminate you from consideration unless and until you get a firm job offer. If you are not sure ask "Is this a job offer?" If it is, and if the pay they offer is low, say something like,

EXAMPLE:

> *"Thank you for the offer. The position is very much what I*
> *wanted in many ways and I am delighted at your interest.*
> *This is an important decision for me and I would like some*
> *time to consider your offer."*

EXAMPLE:

Even if their offer is an insult, do not break their office furniture and stamp out. Be nice (any job offer is good for your ego when you get to turn it down). At worst, you can call them tomorrow and say:

"I am flattered by your job offer but feel that it would not be fair of me to accept. The salary is lower than I would like and that is the one reason I cannot accept it. Perhaps you could reconsider your offer or keep me in mind for future openings that might allow me to be worth more to you?"

COMMENTS :

Even as you say no, leave the door open for negotiation. If the employer wants you, it may be willing to meet your terms. It happens more than you might imagine.

Do not use this example as a technique to get a higher wage. Understand that once you say no to their offer, the deal is off. You must be willing to lose that job forever.

QUESTION 6:

■ **"How does your previous experience relate to the jobs we have here?"**

ANALYSIS:

This is another direct question that requires a direct response. It relates to Employer Expectation #3 (credentials) and your response will be very important if you have created a good impression up to this point. This question does require you to overcome any weaknesses your background might present when you are compared to other job seekers.

Here are some common typical stumbling blocks: You are just out of school and have limited experience in this career; this is your first job or you have not worked for a period of time; your prior work experience was not the same as the tasks required in this job; your previous level of responsibility was lower or higher than this job; you have had lots of jobs but no clear career direction; you do not have the educational or other credentials many other applicants might have.

STRATEGY:

Lead with your strengths. If it is obvious that other job seekers might have more education, more years of experience, or whatever, acknowledge that, then present your strengths. Use the standard Three-Step Approach to answering a problem question. And, again, your JIST Card often will provide a starting point.

EXAMPLE 1:

"As you know, I have just completed an intensive program in the area of computer programming (or whatever). In addition, I have over three years' work experience in a variety of business settings. That work experience included managing a small business during the absence of the owner. I learned to handle money there and a variety of basic bookkeeping tasks. I also inventoried and organized products worth over three hundred thousand dollars. These experiences helped me understand the consequences of computer programming in a business setting. While I am new to the career of programming, I am familiar with computer language. My educational experience was very thorough and I have over 300 hours of interactive computer time as part of my course work. Because I am new, I plan to work harder and will spend extra time as needed to meet any deadlines."

COMMENTS:

This response emphasizes transferable skills (knowledge of accounting procedures) and adaptive skills (meeting deadlines and working hard). This is necessary to counter a lack of previous work experience as a programmer. In this situation, what was learned in school is also very important and should be emphasized as the equivalent of "real" work.

EXAMPLE 2:

"In my previous position I used many of the same skills needed to do this job well. Even though it was in a different industry, managing a business requires the types of organizational and supervisory skills that I possess. Over the past seven years I guided my region to become one of the most profitable in our company. Sales expanded an average of 30 percent per year during the years I worked there, and profits rose at a similar rate. Since this was a mature company, such performance was highly unusual. I received two promotions during those seven years and rose to the executive level at a pace, I was later told, no one had previously achieved. I am now seeking a challenge in a smaller, growth-oriented company such as yours. I feel my experience and contacts have prepared me for this step in my career."

COMMENTS :

This response acknowledges that the previous career field differed from the one now being considered, but emphasizes achievements and prior success. To accomplish this, all sorts of executive skills would have had to be used. The response also includes the motivation to move on to the challenge of a smaller organization.

QUESTION 7:

■ **"What are your plans for the future?"**

ANALYSIS :

This question really explores your motives for working. It is asking whether you can be depended on to stay on at this job and work hard at it.

STRATEGY:

As always, your best approach is an honest one. I'm not encouraging you to reveal negative information, but you should be prepared to answer the employer's concern in a direct and positive way. Which issues are of concern to an employer will depend on the details of your background.

For example:

Will you be happy with the salary? (If not, might you leave?)

Will you want to have a family? (If so, will you quit to raise children?)

Do you have a history of leaving jobs after a short period of time? (If so, why won't you leave this one too?)

Have you just moved to the area and appear to be a temporary or transient resident? (If so, you probably won't stay here long either, right?)

Are you overqualified? (If so, what will keep you from going to a better job as soon as you find one?)

Do you have the energy and commitment to advance in this job? (If not, who needs someone without energy and drive?)

Might you appear to have some other reason to eventually become dissatisfied? (If so, the employer will certainly try to figure out what it is.)

Any of these reasons, and others, can be of concern to an employer. If your situation presents an obvious problem, use the standard Three-Step Approach to answering problem interview questions. If you feel you do not have any problem to defend, use steps #2 and #3 of the Three-Step Approach to assure the employer that, in effect, this is the precise organization you want to stay with and do well for—for at least the rest of your adult life.

EXAMPLE 1:

For a younger person or one just entering a new career:

"I realize I need to establish myself in this field and am very willing to get started. I've thought about what I want to do and am very sure my skills are the right ones to do well in this career. For example, I am good at dealing with people. In one position, I provided services to over 1,000 different people a week. During the 18 months I was there, I served well over 72,000 customers and not once did I get a formal complaint. In fact, I was often complimented on the attention I gave them. There I learned that I enjoy public contact and am delighted at the idea of this position for that reason. I want to learn more about the business and grow with it. As my contributions and value to the organization increase, I hope to be considered for more responsible positions."

COMMENTS:

The employer wants to know that you will stay on the job and work hard for your pay. This response helps the employer feel more comfortable with that concern. (Note that this response could be based on work experiences gained in a fast-food job!)

EXAMPLE 2:

For a person with work history gaps or various short-term jobs:

"I've had a number of jobs (or one, or have been unemployed) and I have learned to value a good, stable position. The variety of my experiences are an asset since I have learned so many things I can now apply to this position. I am looking for a position where I can settle in, work hard, and stay put."

COMMENTS:

This would be an acceptable response, except it is too short and no proof was offered. The ideal place to introduce a story would have been right before the last sentence. Some positions, such as sales-oriented ones, require you to be ambitious and perhaps aggressive. Other jobs have requirements particular to the career field or specific organization. You can't always predict what an employer might want, but you should have a good idea based on the work you will do in Section 2 of this book. If you do it correctly, you have what the position requires. You will simply need to say so.

| QUESTION 8: | ■ "What will your former employers (or teachers, references, warden, or keeper …) say about you?" |

ANALYSIS:

This question again refers to Employer Expectation #2. The employer wants to know about your adaptive skills—are you easy to get along with, are you a good worker, etc.? Your former employers may tell of any problems you had—or they may not. As you know, many employers will check your references before they hire you, so if anything you say here does not match what a former employer says, it could be bad news for you.

STRATEGY:

Be certain to discuss your job-search plans with former employers. Do the same with anyone else who may be contacted for a reference. Clearly tell them the type of job you now seek and why you are prepared to do well in it. If a previous employer may say something negative, discuss this openly with your former supervisor and find out what he or she will say in advance. If you were fired or resigned under pressure, you can often negotiate what would be said to a prospective employer. Lots of successful people have had personality conflicts with previous employers. If these conflicts are presented openly and in the best light possible, many interviewers are likely to understand. It may also be wise to get a written letter of reference, particularly from a not-too-enthusiastic employer. They will rarely be brave enough to write you a totally negative letter. And the letter may be enough to satisfy a potential employer. Larger organizations often don't allow phone references to be given, and this may be a great relief to you. Check it out by calling them and finding out.

If possible, use references that will say nice things about you. If your ex-boss won't, find someone who will. Often, an interviewer appreciates an honest response. If you failed in a job, telling the truth is sometimes the best policy. Tell it like it was but DO NOT be too critical of your old boss. Doing that will make you sound like a person who blames others and does not accept responsibility. Besides, you *were* partly at fault. Admit it, but quickly take the opportunity to say what you learned from the experience.

EXAMPLE:

"My three former employers will all say I work hard, am very reliable, and loyal. The reason I left my previous job, however, is the result of what I can only call a personality conflict. I was deeply upset by this, but decided that it was time I parted with my former employer. You can call and get a positive reference, but I thought it only fair to tell you. I still respect (that old hog). While there, I received several promotions and as my authority increased, there were more conflicts. Our styles were just not the same. I had no idea the problem was so serious because I was so involved in my work. That was my error and I have since learned to pay more attention to interpersonal matters."

COMMENTS:

This response could be strengthened by some introduction of positive skills along with a story to support them.

QUESTION 9:

■ **"Why are you looking for this sort of position and why here?"**

ANALYSIS:

The employer wants to know if you are the sort of person who is looking for any job, anywhere. If you are, she or he will not be impressed. Employers look for people who want to do what needs to be done. They rightly assume that such a person will work harder and be more productive than one who simply sees it as "just a job." People who have a good reason to seek a particular sort of position will be seen as more committed and more likely to stay on the job longer. The same is true for people who want to work in a particular organization.

STRATEGY:

It is most important that you know in advance which jobs are a good match for your skills and interests. Section 2 of this book will help you clarify and explain your assets. In responding to the question, mention your motivations for selecting this career objective, the special skills you have that the position requires, and any special training or credentials you have which relate to the position.

The question actually has two parts. The first is why this position, and the second is why here? If you have a reason for selecting the type of organization you are considering or have even selected this particular organization as highly desirable, be prepared to explain why. If at all possible, learn as much as you can about the organizations you interview with in advance. Call other people to get details, use the library, ask for an annual report, or whatever else it takes to become informed.

EXAMPLE:	*"I've spent a lot of time considering various careers and I think that this is the best area for me. The reason is that this career requires many of my strongest skills. For example, my abilities in analyzing and solving problems are two of the skills I enjoy most. In a previous position, I would often become aware of a problem no one had noticed and develop a solution. In one situation, I suggested a plan that resulted in reducing customer returns of leased equipment by 15 percent. That may not sound like much, but the result was an increase in retained leases of over $250,000 a year. The plan cost about $100 to implement. This particular organization seems to be the type that would let me develop my problem-solving skills. It is well run, growing rapidly, and open to new ideas. Your sales went up 30 percent last year and you are getting ready to introduce several major new products. If I work hard and prove my value here, I feel I would have the opportunity to stay with the business as it grows—and grow with it."*
COMMENTS:	This response uses "Prove It" nicely. It could have been said by an experienced manager or a good secretary.
QUESTION 10:	■ **"Why don't you tell me about your personal situation?"**
ANALYSIS:	A good interviewer will rarely ask this question so directly. Casual, friendly conversation will often provide the information sought. In most cases, the interviewer is digging for information that would indicate you are unstable or undependable. For instance:

THE ISSUE	THE REASON
Do you have marital or family troubles?	Missed work, poor performance, poor interpersonal skills
Do you handle money and personal responsibilities poorly?	Theft of property, irresponsible job-related decisions
Do you live in a good, stable home?	Socio-economic bias, renters less stable than owners
How do you use leisure time?	Drinking, socially unacceptable behavior
Do you have young children?	Days off and child care problems
Marital status?	If single, will you stay? If married, will you devote the necessary time?

STRATEGY:

There are other issues that may be of concern to an employer. Often, these are based on assumptions the person has about people with certain characteristics. These beliefs are often irrelevant, but if the employer wonders whether you can be depended upon, it is in your own best interest to deal with these doubts. Be aware that even your casual conversation should always avoid reference to a potential problem area. In responding to a question about your personal situation, be friendly but positive.

EXAMPLES:

Young children at home:

"I have two children, both in school. Child care is no problem since they stay with a good friend."

EXAMPLES:

Single head of household:

"I'm not married and have two children at home. It is very important to me to have a steady income and so child care is no problem."

Young and single:

"I'm not married and if I should marry, that would not change my plans for a full-time career. For now, I can devote my full attention to my career."

Just moved here:

"I've decided to settle here in Depression Gulch permanently. I've rented an apartment and the six moving vans are unloading there now."

Relatives, upbringing:

"I had a good childhood. Both of my parents still live within an hour's flight from here and I see them several times a year."

Leisure time:

"My time is family-centered when I'm not working. I'm also active in several community organizations and spend at least some time each week in church activities."

COMMENTS:

While all of these responses could be expanded, they should give you an idea of the sorts of approaches you can take with your own answers. The message you want to give is that your personal situation will not hurt your ability to work and, indeed, could help it. If your personal life does disrupt your work, expect most employers to lose patience quickly. It is not their problem, nor should it be.

HANDLING OBVIOUS AND NOT-SO-OBVIOUS "PROBLEMS"

Quick Fact

Most job seekers have at least one problem which they fear will cause an employer to respond negatively. Some of these are obvious, that is, they can be seen by an employer during an interview; others are not so obvious but are the sort of thing an employer might not be enthusiastic about. How you handle these or similar problems differs depending on the situation. Many employers will not react in the way you expect and will give you a fair chance. They will be interested in your ability to do the job you seek. Your task is to convince them that your problem will not be an issue. Here are some considerations:

Quick Tip

There are a variety of legal issues that regulate how an employer can make decisions in hiring one person over another. Check out Section 4 for more details on this topic. This section provides tips on answering questions related to a variety of specific problems that you may have.

Does the problem affect your ability to do the work you seek? If it is a serious limitation or safety hazard, you should consider this in your selection of a position and consider changing your objectives. This does not necessarily mean you need to change careers, but it does mean that you should look for a position where the limitation is not serious. For example, a person with a prison record should not seek a job as a bank teller. A person with seizures should not paint tall houses. A person with back problems should not dig ditches.

Avoid being screened out early.
Assuming your job objective is reasonable, but you still are concerned that you won't be seriously considered because of your problem, use job-search techniques that don't require you to reveal it too early.

Quick Fact

If the problem is obvious or comes up in the interview, deal with it.
Use the standard Three-Step Approach to Answering an Interview Question. If the problem is not obvious and won't seriously affect your ability to do the job, don't bring it up. Do not discuss your problem unless

---

Quick Case Study

Some time ago, I was helping a man who used a wheelchair to find a job. He wanted to work as a dispatcher. This position used his voice and his mind but not his legs, and was a good job objective for him. Yet employers were often unwilling to hire him. The wheelchair probably was an issue. I helped him learn to get interviews by using the phone rather than filling out applications. Employers had no idea he was in a wheelchair until he came for the interview. He was direct about the problem and said he got there for the interview and would do the same every day. He then presented his skills and abilities to do the job well. This approach forced the employer to focus on his ability to do the job rather than on the fact that he was in a wheelchair. He quickly got a job as a dispatcher and was still there three years later.

---

you fear you will eventually lose your job if it is found out. Wait until you have received or are negotiating a job offer. Too many job seekers reveal a problem on an application when they could have simply left the space blank. Too many bring up a problem that is not a problem at all in a preliminary interview ("I want you to know, madam, that a great aunt, once removed, had some odd habits.") Save your secret until after they like you and want to hire you.

SOME TOPICS THAT SHOULD NOT BE AN ISSUE— BUT SOMETIMES ARE

Quick Reference

Employers are people. They often want to know things about your personal situations that, perhaps, you think they have no right to know. Or perhaps you wonder whether an employer will treat you differently because of your status or some other factor that does not seem to affect your ability to do the job. For example, the following topics are sometimes an issue, even though they shouldn't be.

Age

Arrest record

Disabilities or limitations

Being unemployed

Being fired

Being overweight

Gender

Race or ethnicity

Religion

Your plans to have children

I review these and other issues in chapters 14 and 15, always trying to give you a productive way to deal with them. There are laws that are designed to protect you from being treated unfairly in the hiring process. You can learn more about these in chapter 14. But the more important issue is how you can overcome whatever obstacle may be put before you so that you can get the best job you can handle. That is what this book is really about.

SOME FINAL INTERVIEW TIPS

Quick Reference

You can't prepare for everything that might happen in an interview. But you will find that interviewing for jobs before they are advertised will be much easier and more comfortable than the traditional interview setting. But whatever interview you find yourself in, remember to be yourself and tell the employer why she or he should hire you.

You are now much better prepared to do well in the interview than most job seekers. And, if you read the rest of this book, you will be even better prepared ...

JOB SEEKING SKILLS—

YOU HAVE TO

GET INTERVIEWS

BEFORE YOU

CAN DO WELL

IN THEM

Introduction

This a short but very important section of this book because it presents the basics of how to go about looking for a job. Doing well in interviews only has value if you get interviews—and getting and doing well in interviews are the two most important elements of a successful job search.

Many books on interviewing do not do a good job of providing advice about how to *get* interviews. In fact, many such books provide bad advice. For example, they will often tell you that you need to send out lots of resumes and get them into stacks on some employers' desks. Then, if your resume and/or cover letter is good enough, they will pick yours out of the pile and ask you in for an interview. These types of job search books will encourage you to think of an interview in its traditional sense—an advertised opening that you are competing for with many others.

These are, in my opinion, old-fashioned notions of how to look for a job. These techniques put you at the mercy of some employer whose mindset is to screen people out. They encourage you to be passive and wait for the employer to call you. And, worst of all, they assume that the job search is limited to talking to employers who have a job opening now, and exclude all those who do not—but who might soon.

So, the traditional advice on interviewing and job seeking is (to put it kindly) not good. There are techniques that you can use that

are far more effective than the traditional ones. I've been working on these techniques for more than 20 years now, and the best tactics and techniques are common sense. They encourage you to be clear about what you want and then to actively go out and look for it. It does take some nerve, but the people who have used the techniques presented in here have proven that they do work. They tend to help you find better jobs in less time. And that is what it should be all about.

While this section is short, it does present the basic job search methods that I have developed and found to be most effective. If you try these methods, you can cut the amount of time it takes to find a job by quite a bit. In demonstration projects using these basic techniques, the time required to find a job has been cut in half or less than half. And, with the average length of unemployment often exceeding three months or more, this is not a trivial matter.

The material in this section is based on a job search booklet I wrote entitled *The Quick Job Search*. It is also published by JIST and I have adapted it for use here. If you are planning your career or need to know more about finding a job, I strongly encourage you to learn and do more. A book I wrote entitled *The Very Quick Job Search*, also published by JIST, covers the techniques in this section in much greater depth and provides lots of other information as well. It is available through most bookstores and libraries.

Chapters in This Section

There are only two chapters in this section but they provide enough information to give you a good start on your job search.

Chapter 6: How to Get a Good Job in Less Time

As I mentioned earlier, I originally wrote the material in this chapter as a small book. My concept was to present the essential information I felt was needed to get a better job and the techniques to do so in less time. While this book is on interviewing, getting a good job is what you are really after, and this chapter will give you the basics for doing that.

Chapter 7: Quick Resume Tips and Samples

This chapter presents information on doing a resume. As you know, there are many resume books out there but I think that what I have included in this chapter is enough for most situations. I suggest that you write a decent resume and get started on your job search without delay. Should you want more information on resumes, you might find the companion book to this one, titled *The Quick Resume and Cover Letter Book — Write and Use an Effective Resume in Only One Day*, of interest. It provides much additional information on writing resumes, from simple to sophisticated, and many examples.

6

HOW TO GET A GOOD JOB IN LESS TIME

Quick
Tip

This chapter is a VERY important one to read because it will give you the basic techniques to find a better job in less time. Some of the information it contains is covered in more detail in other sections of the book, but here you have an overview of the entire process. Keep in mind that getting interviews is a necessary step in doing well in them ...

CHANGING JOBS AND CAREERS IS OFTEN HEALTHY

Most of us were told from an early age that each career move must be up, involving more money, responsibility, and prestige. Yet research indicates people change careers for many other reasons as well.

In a survey conducted by the Gallup Organization for the National Occupational Information Coordinating Committee, 44 percent of the working adults surveyed expected to be in a different job within three years. This is a very high turnover rate, yet only 41 percent had a definite plan to follow in mapping out their careers.

Logical, ordered careers are found more often with increasing levels of education. For example, while 25 percent of high school dropouts took the only job available, this was true for only 8 percent of those with at least some college. But you should not assume that this means such occupational stability is healthy. Many adult developmental psychologists believe occupational change is not only normal but may even be necessary for sound adult growth and development. It is common, even normal, to reconsider occupational roles during your twenties, thirties, and forties, even in the absence of economic pressure to do so.

One viewpoint is that a healthy occupational change is one that allows some previously undeveloped aspect of the self to emerge. The change may be as natural as from clerk to supervisor or as drastic as from professional musician to airline pilot. Although risk is always a factor when change is involved, reasonable risks are healthy and can raise self-esteem.

A REVIEW OF THE SEVEN STEPS FOR GETTING THE JOB YOU WANT—EMPHASIZING JOB SEEKING SKILLS

Chapter 1 presented seven steps that I feel are essential in getting the job you want. Let's review them again before we go on.

The Seven Steps for Getting the Job You Want

1. Know your skills.
2. Have a clear job objective.
3. Know where and how to look.
4. Spend at least 25 hours a week looking.
5. Get two interviews a day.
6. Do well in interviews.
7. Follow up on all contacts.

Quick Reminder

Various chapters provide substantial information on many of these steps and it is not my intent to try to summarize that information here. Instead, much of this chapter will provide information on those steps that are not covered elsewhere. To help you understand how all the information fits together, I have kept the information presented here in the seven-step format. Where appropriate, I refer you elsewhere in this book for additional details.

STEP 1: KNOW YOUR SKILLS

I have already emphasized the importance of knowing what you are good at in Section 1 and several chapters in Section 3 provide thorough information on this. It is very important that you develop a language to describe your skills because it is a most important issue in handling an interview.

Quick Reminder

STEP 2: HAVE A CLEAR JOB OBJECTIVE

This subject is also covered in Section 3. It is an important issue to resolve before you begin your job search or you will simply be looking for "a" job rather than "the" job that you would most enjoy.

STEP 3: KNOW WHERE AND HOW TO LOOK

This is one of the key steps that I will cover in some detail in this chapter because it is not covered elsewhere in this book.

There is a good deal of research available on how people actually find jobs. While there are study-to-study differences, it is clear that only about 25 percent of all jobs are obtained through publicly advertised sources. About 15 percent of us find jobs through the want ads, and other publicly available sources—such as signs in windows—account for another 10 percent. That leaves about 75 percent of us finding our jobs through some unadvertised source.

The chart that follows will provide you some visual sense of how people find jobs.

HOW MOST JOBS ARE FOUND

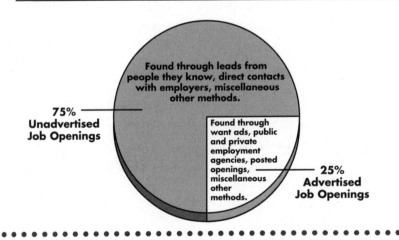

75%
Unadvertised
Job Openings

Found through leads from people they know, direct contacts with employers, miscellaneous other methods.

Found through want ads, public and private employment agencies, posted openings, miscellaneous other methods.

25%
Advertised
Job Openings

MOST JOBS OPENINGS ARE HIDDEN

One survey found that 85 percent of all employers don't advertise at all. They hire people they already know, people who find out about the jobs through word of mouth, or people who simply happen to be at the right place at the right time. These jobs are hidden from job seekers who use conventional job search techniques such as want ads. Yet it is this hidden job market where most of us actually get our jobs. In many cases, we attribute this to "luck" and this is often partly true. However, there are certain things you can do that increase your "luck" in finding job openings.

TRADITIONAL JOB SEARCH METHODS

There are a variety of techniques that most of us know about and use in our search for a job. Some of these are ones that have been used for many years and are known to virtually everyone. Let's take a look at some of these traditional job search methods.

HELP WANTED ADS

The chart I presented earlier indicates that about 15 percent of us get our jobs through the want ads. Everyone who reads the paper knows about these job openings, so competition for these jobs is fierce.

For example, about 10 percent of the working population reads the want ads each week—that number is higher when unemployment rates are high. Consider how many people are served by your local newspaper and you will begin to see the problem. A newspaper that serves an area with a population of 250,000 has a working population of more than 125,000 and you can count on about 12,500 of them reading the want ads. It is no wonder that people who use want ads get discouraged since, invariably, they compete with literally anyone in the job market for those relatively few jobs that get advertised.

Still, some people do get jobs this way, so go ahead and apply. Just be sure to spend most of your time using more effective methods.

THE STATE EMPLOYMENT SERVICE

Often called the "Unemployment Office," it offers free job leads and other services in addition to unemployment compensation checks for the unemployed. Each state has a network of these offices (and may use a different name, such as Department of Labor) but only about 5 percent of all job seekers get their jobs here. This service usually knows of only one-tenth (or fewer) of the available jobs in your area.

While this sounds quite negative, some states do provide substantial assistance to job seekers although funding cuts have forced many to cut back. In most cases, their ability to "find you a job" is quite limited. This is even more so if you are looking for jobs other than labor or entry-level positions.

Still, it is worth a weekly visit. If you ask for the same counselor, you might impress the person enough to remember you and refer you to the better openings.

"Private agencies charge fees as high as 20 percent of your annual salary."

PRIVATE EMPLOYMENT AGENCIES

These are for-profit businesses that charge a fee to either you or to the employer. Recent studies have found that private agencies work reasonably well for those who use them. But there are caveats to consider. For one thing, these agencies work best for entry-level positions or for those with specialized skills that are in demand. Most people who use a private agency find their jobs using some other source, so the success record of these firms is quite modest.

Private agencies also charge a fee to either you (as high as 20 percent of your annual salary!) or the employer. Most of them call employers asking

Quick Reference

if they have any openings—something you could do yourself. Unless you have skills that are in high demand, you may do better on your own— AND save money. At the least, you should only use a private agency as just *one* of the techniques you use and not rely on it too heavily. And do not sign any agreements if you feel pressured to do so, as this could end up costing you big money at a time you can least afford it.

TEMPORARY AGENCIES

Some state employment service offices provide leads for temporary employment, but most temporary jobs are now provided by for-profit businesses. These agencies typically do not charge you for their services but do charge your hourly rate to your employer, plus an additional charge for the agency.

Temporary agencies have become an increasingly important source of job leads over the years. I often recommend that job seekers consider their services to help them make a transition to a new job. Doing so can bring in some income as well as give you experience in a variety of settings—something that can help you land full-time jobs later. More and more employers are also using these agencies as a way to evaluate workers for permanent jobs. So consider using them if it makes sense to do so, but make certain that you continue an active search for a full-time job as you do.

SENDING OUT RESUMES

A resume is not a particularly effective tool for getting interviews. One survey found that you would have to mail more than 500 unsolicited resumes to get one interview! A much better approach is to phone the person who might hire you to set up an interview directly, and *then* send a resume. If you insist on sending out unsolicited resumes, do this on weekends. Save your "prime time" for more effective job search techniques.

FILLING OUT APPLICATIONS

Most applications are designed and used to screen you out. Larger organizations may require them, but remember that your task is to get an interview, not fill out an application. If you do complete them, make them

**Quick
Reference**

neat, error free, and do not include anything that could get you screened out. If necessary, leave a problem section blank. It can always be explained after you get an offer.

High turnover jobs and those that don't require much training most often require you to complete an application. This is so that employers can quickly screen out those applicants who do not meet their needs. This saves time by limiting the number of people who get interviews. Young people, because they are most likely to seek these types of jobs, are most often expected to complete applications. And they also have the most success in using them to get interviews, although simply asking for an interview would be more effective in most settings.

PERSONNEL DEPARTMENTS

Hardly anyone gets hired by people in a personnel department. Their job is to screen you and refer the "best" applicants to the person who would actually supervise you. You may need to cooperate with them,

**Quick
Fact**

According to the Society for Human Resource Management, here are the common types of facts companies try to gather about their employees, either at the interview stage or later:

Education	88.5%
Salary history	85.5%
Age	84.9%
Attendance	83.1%
Citizenship	80.9%
Marital status	78.6%
Medical records	49.0%
Criminal record	36.3%
Hobbies	17.5%
Credit history	15.6%
Substance abuse history	12.9%
Religion	3.5%
Political affiliation	0.4%
None	0.4%

Quick Reference

but it is often better to go directly to the person who is most likely to supervise you, even if there is no job opening just now.

INFORMAL JOB SEARCH METHODS

Most people get their jobs using informal methods. These jobs often are not advertised and are part of the "hidden" job market. How do you find them?

There are two basic informal job search methods: networking with people you know (I call these "warm contacts"), and making direct contact with an employer. They are both based on the most important job search rule of all:

Don't wait until the job is open!

Most jobs are filled by someone the employer meets before a job is formally "open." So the trick is to meet people who can hire you *before* a job is available! Instead of saying "Do you have any jobs open?" say "I realize you may not have any openings now, but I would still like to talk to you about the possibility of future openings."

☑ DEVELOP A NETWORK OF "WARM CONTACTS" AMONG PEOPLE YOU KNOW

One study found that 40 percent of all people found their jobs through a lead provided by a friend, a relative, or an acquaintance. Because you already know these people, I call them warm contacts, and they are the most important (though often overlooked) group of people in your job search. If you are organized in asking them to help you, they can lead you to many jobs that you will not find in any other way. They can also lead you to other people they know. Developing new contacts from people you know is called "networking" and here's how it works:

☑ MAKE LISTS OF PEOPLE YOU KNOW

Develop a list of anyone you are friendly with, and then make a separate list for all your relatives. These two lists alone often add up to 25 to 100 people or more. Then think of other groups of people with whom you have something in common, like people you used to work with, people who went to your school, people in your social or sports groups, members of your professional association, former employers, and members of your

**Quick
Reference**

religious group. You may not know many of these people personally, but most will help you if you ask them.

☑ CONTACT THEM IN A SYSTEMATIC WAY

Each of these people is a contact for you. Obviously, some lists and some people on those lists will be more helpful than others, but almost any one of them could help you find a job lead.

☑ PRESENT YOURSELF WELL

Start with your friends and relatives. Call them up and tell them you are looking for a job and need their help. Be as clear as possible about what you are looking for and what skills and qualifications you have. Look at the sample JIST Card and phone script later in this chapter for presentation ideas.

☑ ASK THEM FOR LEADS

It is possible that they will know of a job opening just right for you. If so, get the details and get right on it! More likely, however, they will not, so following are three questions you should ask.

☑ THE THREE MAGIC NETWORKING QUESTIONS

1. "Do you know of any openings for a person with my skills?"

If the answer is no, then ask:

2. "Do you know of someone else who might know of such an opening?"

If they do, get that name and ask for another one. If they don't, then ask:

3. "Do you know of anyone who might know of someone else who

NETWORKING:

ONE PERSON REFERS YOU TO TWO OTHERS

Person You Know

Fred   **Susan**

**By the tenth level of contact, you will have been
put in touch with more than 1,000 people.**

**Quick
Reference**

might?" Another way to ask this is, "Do you know someone else who knows lots of people?" If all else fails, this will usually get you a name.

☑ CONTACT THESE REFERRALS AND ASK THEM THE SAME QUESTIONS

For each original contact, you can extend your network of acquaintances by hundreds of people. Eventually, one of these people will hire you—or refer you to someone who will!

Quick
Reference

☑ USE "COLD CONTACTS"—CONTACT EMPLOYERS DIRECTLY

It takes more courage, but contacting an employer directly is a very effective job search technique. Next to getting leads from people you know, direct contacts with employers account for about 30 percent of how all people find jobs, which makes this technique the second most effective source of job leads.

☑ THE TWO BASIC COLD CONTACT TECHNIQUES

There are two basic techniques for contacting employers directly.

1. Call them: Use the *Yellow Pages* to identify types of organizations that could use a person with your skills. Then call the organizations listed and ask to speak to the person who is most likely to hire you. There is a sample telephone script later in this chapter to give you ideas about what to say.

2. Drop in: You can also just walk in and ask to speak to the person in charge. This is particularly effective in small businesses, but it works surprisingly well in larger ones, too. Remember, you want an interview even if there are no openings now. If your timing is inconvenient, ask for a better time to come back for an interview.

You might think that sending a resume to an employer would also count as a direct contact technique. I don't include it in this category because it is not a direct contact at all, but an indirect one. That is why sending out resumes was mentioned among the traditional—and more passive—techniques covered earlier.

WHERE THE JOBS ARE—SMALL BUSINESS!

About 70 percent of all nongovernment workers now work for small businesses. While the largest corporations have reduced the number of employees, small businesses have been creating as many as 80 percent of the new jobs. There are many opportunities to obtain training and advance in smaller organizations, too. Many do not even have a personnel department, so nontraditional job search techniques are particularly effective with these companies.

WHERE PEOPLE WORK

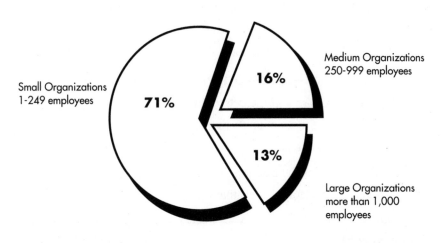

Small Organizations
1-249 employees

71%

16% Medium Organizations
250-999 employees

13%

Large Organizations
more than 1,000
employees

COMPUTERIZED JOB SEEKING

Electronic bulletin board systems are virtual hotbeds of job information in a variety of ways. Most of the nationally recognized networks such as CompuServe, e World, GEnie, America Online, and Prodigy have formally designated areas to post jobs available and jobs wanted—and they do generate inquiries! But opportunities abound even outside these formal job-related areas. Don't overlook local bulletin board systems, either. Their operators generally post notices in libraries, business or

---

Quick Case Study

Cindy Ludlow provides one example of how computerized bulletin boards can be used. This Columbus, Ohio, journalist spent her online hours chatting with fellow scribblers in the Writing Club hobby area, seeking new opinions and insight into her field. She struck up a typing friendship with a business editor, who, two weeks after their first correspondence, needed an editor in that city. Ludlow was invited to interview for the position, and thanks in part to the former relationship, was offered the job. So take a few minutes to converse with other professionals in your field, even if it's not about a job position directly—the resulting online charge is well worth the cost!

Quick Reference

hobby magazines, and in computer publications (*Computer User* magazine is one such source, if it is available in your city. Best of all, it's free at local grocery and drug store stands.) These hometown networks buzz with the same type of generous advice and professional camaraderie as the national systems—and many times, they're free.

JIST CARDS—AN EFFECTIVE MINI-RESUME

JIST Cards are a job search tool that get results. Because they work so well, I want to mention them briefly here.

Typed, printed, or even neatly written on a three-by-five-inch card, a JIST Card contains the essential information most employers want to know. Look at the sample cards that follow:

Sandy Zaremba   Home: (512) 232-7608
Message: (512) 234-7465

Position: General Office/Clerical

Over two years' work experience plus one year of training in office practices. Type 55 wpm, trained in word processing operations, post general ledger, interpersonal skills and get along with most people. Can meet deadlines and handle pressure well.

Willing to work any hours

Organized, honest, reliable, and hardworking

Thomas Welborn   Home: (602) 253-9678
Message: (602) 257-6643

Objective: Electronics—installation, maintenance and sales

SKILLS: Four years work experience plus two years advanced training in electronics. A.S. degree in Electronic Engineering Technology. Managed a $300,000/yr. business while going to school full-time, with grades in the top 25%. Familiar with all major electronic diagnostic and repair equipment. Hands-on experience with medical, consumer, communication, and industrial electronics equipment and applications. Good problem-solving and communication skills. Customer service oriented.

Willing to do what it takes to get the job done.

Quick Reference

JIST Cards are an effective job search tool! Give one to friends and network contacts. Attach it to a resume. Enclose one in your thank-you notes before or after an interview. Leave it with employers as a business card. Use them in many creative ways. Even though they can be typed or even handwritten, it is best to have 100 or more printed so you can put lots of them into circulation. Thousands of job seekers have used them and they get results.

USE A SCRIPT TO MAKE TELEPHONE CONTACTS

Once you have your JIST Card, it is easy to create a telephone contact "script" based on it. Adapt the basic script to call people you know or your *Yellow Pages* leads. Just pick out *Yellow Page* index categories that might use a person with your skills. Then ask for the person who is most likely to supervise you and present your phone script.

While it doesn't work all the time, with practice, most people can get one or more interviews in an hour by making these cold calls. Here is a phone script based on another JIST card:

"Hello, my name is Pam Nykanen. I am interested in a position in hotel management. I have four years' experience in sales, catering, and accounting with a 300-room hotel. I also have an associate degree in Hotel Management plus one year with the Bradey Culinary Institute. During my employment, I helped double revenue from meetings and conferences and increase bar revenues by 46 percent. I have good problem-solving skills and am good with people. I am also well organized, hard working, and detail oriented. When can I come in for an interview?"

Quick Fact

STEP 4: SPEND AT LEAST 25 HOURS A WEEK LOOKING

On average, most job seekers spend about five hours a week actually looking for work. They are also unemployed an average of three or more months! People who follow my advice spend much more time on their job search each week. They also often get jobs in less than half the average time. Time management is the key.

Decide how many hours per week you plan to look for a job. I suggest

**Quick
Fact**

at least 25 hours per week if you are unemployed and are looking for a full-time job. The most important thing is to decide how many hours you can commit to your job search, and stay with it.

Decide on which days you will look for work. How many hours will you look each day? At what time will you begin and end your job search on each of these days? Look at the sample job search schedule that follows to see how one person planned her time. Create your own schedule on a sheet of paper or, better yet, set up your schedule in advance on a daily planner. You can buy a daily/weekly/monthly planner at many department or stationery stores.

SAMPLE WEEKLY JOB SEARCH SCHEDULE

Here is a simple schedule showing you how one person organized her week into major blocks of time spent on the job search. You should use a similar form for planning your own job search schedule.

SAMPLE WEEKLY JOB SEARCH SCHEDULE		
Days	**Job search schedule**	**No. of Hours**
Monday	8:00 am - Noon, 1-4 pm	7
Tuesday	8:00 am - Noon	4
Wednesday	8:00 am - Noon, 1-4 pm	7
Thursday	8:00 am - Noon	4
Friday	8:00 am - 11:00 am	3
Saturday		
Sunday		
Total Hours Per Week		25

Schedule how to spend your time each day. This is very important because most job seekers find it hard to stay productive each day. You already know which job search methods are most effective and you should plan on spending more of your time using these methods. The sample daily schedule that follows has been very effective for people who have used it, and will give you ideas for your own schedule.

SAMPLE DAILY SCHEDULE

7:00 to 8:00	Get up, shower, dress, eat breakfast.
8:00 to 8:15	Organize work space, review schedule for interviews or follow ups, update schedule.
8:15 to 9:00	Review old leads for follow up, develop new leads (want ads, *Yellow Pages*, networking lists, etc.).
9:00 to 10:00	Make phone calls, set up interviews.
10:00 to 10:15	Take a break!
10:15 to 11:00	Make more calls.
11:00 to noon	Make follow-up calls as needed.
noon to 1:00	Lunch break.
1:00 to 5:00	Go on interviews, make cold contacts in the field, research at the library.

Quick Fact

STEP 5: GET TWO INTERVIEWS A DAY

I pointed out in chapter 1 that getting two interviews a day is far more than the one or two interviews a week that most job seekers get. The reason they don't do better is because they are not using effective techniques to get interviews. And the biggest problem is often their limited definition of what counts as an interview.

So, because of its importance, here is a review of the new definition of an interview that I encourage you to use:

A New Definition of an Interview

An interview is any face-to-face contact with someone who has the authority to hire or supervise a person with your skills. This person may or may not have a job opening at the time you interview with them.

If you use this definition, it will be much easier to get interviews.

STEP 6: YOU MUST DO WELL IN THE INTERVIEW

It should seem obvious to you that you need to do well in an interview in order to be offered a job. Many of the chapters in this book provide details on how to improve your interviewing skills, so let me just present a few essentials here.

One study indicated that, of those who made it as far as the interview (many others were screened out beforehand), about 40 percent created a bad first impression, mostly based on their dress and grooming. First impressions *do* count and, if you make a bad one, you will never get a chance to recover. While there is more to making a good first impression than your dress and grooming, this is, fortunately, something that you can change. So, for this reason, remember the following rule, already discussed in chapter 4.

FARR'S DRESS AND GROOMING RULE

> *Dress like you think the boss is most likely to dress—only neater.*

Also, keep in mind the importance of answering problem questions, which was also discussed in detail in chapter 4.

Quick Reminder

STEP 7: FOLLOW UP ON ALL CONTACTS

People who follow up with potential employers and with others in their network get jobs faster than those who do not. It is as simple as that. Here are three guidelines to follow to get the best results from contacts with people in your network:

1. Send a thank-you note to every person who helps you in your job search.

2. Send the thank-you note within 24 hours after you speak with them.

3. Develop a system to continually follow up on all good contacts.

SEND LOTS OF THANK-YOU NOTES

While this seems a small thing, sending thank-you notes can make a big difference. Handwritten notes are acceptable if your handwriting is neat but, if not, typed ones are fine too. Keep them simple, neat, and error free. See the following sample note.

Cynthia Kijek,

Thanks so much for your willingness to see me next Wednesday at 9:00 a.m. I know that I am one of many who is interested in working with your organization and appreciate the opportunity to meet you and learn more about the position.

I've enclosed a JIST Card that presents the basics of my skills for this job and will bring a copy of my resume to the interview. Please call me if you have any questions at all.

Sincerely,

Bruce Vernon

Quick Reminder

USE JOB LEAD CARDS TO ORGANIZE YOUR CONTACTS

If you do as I suggest and make lots of contacts with lots of people, you will soon begin to forget just who is whom (or who suggested you contact whom...). For this reason, you'll need a simple system to organize your many contacts. You could use a computer to do this, but you can also use a simple three-by-five-inch card to keep essential information on each person in your network.

Buy a three-by-five-inch card file box and tabs for each day of the month. File the cards under the date you want to contact the person, and the rest is easy. I've found that staying in touch with a good contact every other week can pay off big. Here's a sample card to give you ideas on how to create your own:

Organization: Mutual Health Insurance

Contact Person: Anna Tomey   **Phone:** (317) 355-0216

Source of Lead: Steve Wiley

Notes: 4/10-called. Anna on vacation. Call back 4/15.

4/15-Interview on 4/20 at 1:30. 4/20 Anna showed

me around. They use the same computer we used in

school! Friendly people. Sent thank-you note & JIST

Card. Call back 5/1-2nd interview on 5/8 at 9 am.

THE QUICK JOB SEARCH REVIEW

To wrap up this chapter, here are a few of its most important points:

☞ Go at your job search as if it were a job itself.

☞ Get organized and spend at least 25 hours per week actively looking for a job.

☞ Know your skills and have a clear job objective.

☞ Believe in yourself and ask people to help you.

☞ If you want to get a good job quickly, get lots of interviews!

☞ Pay attention to all the details, and then be yourself in the interview. Remember that employers are people, too. They will hire someone they feel will do the job well, who will be reliable, and who will fit easily into their work environment.

☞ Be able to answer the ultimate interview question: "Why should I hire you?"

☞ When you want the job, tell the employer why they should hire you. Tell them you want the job and why.

☞ Follow up on all the leads you generate and send thank-you notes.

☞ Keep following up and don't quit!

7

QUICK RESUME TIPS AND SAMPLES

Quick Tip

While this is a book on interviewing, you probably also have concerns about your resume. This chapter will provide you with the basics for a good resume. It gives advice on writing a resume, explains the different kinds, includes samples and a resume writing worksheet.

There is entirely too much importance placed on the resume in the job search. If you are looking for a job where an employer will expect you to have a resume, write one. But the problem is that many people believe a resume should be used to get interviews. That is a very old-fashioned idea.

Unfortunately, too many people write resume and job search books that provide bad advice. Their idea of the job search is the traditional one, where a job is advertised and people are screened in or out of an interview based on an application or a resume. In that context, the advice is to have a great looking resume that will somehow stand out from the others and get you an interview.

While that makes sense from the personnel manager's point of view, it is not a helpful mindset for you to adopt. It encourages you to be passive and completely dependent on someone else to evaluate your merits without ever meeting you.

In an environment where most people are working for smaller employers who don't have a personnel department, the passive and traditional approach of sending in an unsolicited resume just does not make good sense. Even where there *is* a personnel office and a traditional interview/screening situation, you would be far better off calling up the supervisor directly and asking for an interview. How could it hurt? While others are dutifully (and passively) sending in their resumes, you have made direct contact and now have a direct shot at an interview.

So, my advice is to go ahead and do a resume but to use it as a support tool *after* you get an interview. Don't expect it to get an interview for you, no matter how "good" it is.

● ●

QUICK RESUME WRITING TIPS

Quick Reference

Here are some general guidelines for writing your resume.

Write it yourself. It's OK to look at other resumes for ideas, but write yours yourself. It will force you to organize your thoughts and background.

Make it error free. One spelling or grammar error will create a negative impression. Get someone else to review your final draft for any errors. Then review it again!

Make it look good. Poor copy quality, cheap paper, bad type quality, or anything else that creates a poor physical appearance will turn off employers—even to the best resume content. Get professional help with typing and printing if necessary. Most print shops can do it all for you.

Be brief, be relevant. Many good resumes fit on one page—few justify more than two. Include only the most important points. Use short sentences and action words. If it doesn't relate to and support your job objective, cut it!

Be honest. Don't overstate your qualifications. Most employers will see right through it and not hire you. If you end up getting a job you can't handle, it will *not* be to your advantage.

Be positive. Emphasize your accomplishments and results. This is no place to be too humble or to display your faults.

Be specific. Rather than "I am good with people," say, "I supervised four people in the warehouse and increased productivity by 30 percent." Use numbers whenever possible, such as the number of people served, percent of increase, or dollar increase.

You should also know that everyone feels he or she is a resume expert. Whatever you do, someone will tell you it is wrong. For this reason, it is important to understand that a resume is a job search tool. You should never delay or slow down your job search because your resume is not "good enough." The best approach is to create a simple and acceptable resume as soon as possible, then use it! As time permits, make a better one if you feel it's necessary.

References. Contact your references and let them know what type of job you want and why you are qualified. Be sure to review what they will say about you! Because some employers will not give out references by phone or in person, have previous employers write a letter of reference for you in advance. You can then make copies of these letters to give to potential employers, if asked. If you feel you'll get a bad reference from a previous employer, negotiate what they will say about you, or get written references from other people you worked with at that company. When creating your list of references, be sure to include your reference's name and job title, where he or she works, a business address and phone number, how that person knows you, and what your reference will say about you.

WRITING A SIMPLE CHRONOLOGICAL RESUME

The simple chronological approach is the resume format most people use. It is a quick and relatively easy resume that presents previous experience in the order of your most recent experience listed first, followed by each previous job. Look at the sample resumes of Judith Jones on the next few pages. Both are chronological resumes, but notice that the second resume includes some improvements over her first. The improved resume is clearly better, but both would be acceptable to most employers.

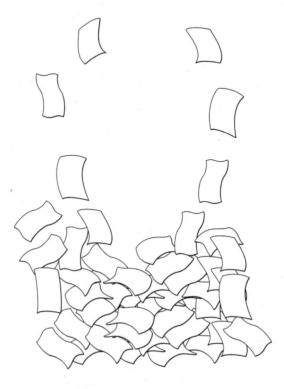

FIGURE 7-1 Simple Chronological Resume.

Judith J. Jones

115 South Hawthorne Avenue
Chicago, Illinois 46204
(317) 653-9217 (home)
(317) 272-7608 (message)

JOB OBJECTIVE

Desire a position in the office management, secretarial, or clerical area. Prefer a position requiring responsibility and a variety of tasks.

EDUCATION AND TRAINING

Acme Business College, Indianapolis, Indiana
Graduate of a one-year business/secretarial program, 1995.

John Adams High School, South Bend, Indiana
Diploma, business education.

U.S. Army
Financial procedures, accounting functions. Other: Continuing education classes and workshops in Business Communication, Scheduling Systems, and Customer Relations.

EXPERIENCE

1994–1995—Returned to school to complete and update my business skills. Learned word processing and other new office techniques.

1992–1994—Claims Processor, Blue Spear Insurance Co., Indianapolis, Indiana. Handled customer medical claims, used a CRT, filed, miscellaneous clerical duties.

1990–1992—Sales Clerk, Judy's Boutique, Indianapolis, Indiana. Responsible for counter sales, display design, and selected tasks.

1988–1990—E4, U.S. Army. Assigned to various stations as a specialist in finance operations. Promoted prior to honorable discharge.

Previous jobs—Held part-time and summer jobs throughout high school.

PERSONAL

I am reliable, hardworking, and good with people.

FIGURE 7-2 Improved Chronological Resume.

Judith J. Jones

115 South Hawthorne Avenue
Chicago, Illinois 46204
(317) 653-9217 (home)
(317) 272-7608 (message)

JOB OBJECTIVE

Seeking position requiring excellent management and secretarial skills in office environment. Position should require a variety of tasks including typing, word processing, accounting/book-keeping functions, and customer contact.

EDUCATION AND TRAINING

Acme Business College, Indianapolis, Indiana.
Completed one-year program in Professional Secretarial and Office Management. Grades in top 30 percent of my class. Courses: word processing, accounting theory and systems, time management, basic supervision, and others.

John Adams High School, South Bend, Indiana.
Graduated with emphasis on business and secretarial courses. Won shorthand contest.

Other: Continuing education at my own expense (Business Communications, Customer Relations, Computer Applications, other courses).

EXPERIENCE

1994-1995 — Returned to business school to update skills. Advanced course work in accounting and office management. Learned to operate word processing and PC-based accounting and spreadsheet software. Gained operating knowledge of computers.

1992-1994 — Claims Processor, Blue Spear Insurance Company, Indianapolis, Indiana. Handled 50 complex medical insurance claims per day — 18 percent above department average. Received two merit raises for performance.

1990-1992 — Assistant Manager, Judy's Boutique, Indianapolis, Indiana. Managed sales, financial records, inventory, purchasing, correspondence, and related tasks during owner's absence. Supervised four employees. Sales increased 15 percent during my tenure.

1988-1990 — Finance Specialist (E4), U.S. Army. Responsible for the systematic processing of 500 invoices per day from commercial vendors. Trained and supervised eight employees. Devised internal system allowing 15 percent increase in invoices processed with a decrease in personnel.

1984-1988 — Various part-time and summer jobs through high school. Learned to deal with customers, meet deadlines, work hard and other skills.

SPECIAL SKILLS AND ABILITIES

Type 80 words per minute and can operate most office equipment. Good communication and math skills. Accept supervision, able to supervise others. Excellent attendance record.

TIPS FOR WRITING A CHRONOLOGICAL RESUME

Quick Reference

Here are some tips for completing your basic resume.

Name: Use your formal name rather than a nickname. It sounds more professional.

Address: Be complete. Include zip code and avoid abbreviations. If you may move sometime during your job search, use the address of a friend or relative, or be certain to include a forwarding address.

Telephone Number: If your home number is often left unanswered during the day, include an alternate number where a message can be left. A reliable friend or relative will usually agree to this, but consider getting an answering machine. Employers are most likely to try to reach you by phone, so having a reliable way to be reached is very important.

Job Objective: This is optional for a very basic resume but is still important to include. Notice that Judy is keeping her options open with her objective. Saying "Secretary" or "Clerical" might limit her to lower paying jobs, or even prevent her from being considered for higher-level jobs for which she might be qualified.

Education and Training: Include any formal training you've had plus any training that supports the job you seek. If you did not finish a formal degree or program, list what you did complete. Include any special accomplishments.

Previous Experience: The standard approach is to list employer, job title, dates employed, and responsibilities. But there are better ways of presenting your experience. Look over the "Improved Chronological Resume" for ideas. The improved version emphasizes results, accomplishments, and performance.

Personal Data: Neither of the sample resumes includes the height, weight, or marital status included on so many resumes. That information is simply not relevant! If you do include some personal information, put it at the bottom and keep it related to the job you want.

References: There is no need to list references. If employers want them, they will ask. If your references are particularly good, it's OK to say so.

"New graduates should emphasize their recent training and education."

Quick Reference

TIPS FOR WRITING AN IMPROVED CHRONOLOGICAL RESUME

Once you have a simple, error-free and eye-pleasing resume, get on with your job search. There is no reason to delay! But you may want to create a better one in your spare time (evenings and/or weekends). If you do, here are some tips.

Job Objective: Job objectives often limit the types of jobs for which you will be considered. Instead, think of the type of work you want to do and can do well and describe it in more general terms. For example, instead of "Restaurant Manager," say "Managing a small to mid-sized business" (as long as that is what you are qualified to do).

Education and Training: New graduates should emphasize their recent training and education more than those with five years or more of related work experience. Mention any special accomplishments you had while in school if they relate to the job. Did you work full-time while in school? Did you do particularly well in work-related classes, get an award, participate in sports?

Skills and Accomplishments: Employers are interested in what you did well. Include those things that relate to doing well in the job you are seeking now. Even small things count. Perhaps your attendance was perfect,

Quick
Reference

you met a tight deadline, did the work of others during vacations, etc. Be specific and include numbers—give an accurate estimate, if need be.

Job Titles: Many job titles don't accurately reflect the job you did. For example, your job title may have been "cashier" but you also opened the store, trained new staff, and covered for the boss on vacations. Perhaps "Head Cashier and Assistant Manager" would be more accurate. Check with your previous employer if you're not sure.

Promotions: If you were promoted or got good evaluations, say so. A promotion to a more responsible job can be handled as a separate job if this makes sense.

Problem Areas: Employers look for any sign of instability or lack of reliability. It is very expensive to hire and train someone who won't work out or stay on the job very long. Gaps in employment, jobs held for short periods of time, or a lack of direction in the jobs you've held are all things that employers are concerned about. If you have a legitimate explanation, use it. For example:

- ✔ Continued my education at...
- ✔ Traveled extensively throughout the United States
- ✔ Self-employed barn painter and widget maker
- ✔ Had first child, took year off before returning to work

Use entire years or even seasons to avoid displaying a shorter gap you can't explain easily: "Spring 1995 to Fall 1995" will not emphasize unemployment from January to March, for example.

Remember that a resume can get you screened out, but it is up to you to get the interview and the job. So, cut anything negative from your resume!

WRITING A SKILLS OR COMBINATION RESUME

Quick
Fact

There are no firm rules about how you should do your resume. Different formats make sense for different people. Besides the chronological format, the functional or "skills" resume is often used. This resume emphasizes your most important skills, supported by specific examples of how you have used them. This approach allows you to use any part of your life

Quick Fact

history to support your ability to do the job you want.

While the skills resume can be very effective, it does require more work to create. And some employers don't like them because they can hide a job seeker's faults better than a chronological resume (such as job gaps, lack of formal education, or no related work experience).

Still, a skills resume may make sense for you. Look over the sample resumes provided at the end of this chapter for ideas. Notice that one resume includes elements of a skills *and* a chronological resume. This is called a "combination" resume—an approach that makes sense if your previous job history or education and training lends itself to a more diversified format.

Quick Tip

I recommend that you put together a simple resume of some kind as soon as you can. It must be neat, stress accomplishments, and be error free. Use it early in your job search without delay. Later, when you have time, you can create a a "better" one.

"INSTANT RESUME" WORKSHEET

This worksheet will help you organize the information needed to complete a simple chronological resume. Several worksheets can be found in chapter 10 which will be helpful in identifying information needed for a skills resume.

Key Accomplishments

List the three accomplishments that best prove your ability to do well in the kind of job you want

1. _____

2. _____

3. _____

Education & Training

Name of high school(s)/years attended _____

_____

_____

_____

Subjects related to job objective _____

_____

_____

_____

Extracurricular activities/hobbies/leisure activities _____

_____

_____

_____

Accomplishments/things you did well _____

_____

_____

_____

Schools you attended after high school, years attended, degrees/certificates earned _____

_____

_____

_____

Courses related to job objective _____

_____

_____

_____

Extracurricular Activities/Hobbies/Leisure Activities

Accomplishments/things you did well _____

_____

_____

_____

Military Training/On-the-Job/or Informal Training
(Include hobbies; also include dates of training
and type of certificate earned.)

_____

_____

_____

_____

_____

_____

_____

_____

Specific things you can do as a result _____

_____

_____

_____

_____

WORK AND VOLUNTEER HISTORY

List your most recent job first, followed by each previous job. Include military experience and unpaid work here, too. Use additional sheets to cover *all* your significant jobs or unpaid experiences. Whenever possible, provide numbers to support what you did: number of people served over one or more years, number of transactions processed, percent of sales increase, total inventory value you were responsible for, payroll of the staff you supervised, total budget you were responsible for, etc. These results can be very impressive to a prospective employer.

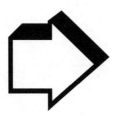

JOB / VOLUNTEER WORKSHEET

. . . .

Job #1

Name of organization: _____

Address: _____

_____

Phone number: (   ) _____

Dates employed: _____ **to:** _____

Job title(s): _____

Supervisor's name: _____

Details of any raises or promotions: _____

_____

_____

_____

Machinery or equipment you used: _____

_____

_____

_____

Special skills this job required: _____

_____

_____

_____

List what you accomplished or did well: _____

_____

_____

_____

_____

_____

JOB / VOLUNTEER WORKSHEET

Job #2

Name of organization: _____

Address: _____

_____

Phone number: (   ) _____

Dates employed: _____ **to:** _____

Job title(s): _____

Supervisor's name: _____

Details of any raises or promotions: _____

_____

_____

_____

Machinery or equipment you used: _____

_____

_____

_____

Special skills this job required: _____

_____

_____

_____

List what you accomplished or did well: _____

_____

_____

_____

_____

_____

JOB / VOLUNTEER WORKSHEET

Job #3

Name of organization: _____

Address: _____

_____

Phone number: (   ) _____

Dates employed: _____ **to:** _____

Job title(s): _____

Supervisor's name: _____

Details of any raises or promotions: _____

_____

_____

_____

Machinery or equipment you used: _____

_____

_____

_____

Special skills this job required: _____

_____

_____

_____

List what you accomplished or did well: _____

_____

_____

_____

_____

JOB / VOLUNTEER WORKSHEET

Job #4

Name of organization: _____

Address: _____

_____

Phone number: ( ) _____

Dates employed: _____ **to:** _____

Job title(s): _____

Supervisor's name: _____

Details of any raises or promotions: _____

_____

_____

_____

Machinery or equipment you used: _____

_____

_____

_____

Special skills this job required: _____

_____

_____

_____

List what you accomplished or did well: _____

_____

_____

_____

_____

SAMPLE RESUMES

DARREL CRAIG'S RESUME AND JIST CARD

Comments on Darrel's Resume:

This is a resume of a career changer. After working in a variety of jobs, Darrel went to school and learned computer programming. The skills format allows him to emphasize the business experiences in his past to support his current job objective. There is no chronological listing of jobs and no dates are indicated related to his education, so it is not obvious that he is a recent graduate with little formal work experience as a programmer.

Darrel does a good job of presenting his previous work experience and includes numbers to support his skills and accomplishments. Even so, the relationship between his previous work and current objective could be improved. For example, collecting bad debts requires discipline, persistence, and attention to detail— the same skills required in programming. And, while he is good at sales, how does this relate to programming?

To correct this, he might consider modifying his job objective to include the use of his sales skills (such as selling technological services) or emphasizing other skills from his previous work experience. Still, his resume is reasonably effective and does a decent job of relating past business experience to his ability to be an effective programmer in a business environment. He did get a job as a programmer and is doing just fine in his new career.

DARREL'S JIST CARD

Darrel Craig   (412) 437-6217

                                        Message: (412) 464-1273

Position Desired: PROGRAMMER/SYSTEMS MANAGEMENT

Skills: Over 10 years combined education and experience in data processing, business, and related fields. Programming ability in COBOL, RPG, BASIC, and FORTRAN. Knowledge of various data base and applications programs in networked PC, Mac, and mainframe environments. Substantial business experience including accounting, management, sales, and public relations.

Dedicated, self-starter, creative, dependable, and willing to relocate.

FIGURE 7-3 Darrel's Resume.

Darrel Craig

Career Objective
Challenging position in programming or related areas which would best utilize expertise in the business environment. This position should have many opportunities for an aggressive, dedicated individual with leadership abilities to advance.

Programming Skills
Include functional program design relating to business issues including payroll, inventory and data base management, sales, marketing, accounting and loan amortization reports. In conjunction with design would be coding, implementation, debugging, and file maintenance. Familiar with distributed network systems including PC's and Mac's and working knowledge of DOS, UNIX, COBOL, Basic, RPG and FORTRAN. Also familiar with mainframe environments including DEC, Prime, and IBM including tape and disk file access, organization and maintenance.

Areas of Expertise
Interpersonal communication strengths, public relations capabilities, innovative problem solving and analytical talents.

Sales
A total of nine years experience in sales and sales management. Sold security products to distributors and burglar alarm dealers. Increased company's sales from $16,000 to over $70,000 per month. Creatively organized sales programs and marketing concepts. Trained sales personnel in prospecting techniques while also training service personnel in proper installation of burglar alarms. Result: 90% of all new business was generated through referrals from existing customers.

Management
Managed burglar alarm company for four years while increasing profits yearly. Supervised office, sales, and installation personnel. Supervised and delegated work to assistants in accounting functions and inventory control. Worked as assistant credit manager, responsible for over $2 million per month in sales. Handled semi-annual inventory of five branch stores totaling millions of dollars and supervised 120 people.

Accounting
Balanced all books and prepared tax forms for burglar alarm company. Eight years experience in credit and collections, with emphasis on collections. Collection rates were over 98% each year and was able to collect a bad debt deemed "uncollectible" by company in excess of $250,000.

Education
School of Computer Technology, Pittsburgh, PA
Business Application Programming/TECH EXEC- 3.97 GPA

Robert Morris College, Pittsburgh, PA
Associate degree in Accounting, Minor in Management

2306 Cincinnati Street, Kingsford, PA 15171 (412) 437-6217
Message: (412) 464-1273

THOMAS MARRIN'S RESUME AND JIST CARD

Comments on Thomas' Resume:

This is one of those resumes that is hard to put into a category because it is neither a skills nor a chronological resume—but combines elements of both. Remember that I have suggested that you can break any rule that you want in putting together your own resume if you do so for a good reason. Thomas' resume does break some rules, but he does so for good reasons and the resume presents him well.

Thomas has kept his job objective quite broad and does not limit it to a particular type of industry or job title. Because he sees himself as a business manager, it does not matter to him much just what kind of business, though he prefers to work in a larger organization, as his job objective indicates.

His education is towards the top of his resume because he thought it would be a strength. His military experience, while not recent, is also listed towards the top because he also felt that would help him. Note how he presented his military experience using civilian language such as annual budgets and staff size, things that are easy to relate to a business environment.

Thomas has work experience with one employer for many years, but he presents each job he held there as a separate one. This approach allows him to provide more details about his accomplishments within each job and also clearly points out that these were promotions. This shows a progression of increasingly responsible jobs nicely.

This resume could easily have been a two-page resume and doing so would allow him to provide additional details on his job at Hayfield Publishing and in other areas. The extra space could also be used to provide more white space and a less crowded look, though it works fine as it is.

Thomas got a job in a smaller company (50 employees) as a vice president of operations and is as happy as a clam.

THOMAS' JIST CARD

Thomas Marrin   Answering Service: (716) 223-4705

Objective: Business management position requiring skills in problem solving, planning, organizing, and cost management.

Skills: B.A. degree in Business Administration and over ten years of management experience in progressively responsible positions. Responsible for as many as 40 staff and budgets in excess of $6 million. Consistent record of getting results. Excellent communication skills. Thorough knowledge of budgeting, cost savings, computerized database and spreadsheet programs. Like challenges and accept responsibility.

Willing to relocate
Results-oriented, good problem-solving skills, energetic

FIGURE 7-4   Thomas' Resume.

THOMAS P. MARRIN
80 Harrison Avenue
Baldwin L.I., New York 11563
Answering Service: (716) 223-4705

OBJECTIVE:
A middle/upper level management position with responsibilities including problem solving, planning, organizing, and budget management.

EDUCATION:
University of Notre Dame, BS in Business Administration. Course emphasis on accounting, supervision, and marketing. Upper 25% of class. Additional training: Advanced training in time management, organization behavior, and cost control.

MILITARY:
US Army — 2nd Infantry Division, 1984 to 1987. 1st Lieutenant and platoon leader —stationed in Korea and Ft. Knox, Kentucky. Supervised an annual budget of nearly $4 million and equipment valued at over $40 million. Responsible for training, scheduling, and activities of as many as 40 people. Received several commendations. Honorable discharge.

BUSINESS EXPERIENCE:

Wills Express Transit Co., Inc., Mineola, New York

Promoted to Vice President, Corporate Equipment — 1992 to Present
Controlled purchase, maintenance and disposal of 1100 trailers and 65 company cars with $6.7 MM operating and $8.0 MM Capital expense responsibilities

· Scheduled trailer purchases, 6 divisions
· Operated 2.3% under planned maintenance budget in company's second best profit
  year while operating revenues declined 2.5%.
· Originated schedule to correlate drivers' needs with available trailers.
· Developed systematic Purchase and Disposal Plan for company car fleet.
· Restructured Company Car Policy, saving 15% on per car cost.

Promoted to Asst. Vice President, Corporate Operations — 1991 to 1992
Coordinated activities of six sections of Corporate Operations with an operating budget over $10 million.

· Directed implementation of zero base budgeting.
· Developed and prepared Executive Officer analyses detailing achievable cost reduction
  measures. Resulted in cost reduction of over $600,000 in first two years.
· Designed policy and procedure for special equipment leasing program during peak
  seasons. Cut capital purchases by over $1 million.

Promoted to Manager of Communications — 1989 to 1991
Directed and Managed $1.4 MM communication network involving 650 phones, 150 WATS lines, 3 switchboards, 1 teletype machine, 5 employees.

· Installed computerized WATS Control System. Optimized utilization of WATS lines
  and pinpointed personal abuse. Achieved payback earlier than originally projected.
· Devised procedures that allowed simultaneous 20% increase in WATS calls and a
  $75,000/year savings.

Hayfield Publishing Company, Hempstead, New York.

Communications Administrator — 1987 to 1989

Managed daily operations of a large communications center. Reduced costs and improved services.

PETER NEELY'S RESUME AND JIST CARD

Comments on Peter's Resume:

Peter lost his factory job when the plant closed in the early 1990s. He had picked up a survival job as a truck driver and now wants to make this his career because it allows him to earn good money and he likes the work.

Notice how his resume emphasizes skills from previous experiences that are essential for success as a truck driver. This resume uses a "combined" format because it includes elements from both the skills and chronological resume formats. The skills approach allows him to emphasize specific skills that support his job objective and the chronological listing of jobs allows him to display his stable work history.

The miscellaneous jobs he had before 1977 are simply clustered together under one grouping, because they are not as important as more recent experience—and because doing this does not display his age. For the same reasons, he does not include dates for his military experience or high school graduation, nor does he separate them into different categories such as "Military Experience" or "Education." They just aren't as important in supporting his current job objective as they might be for a younger person. An unusual element here is his adding comments about not smoking or drinking, although it does work, as do his comments about a stable family life.

Peter also has another version of this resume that simply changed his job objective to include supervision and management of trucking operations and added a few details to support this. When it made sense, he used the other version.

He got a job in a smaller long distance trucking company driving a regular trip and now supervises other drivers.

PETER'S JIST CARD

Peter Neely

Messages: (237) 649-1234
Beeper: (237) 765-9876

Position: Truck Driver

Background and Skills: Over twenty years of stable work history including no traffic citations or accidents. Formal training in diesel mechanics and electrical systems. Am familiar with most major destinations and have excellent map-reading and problem-solving abilities. I can handle responsibility and have a track record of getting things done.

Excellent heath, good work history, dependable

FIGURE 7-5 Peter's Resume.

Peter Neely
203 Evergreen Road
Houston, Texas 39127
Messages:(237) 649-1234   Beeper:(237) 765-9876

POSITION DESIRED: Truck Driver

Summary of Work Experience:	Over twenty years of stable work history, including substantial experience with diesel engines, electrical systems, and truck driving.

SKILLS

Driving Record/ Licenses:	Chauffeur's license, qualified and able to drive anything that rolls. No traffic citations or accidents for over 20 years.
Vehicle Maintenance:	I maintain correct maintenance schedules and avoid most breakdowns as a result. Substantial mechanical and electrical systems training and experience permits many breakdowns to be repaired immediately and avoid towing.
Record Keeping:	Excellent attention to detail. Familiar with recording procedures and submit required records on a timely basis.
Routing:	Knowledge of many states. Good map-reading and route-planning skills.
Other:	Not afraid of hard work, flexible, get along well with others, meet deadlines, responsible.

WORK EXPERIENCE

1993 - Present	CAPITAL TRUCK CENTER, Houston, Texas Pick up and deliver all types of commercial vehicles from across the United States. Am trusted with handling large sums of money and handling complex truck purchasing transactions.
1983 - 1993	QUALITY PLATING CO., Houston, Texas Promoted from production to Quality Control. Developed numerous production improvements resulting in substantial cost savings.
1981 - 1983	BLUE CROSS MANUFACTURING, Houston, Texas Received several increases in salary and responsibility before leaving for a more challenging position.
1977 - 1981	Truck delivery of food products to destinations throughout the south. Also responsible for up to 12 drivers and equipment maintenance personnel.
Prior to 1977	Operated large diesel-powered electrical plants. Responsible for monitoring and maintenance on a rigid schedule.

OTHER

Four years experience in the U.S. Air Force operating power plants. Stationed in Alaska, California, Wyoming, and other states. Honorable discharge. High school graduate plus training in diesel engines and electrical systems. Excellent health, love the outdoors, stable family life, nonsmoker and nondrinker.

ANDREA ATWOOD'S RESUME AND JIST CARD

Comments on Andrea's Resume:

This resume uses few words and lots of white space. It looks better, I think, than more crowded resumes. I would like to see more numbers used to indicate performance or accomplishments. For example, what was the result of the more efficient record-keeping system she developed? And why did she receive the Employee-of-the-Month awards?

Andrea does not have substantial experience in her field, having had only one job. For this reason, this skills format allows her to present her strengths better than a chronological resume. Because she has formal training in retail sales and is a recent graduate, she could have given more details about specific courses she took or other school-related activities that would support her job objective. Even so, her resume does a good job of presenting her basic skills to an employer in an attractive format.

ANDREA'S JIST CARD

Andrea Atwood   Home: (303) 447-2111
                                                                Message: (303) 547-8201

Position Desired: Copywriter or Account Executive in Advertising or
Public Relations Agency

Skills: Two years of retail sales training including accounting, promotional writing, and advertising design. Computer skills in desktop publishing, graphics design, accounting, and word processing. Good written and verbal communication skills. Experienced in dealing with customers, direct sales, and in solving problems.

Punctual, honest, reliable, and hard-working

FIGURE 7-6 Andrea's Resume.

ANDREA ATWOOD
3231 East Harbor Road
Grand Rapids, Michigan 41103

Home: (303) 447-2111   Message: (303) 547-8201

Objective: A responsible position in retail sales.

**Areas of
Accomplishment:**

Customer Service	• Communicates well with all age groups.
	• Able to interpret customer concerns to help them find the items they want.
	• Received six Employee-of-the-Month awards in 3 years.
Merchandise Display	• Developed display skills via in-house training and experience.
	• Received Outstanding Trainee award for Christmas Toy Display
	• Dressed mannequins, arranged table displays, and organized sale merchandise.
Stock Control and Marking	• Maintained and marked stock during department manager's 6-week illness.
	• Developed more efficient record-keeping procedures.
Additional Skills	• Operate cash register and computerized accounting systems.
	• Willing to work evenings and weekends.
	• Punctual, honest, reliable, and hard-working.

Experience: Harper's Department Store
Grand Rapids, Michigan
1992 to present

Education: Central High School
Grand Rapids, Michigan
3.6/4.0 grade point average
Honor Graduate in Distributive Education

Two years retail sales training in Distributive
Education. Also courses in Business Writing,
Computerized Accounting and Word Processing.

MORE THOROUGH PREPARATION FOR THE INTERVIEW

Introduction

This is the kind of section that, if you are like me, you will be tempted to skip. There are, after all, lots of details, worksheets, and pages of information to read. I really can't blame you for being a tad intimidated and that is why I've put all this into a separate section. If you want "quick" information, this is probably not the section for you.

On the other hand, those who do take the time to learn more about their skills, define the ideal type of job for them, and better prepare themselves for the interview tend to get better jobs. So, you have to ask, is it worth it?

Look at it this way: Completing this section over the course of a few days won't take any more time than you probably already spend watching TV—yet the potential payoff is much greater. While Sections 1 and 2 do give you enough information to get out and get interviewing, this is the sort of section you should read and work on at night (instead of watching TV). Consider it a form of homework.

Chapters in This Section

While you might not want to read all of the chapters in this section, one or more of them are likely to be particularly important to you. Also note that those who are best prepared for the job search are often those who get the best jobs …

Chapter 8: Develop Your Skills Language

This is a very important chapter because it will help you identify your key skills. This is a most important matter because most job seekers do not do a good job presenting their skills in an interview. Those who do have a distinct advantage.

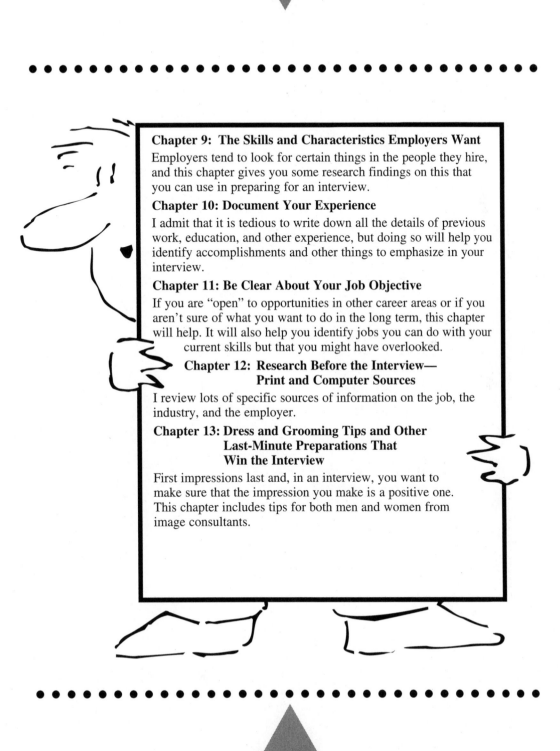

Chapter 9: The Skills and Characteristics Employers Want

Employers tend to look for certain things in the people they hire, and this chapter gives you some research findings on this that you can use in preparing for an interview.

Chapter 10: Document Your Experience

I admit that it is tedious to write down all the details of previous work, education, and other experience, but doing so will help you identify accomplishments and other things to emphasize in your interview.

Chapter 11: Be Clear About Your Job Objective

If you are "open" to opportunities in other career areas or if you aren't sure of what you want to do in the long term, this chapter will help. It will also help you identify jobs you can do with your current skills but that you might have overlooked.

**Chapter 12: Research Before the Interview—
Print and Computer Sources**

I review lots of specific sources of information on the job, the industry, and the employer.

**Chapter 13: Dress and Grooming Tips and Other
Last-Minute Preparations That
Win the Interview**

First impressions last and, in an interview, you want to make sure that the impression you make is a positive one. This chapter includes tips for both men and women from image consultants.

8

DEVELOP YOUR
SKILLS LANGUAGE

• • • • • • • • • • • • • • • • • • • •

**Quick
Tip**

*It is absolutely essential
that you know what you
are good at and enjoy
doing. Being able to pre-
sent skills effectively has
helped many people get
jobs over others with
better credentials. But
this chapter is far more
important than that.
Knowing your skills is
the key to making good
decisions about your
future and finding a job
that matches what you
do well. Developing a
skills language can make
a tremendous difference
to you, so I encourage
you to complete the
activities in this chapter
carefully. Doing so can
pay off in a variety of
ways.*

• • • • • • • • • • • • • • • • • • • •

Knowing what you are good at is an essential part of
doing well in an interview. But it is also important
to you in other ways. For example, unless you use those
skills that you enjoy *and* are good at, it is unlikely that you
will be fully satisfied with your job.

Most people are not good at expressing the skills they have.
I can tell you this based on many years of working with
groups of job seekers. When asked, few can quickly tell me
what they are good at and fewer yet can quickly present the
specific skills they have that are needed to succeed in the
job they want.

Many employers also note that most job seekers don't
present their skills effectively. According to one survey of
employers, more than 90 percent of the people they interview cannot adequately define the skills they have to support their ability to do the job. They may *have* the necessary
skills, but they can't communicate them.

In an exhaustive study titled *Job Search: A Review of the Literature*, Steve Mangum cites a variety of research studies and concludes that "No single factor carries more negative connotations in the interview than an inability to communicate." It is problem number one in the interview process. So, this chapter is designed to help you fix that problem.

●●●●●●●●●●●●●●●●●●●●●●●●●●●●●●

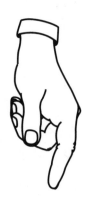

THE SKILLS TRIAD

Quick Fact

Analyzing skills for even a simple task can become quite complicated. But a useful way to organize skills, for our purposes, is to divide them into three basic types. Each of these are explained briefly below. The rest of the chapter will help you identify your own key skills in each of these areas.

ADAPTIVE SKILLS / PERSONALITY TRAITS

These are skills you use every day to survive and get along. They are called adaptive or self-management skills because they allow you to adapt or adjust to a variety of situations. Some of them also could be considered part of your basic personality. Examples of adaptive skills valued by employers include getting to work on time, honesty, enthusiasm, and being able to get along with others.

TRANSFERABLE SKILLS

These are general skills that can be useful in a variety of jobs. For example, writing clearly, good language skills, or the ability to organize and prioritize tasks would be desirable skills in many jobs. These are called transferable skills because they can be transferred from one job—or even one career—to another.

JOB-RELATED SKILLS

These are the skills people typically first think of when asked, "Do you have any skills?" They are related to a particular job or type of job. An auto mechanic, for example, needs to know how to tune engines and repair brakes. Typing or being able to read a micrometer are other examples of job-related skills.

This system of dividing skills into three categories is not perfect. Some things, such as being trustworthy, dependable, or well-organized are really not skills as much as they are personality traits. There is also some overlap between the three skills categories. For example, a skill such as being organized can be considered either adaptive or transferrable. For our purposes, however, the Skills Triad is a very useful system for identifying skills that are important in the job search.

IDENTIFYING YOUR SKILLS

Because it is so important to know your skills, I have included a series of checklists and other activities in this chapter to help you identify the skills that will be most important to emphasize in an interview. Doing this will help you develop a skills language that can also be very helpful to you in writing your resume and conducting your job search.

ADAPTIVE SKILLS—SKILLS THAT ALLOW YOU TO ADAPT TO NEW SITUATIONS

▼▼▼▼▼▼▼▼▼▼▼▼▼▼▼▼▼▼▼▼▼▼▼▼▼▼▼

On the following lines, list three things about yourself that you think make you a good worker. Take your time. Think about what an employer might like about you or the way you work.

1. _____

2. _____

3. _____

The skills you just wrote may be among the most important things that an employer will want to know about you. Most (but not all) people write adaptive skills when asked this question. Whatever you wrote, these are important things to mention in the interview. In fact, presenting these skills well will often allow a less experienced job seeker to get the job over someone with better credentials.

ADAPTIVE SKILLS/PERSONALITY TRAITS CHECKLIST

I have created a list of adaptive skills that tend to be important to employers. The ones listed as "The Minimum" are those that most employers consider essential. They will typically not hire someone who has problems in these areas.

Look over the list and put a checkmark next to each adaptive skill on the list that you have. Put a second checkmark next to those skills that are particularly important for you to use or include in your next job.

ADAPTIVE SKILLS CHECKLIST

The Minimum
- ❑ Good attendance
- ❑ Honesty
- ❑ Arrive on time
- ❑ Follow instructions
- ❑ Meet deadlines
- ❑ Get along with supervisor
- ❑ Get along with co-workers
- ❑ Hardworking, productive

Other Adaptive Skills
- ❑ Able to coordinate
- ❑ Friendly
- ❑ Ambitious
- ❑ Good-natured
- ❑ Assertive
- ❑ Helpful
- ❑ Capable
- ❑ Humble
- ❑ Cheerful
- ❑ Imaginative
- ❑ Competent
- ❑ Independent
- ❑ Complete assignments
- ❑ Industrious
- ❑ Conscientious
- ❑ Informal
- ❑ Creative
- ❑ Intelligent

- ❑ Dependable
- ❑ Intuitive
- ❑ Discreet
- ❑ Learn quickly
- ❑ Eager
- ❑ Loyal
- ❑ Efficient
- ❑ Mature
- ❑ Energetic
- ❑ Methodical
- ❑ Enthusiastic
- ❑ Modest
- ❑ Expressive
- ❑ Motivated
- ❑ Flexible
- ❑ Natural
- ❑ Formal
- ❑ Open-minded
- ❑ Optimistic
- ❑ Sincere
- ❑ Original
- ❑ Solve problems
- ❑ Patient
- ❑ Spontaneous
- ❑ Persistent
- ❑ Steady
- ❑ Physically strong
- ❑ Tactful
- ❑ Practice new skills
- ❑ Take pride in work
- ❑ Reliable
- ❑ Tenacious
- ❑ Resourceful
- ❑ Thrifty

- ❑ Responsible
- ❑ Trustworthy
- ❑ Self-confident
- ❑ Versatile
- ❑ Sense of humor
- ❑ Well-organized

Add any adaptive skills to the list above that were not listed but that you think are important to include.

- ❑ _____
- ❑ _____
- ❑ _____
- ❑ _____
- ❑ _____
- ❑ _____
- ❑ _____
- ❑ _____
- ❑ _____
- ❑ _____
- ❑ _____
- ❑ _____

YOUR TOP ADAPTIVE SKILLS

▼▼▼▼▼▼▼▼▼▼▼▼▼▼▼▼▼▼▼▼▼▼▼▼▼▼▼

Carefully review the checklist you just completed and select the three adaptive skills you feel are most important for you to tell an employer about or that you most want to use in your next job. These three skills are *extremely* important to present to an employer in an interview.

1. _____

2. _____

3. _____

TRANSFERABLE SKILLS—SKILLS THAT TRANSFER TO MANY JOBS

Over the years, I have assembled a list of transferable skills that are important in a wide variety of jobs. In the checklist that follows, the skills listed as "Key Transferable Skills" are those that I consider to be most important to many employers. The key skills are also those that are often required in jobs with more responsibility and higher pay, so it pays to emphasize these skills if you have them.

The remaining transferable skills are grouped into categories that may be helpful to you. Go ahead and check each skill you are strong in, then double-check the skills you want to use in your next job. When you are finished, you should have checked 10 to 20 skills at least once.

TRANSFERABLE SKILLS CHECKLIST

Key Transferable Skills
- ❏ Meet deadlines
- ❏ Plan
- ❏ Speak in public
- ❏ Control budgets
- ❏ Supervise others
- ❏ Increase sales or efficiency
- ❏ Accept responsibility
- ❏ Instruct others
- ❏ Solve problems
- ❏ Manage money or budgets
- ❏ Manage people
- ❏ Meet the public
- ❏ Negotiate
- ❏ Organize/manage projects
- ❏ Written communications

Other Transferable Skills

Dealing with Things
- ❏ Use my hands
- ❏ Assemble or make things
- ❏ Build, observe, inspect things
- ❏ Construct or repair buildings
- ❏ Operate tools and machinery
- ❏ Drive or operate vehicles
- ❏ Repair things
- ❏ Good with my hands
- ❏ Use complex equipment

Dealing with Data
- ❏ Analyze data or facts
- ❏ Investigate
- ❏ Audit records
- ❏ Keep financial records
- ❏ Budget
- ❏ Locate answers or information
- ❏ Calculate, compute
- ❏ Manage money
- ❏ Classify data
- ❏ Negotiate
- ❏ Compare, inspect, or record facts
- ❏ Count, observe, compile
- ❏ Research
- ❏ Detail-oriented
- ❏ Synthesize
- ❏ Evaluate
- ❏ Take inventory

Working with People
- ❏ Administer
- ❏ Patient
- ❏ Care for
- ❏ Persuade
- ❏ Confront others
- ❏ Pleasant
- ❏ Counsel people
- ❏ Sensitive
- ❏ Demonstrate
- ❏ Sociable
- ❏ Diplomatic
- ❏ Supervise
- ❏ Help others
- ❏ Tactful
- ❏ Insightful
- ❏ Teach
- ❏ Interview others
- ❏ Tolerant
- ❏ Kind
- ❏ Tough
- ❏ Listen
- ❏ Trust
- ❏ Negotiate
- ❏ Understand
- ❏ Outgoing

Using Words, Ideas
- ❏ Articulate
- ❏ Inventive
- ❏ Communicate verbally
- ❏ Logical
- ❏ Correspond with others
- ❏ Remember information
- ❏ Research
- ❏ Create new ideas
- ❏ Design
- ❏ Speak in public
- ❏ Edit
- ❏ Write clearly

Leadership
- ❏ Arrange social functions
- ❏ Motivate people
- ❏ Competitive
- ❏ Negotiate agreements
- ❏ Decisive
- ❏ Plan
- ❏ Delegate
- ❏ Run meetings
- ❏ Direct others
- ❏ Self-controlled
- ❏ Explain things to others
- ❏ Self-motivated
- ❏ Get results
- ❏ Solve problems
- ❏ Mediate problems
- ❏ Take risks

Creative, Artistic
- ❏ Artistic
- ❏ Music appreciation
- ❏ Dance, body movement
- ❏ Perform, act
- ❏ Draw, sketch, render
- ❏ Play instruments
- ❏ Expressive
- ❏ Present artistic ideas

Add Any Other Transferable Skills That You Think Are Important
- ❏ _____
- ❏ _____
- ❏ _____
- ❏ _____
- ❏ _____

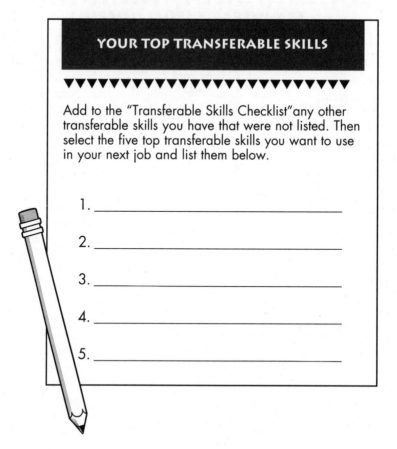

YOUR TOP TRANSFERABLE SKILLS

▼▼▼▼▼▼▼▼▼▼▼▼▼▼▼▼▼▼▼▼▼▼▼

Add to the "Transferable Skills Checklist" any other transferable skills you have that were not listed. Then select the five top transferable skills you want to use in your next job and list them below.

1. _____

2. _____

3. _____

4. _____

5. _____

IDENTIFYING YOUR JOB-RELATED SKILLS

Many jobs require skills that are specific to that occupation. An airline pilot will obviously need to know how to fly an airplane and, thankfully, having good adaptive and transferable skills would not be enough to be considered for that job.

Job-related skills may have been gained in a variety of ways including education, training, work, hobbies, or other life experiences. The next chapter in this book will review your education, work, and other experiences and use this as a basis for identifying your key job-related skills which can then be presented to a potential employer.

9

THE SKILLS AND CHARACTERISTICS EMPLOYERS WANT

Quick Tip

While I rely on common sense to develop much of my advice, I also look for research that gives tips on how to approach the interviewing process. This chapter provides information from various employer surveys. I try to keep my information current by researching various job-search techniques and incorporating them into my teaching strategy. I think that you will find the information in this chapter interesting. It will help you understand what employers look for during the interview process.

Exactly what are employers searching for in the parade of candidates that file through their offices? Among the top traits: education, pride in their work, team orientation, flexibility, enthusiasm, maturity … in a phrase, basic workplace skills. By describing what several studies say employers expect in their future staff, this chapter spells out exactly which skills and experiences equal "basic workplace skills."

THE SKILLS EMPLOYERS WANT—THE RESULTS OF A SURVEY OF EMPLOYERS

In chapters 2 and 8, I suggested that basic skills were very important to employers. There the concept of adaptive skills was presented and I suggested to you that these were very important to emphasize in an interview.

There is substantial support for that suggestion. In an important study entitled *Workplace Basics—The Skills Employers Want*, a large cross-section of employers was surveyed to discover what they wanted in the people they hired. This survey was jointly conducted by the American Society of Training and Development (ASTD) and the U.S. Department of Labor (DOL). It turns out that most of the skills employers want are either adaptive or transferable skills. These are the skills, if you recall, that are basic to your ability to do any job. Of course, specific job-related skills will remain important, but basic skills form an essential foundation for success on the job.

Following are the top skills employers identified in the *Workplace Basics* survey:

THE TOP SKILLS EMPLOYERS WANT

▲ **1. Learning to learn**

▲ **2. Basic academic skills in reading, writing, and computation**

▲ **3. Listening and oral communication**

▲ **4. Creative thinking and problem solving**

▲ **5. Self-esteem, motivation, and goal setting**

▲ **6. Personal and career development**

▲ **7. Interpersonal/negotiation skills and teamwork**

▲ **8. Organizational effectiveness and leadership**

Quick
Fact

Because all of the above are either adaptive or transferable skills, I rest my case regarding their importance. Let's look at each of these skills in a bit more detail.

The ASTD/DOL *Workplace Basics* study discussed American competitiveness and stressed the importance of ensuring basic skills in our workforce in order to be competitive in a global economy. It presented the findings of surveys that indicated the key skills needed for success in the workplace. It also included suggestions for establishing effective programs to improve those skills.

Quick
Tip

Employers value adaptive and transferable skills and it is important to emphasize these skills in your interviews. Once you know what employers want, you can emphasize those skills you have that best meet their needs. If you have been thorough in identifying the kind of work you want to do, the skills an employer needs should closely match those you want to use.

"*Never assume that you are exempt from new training.***"**

Quick
Fact

☑ LEARNING TO LEARN

According to the *Workplace Basics* study, knowing how to learn is the foundation for all future success. With this skill, you can achieve competency in all other areas. Without this skill, you can't learn as rapidly or as efficiently.

You can never assume that you are exempt from new training because your duties involve routine tasks. Competitive pressures compel employers to shift employees between jobs and responsibilities, which places a premium on your ability to absorb, process, and apply new information quickly and effectively.

From the organization's perspective, having an employee who knows how to learn is more cost-effective because it reduces the time and resources spent on training. Your adaptability also means you'll have reason to stay longer, and every employer values the money he or she can save by hiring a long-term employee.

Quick Fact

To enhance your learning skills, first identify the primary sense you rely on to learn: vision, hearing, or touch. Then begin filtering all information that comes your way through that channel. For instance, I learn best by seeing information in print. So whether someone asks a favor of me, needs a file, explains something, etc., I jot it down on a piece of paper. If you learn through hearing, consider dictating manuals and articles into a cassette recorder and playing them back. If you learn by tactile methods, and "feel," print out computer files so that you can hold the paper in your hand while you read, and write out summaries of information as you gather it. How you say it isn't as important at this point as holding a pen, which stimulates your brain to learn.

☑ READING, WRITING, AND COMPUTATION

Employers have long revered basic academic skills: reading, writing, and computation (or arithmetic for those of us who attended school before 1980). Today, as manual labor is increasingly being replaced by automation, basic academic skills are becoming more and more vital to workplace survival.

Now, fortunately, the vast majority of us are literate and numerate. But frequently, employees can't use these skills effectively in the workplace. Sometimes, as the ASTD/DOL study points out, it's because we're "rusty" and are called upon to use mathematical principles we haven't used for years. Sometimes it's because we must use those skills in a different context than what we originally learned. And sometimes we have the base knowledge but no understanding of how to expand and apply it.

Most employers today cannot compete successfully without a workforce that has sound basic academic skills. Workers spend an average of an hour and a half to two hours per work day reading forms, charts, graphs, manuals, and computer terminals. Writing remains the primary form of communication for transmitting policies, procedures, and concepts. Computation is used to conduct inventories, report on production levels, or measure machine parts or specifications, and so on.

Deficiencies in these areas are reflected in productivity decline, increased accident rates, costly production errors, and the inability to implement job retraining. In other words, your inability to efficiently handle basic tasks costs the employer much more than just your wages—it could cost you both your livelihoods.

Quick Tip

Here's how you can reapply "the three Rs" to meet workplace demands:

Reading: The classroom setting taught you to follow directions and internalize data for future recall—in other words, you memorized what you needed to know. Today's work-related reading tasks require you to be analytical, to summarize information, and to monitor your own comprehension. You should focus on reading to locate information and use higher-level thinking strategies to solve problems.

Writing: The classroom setting emphasized creative, descriptive writing, and regurgitation of learned facts and events—the dreaded essay exam. At work, you need to rely on analysis, conceptualization, synthesis, and distillation of information. Practice writing clear, succinct points and proposals.

Arithmetic: In school, math concepts were presented sequentially, beginning with fundamentals such as addition and subtraction and moving on to geometry, trigonometry, and calculus. The learning process involved handing you the problems for independent practice, repeated drills, and standardized tests. Now you need to emphasize reasoning, estimating, and identifying and solving problems.

☑ LISTENING AND ORAL COMMUNICATION

Let's face it—you may not have taken drama or debate electives in school, but on the job you must communicate procedures, information, and problems effectively.

You may be asked to defend your position. And you are always required to listen.

Business leaders estimate that deficiencies in these skills cost employers millions each year in lost productivity and errors. Communications skills are at the heart of getting and keeping customers. Pitching innovation, contributing to quality circles, resolving conflict, and providing meaningful feedback all hinge on oral communication and listening skills.

Quick Fact

The average person spends 8 percent of communications time writing, 13 percent reading, 24 percent speaking, and 55 percent listening. According to a survey by the International Association of Corporate and Professional Recruiters, if two job applicants have equal professional qualifications, employers base their selection on the candidates' energy and verbal skills. So, you see, communication skills pay off in the interview as well as on the job …

To enhance your oral communications skills, study the importance of voice inflection and body language when communicating. Most colleges offer continuing education courses that are easy to grasp and even entertaining. As for listening, you need to concentrate on identifying exactly which of five areas apply to the workplace situation at hand: content, conversation, long-term context, emotional meaning, and following directions.

"Effectiveness in the workplace is linked to positive self-esteem and personal management."

☑ CREATIVE THINKING AND PROBLEM SOLVING

Problem-solving skills include the ability to recognize and define problems, invent and implement solutions, and track and evaluate results. To do this, you need cognitive skills, group interaction skills, and problem-processing skills. That means you need to look at problems in new ways and invent new solutions both on your own and in a group.

Quick Fact

An organization's ability to achieve its strategic objective often depends on the problem solving and creative thinking skills of its workforce. Employers know that unresolved problems create dysfunctional relationships in their workplaces. Ultimately, these problems create barriers to dealing with change in creative ways.

☑ SELF-ESTEEM, MOTIVATION, AND GOAL SETTING

An individual's effectiveness in the workplace can be linked directly to positive self-esteem and personal management. A good self-image means you take pride in your work. Because when you believe in yourself, you are more likely to set goals and achieve them.

Quick Fact

According to Korn/Ferry International in Atlanta, penny-pinchers are out and visionaries are in as companies seek new staff. Companies now look for those who can build organizations and "take them to the next plateau," Alan Neely, managing director of the firm, told the *Wall Street Journal*.

Your ability to set goals and meet them will become evident as you exceed production quotas or meet deadlines. Solid personal and career development skills are apparent when you efficiently integrate new technology or processes, think creatively, display high productivity, and pursue skills enhancement through training or education.

Employees with self-esteem also have laid the groundwork for good interpersonal relationships, negotiation skills, and leadership. Overall, to compete in world markets, employees need people who can operate effectively within the parameters of their organization, assume responsibility willingly, and motivate co-workers toward exemplary performance. These skills, once only identified with those on the "fast track," are now basic ingredients.

Ironically, just as employers are recognizing this need for employees with positive self-esteem, they are faced with a shrinking entry-level labor pool which will propel them toward selecting workers from populations that have been buffeted by poverty, circumstance, and a negative environment—workers who tend to have low self-esteem! And at the same time, the frustrating realities of business today—frequent mergers, downsizing, lay-offs—can erode established workers' self-esteem.

☑ PERSONAL AND CAREER DEVELOPMENT

The *Workplace Basics* study makes it clear that employers want to hire those with a clear sense of where they want their lives/careers to go. They want those who have set goals and are willing to work toward them. They know that those with well-planned career goals are more likely to benefit from related training and to make more successful transitions to higher levels of responsibility. Of course, those career and life goals need to be compatible with the goals of the organization, but few employers are impressed by applicants who don't know what they want to do.

Quick Reference

☑ INTERPERSONAL/NEGOTIATION SKILLS AND LEADERSHIP

The ability to work as part of a team has become increasingly important over the past few decades. The team approach has been proven to result in higher productivity, product quality, and an increased quality of worklife. Team-building skills are important to meeting organizational goals and in adapting quickly to change. Skills such as judging appropriate behavior, coping with undesirable behavior in others, absorbing stress, dealing with uncertainty, inspiring confidence in others, sharing responsibility, and interacting easily with others are becoming increasingly important to employers. These skills allow people to successfully negotiate problems and solutions and more readily accept responsibility and leadership roles.

Quick Tip

Emphasize "Workplace Basics" in the interview. Because the skills mentioned above are among the most important to employers, you can see how vital it is to emphasize those skills you possess.

☑ ORGANIZATIONAL EFFECTIVENESS AND LEADERSHIP

To be effective in an organization, employees need a sense of the workings of the organization and how their actions affect the firm's objectives. An employee who can be an effective problem solver, innovator, and team builder is of great value to an employer. Understanding how things can get done—and making things happen without undue disruption in operations—makes you a great asset to the company as well as a potential leader.

SOME TIPS ON CREATING A POSITIVE IMPRESSION

Most interviews are quite subjective and few interviewers have received training in how to conduct an interview. However, attempts have been made to make interviewers a bit more objective in their evaluations.

Quick
Fact

In a book by Arthur Bell entitled *Extraviewing*, he points out that American managers typically tend to trust subjective impressions over objective data when appraising you. This is otherwise known as "gut instinct" and is an important element in the interview process. But just what affects this reaction? Bell includes a list of traits employers react to during an interview. The traits were gathered in a survey of employers conducted by Baylor University researchers Joe Cox and David Schlueter.

TRAITS THAT TEND TO CREATE POSITIVE IMPRESSIONS IN AN INTERVIEW

- ✔ Appropriate responses to questions
- ✔ Enthusiasm
- ✔ Maturity
- ✔ Confidence
- ✔ Emotional stability
- ✔ Appropriate appearance
- ✔ Intelligence
- ✔ Work experience
- ✔ Language fluency/verbal skills
- ✔ Potential for advancement
- ✔ Initiative
- ✔ Controlled energy
- ✔ Body language
- ✔ Clear career goals
- ✔ Good grades
- ✔ Outside activities

☑ BEHAVIORAL MEASURES THAT CAN AFFECT YOUR INTERVIEW IMPRESSION

While we all react to subtle cues when evaluating other people, there are some cues that interviewers react to. In a book entitled *The Speaker's Edge*, the authors Bell and Skopec list a score sheet to evaluate candidates' presentation skills. Here are some of the positive behavioral details it includes:

● ●

Posture and Dress

Stood up straight

Held head at appropriate angle

Didn't play with clothing

Gestures and movement

Used natural hand/arm movements

Did not sway

Did not shift

Eyes and expression

Sustained eye contact

Directed and distributed eye contact appropriately

Did not blink excessively

Voice

Used a comfortable pace for conversation/comprehension

Employed appropriate variety in pace

Used correct pronunciation

● ●

KEY EVALUATION FACTORS FOR SELECTING MANAGERS AND EXECUTIVES

When the International Association of Corporate and Professional Recruiters in Louisville, Kentucky, asked its members to name the single most important characteristic of a top executive in today's business environment, the results were split. Fifty percent said that decisiveness is the key to the executive suite, while 24 percent felt that experience was the vital ingredient. Low marks went to determination (14 percent), fairness (4 percent), aggressiveness (3 percent), tolerance (1 percent), sense of humor (1 percent), and a mix of other responses.

What was the most important factor in the decision to hire an executive job candidate? Opinion was almost equally divided between career track record (46 percent) and the ability to fit into the company's corporate culture (42 percent). Only 10 percent said that relevant experience in the company's field was the decisive factor.

What if two job applicants had equal professional qualifications? The candidates' energy (46 percent) and verbal skills (24 percent) topped the list of hiring selection traits. Other qualities, such as extroverted personality, sense of humor, friendliness, and appearance had little effect on the final decision, according to this survey.

WHAT EMPLOYERS DON'T WANT UNDER ANY CIRCUMSTANCES

Quick Reference

Interviewers are constantly on the lookout for unethical persons who deny their tactics are anything less than above-board. Behavioral scientists George Dudley and Shannon Goodson have devoted 20 years of research and 700 studies to outlining a method to recognize such people, which they present in a book entitled *Earning What You're Worth?* If any of these traits fit you, I recommend you seek professional career counseling to augment your chances of landing a job:

- ☛ Inappropriately calm and poised, even when caught in a lie
- ☛ Explain being caught in a lie as a "harmless misunderstanding"
- ☛ Melodramatic use of righteous indignation to overassert character, credibility, values, or integrity
- ☛ Concealed history of legal problems and financial "misunderstandings"
- ☛ Deal with shady ethical issues with phrases such as "It's just how you look at it" or "Everybody does it"
- ☛ Use simplistic, manipulative techniques to gain rapport and advantage
- ☛ Rely on words such as "integrity," "openness," and "trust" to deflect requests for proof of character
- ☛ Use verbal ambiguity as a manipulative technique

THE LAST WORD

Quick Reminder

What really wins that job offer? The outplacement firm Swain & Swain of New York City sums it up: Your particular job market situation and whether you are moving on in your field or changing careers counts for 20 percent of a successful job search. Your resources and background account for 30 percent. But a full 50 percent is your own attitude and job search skills—the very things you can do the most about.

10

DOCUMENT YOUR EXPERIENCE

Quick Tip

I admit that this is a tedious chapter, with lots of forms to complete. And, for that reason, you would be forgiven for not wanting to complete them all. But the details this chapter asks for will help you recollect skills, accomplishments, competencies, and results that can later help you to handle an interview more effectively, write a better resume, and get a better job. All the information will give you a chance to reflect on your varied experiences and gather up those that best support what you want to do next.

An interview requires you to provide information about what you have done in the past. This chapter will help you collect the basic information needed to do that but it will also encourage you to consider your accomplishments, identify additional skills, and develop specific examples of when and where you used those skills. These additions to the dry facts can help you present yourself far more effectively in an interview. This thorough review of your history will also prepare you to better complete applications and write a better resume.

A series of forms will ask you for information on your education, training, work and volunteer history, and other life experiences. While you may have already completed some of this information in previous sections of this book, the forms that follow are considerably more detailed.

When completing the forms in this chapter, emphasize the key skills you have identified from the previous chapters. Those skills, as well as your accomplishments and results, are of particular interest to most employers.

Pay special attention to those experiences and accomplishments that you really enjoyed—these often demonstrate skills that you should try to use in your next job. When possible, include numbers to describe your activities or their results. For example, saying "spoke to groups as large as 200 people" has more impact than "did presentations."

In some cases, you may want to write a draft on a separate sheet of paper before completing the form in this book. Use an erasable pen or pencil on the worksheets to allow for changes. In all sections, emphasize the skills and accomplishments that best support your ability to do the job you are seeking. If you completed the worksheets in chapter 7, you may wish to refer back to those to help with your responses here.

● ●

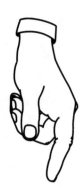

EDUCATION AND TRAINING WORKSHEET

Most of us, in our early years of schooling, managed to acquire some basic skills that are important in most jobs: getting along with others, reading instructions, and accepting supervision. Later on, courses became more specialized and relevant to potential careers.

Use this worksheet to review your educational experiences. Some courses may seem more important to certain careers than others. But even courses that don't seem to support a particular career choice can be an important source of certain skills.

EDUCATION WORKSHEET

High School Worksheet

Unless you are a recent high school graduate, most employers won't be interested in too many details related to your work in high school. Still, it can be worthwhile to emphasize highlights, particularly if you are a recent graduate.

Name of school(s)/years attended: _____

_____

Subjects you did well in or might relate to the job you want: _____

_____

_____

_____

_____

_____

Extracurricular activities/hobbies/leisure activities: _____

_____

_____

_____

_____

_____

Accomplishments/things you did well (in or out of school): _____

_____

_____

_____

_____

_____

College Worksheet

If you graduated from college or took college classes, this is often of interest to an employer. If you are a new graduate, these experiences can be particularly important. Consider those things that directly support your ability to do the job. For example, working your way through school supports your being hardworking. If you took courses that specifically support your job, you can include details on these as well.

Name of school(s)/years attended: _____

_____

Courses related to job objective: _____

_____

_____

_____

_____

Extracurricular activities/hobbies/leisure activities: _____

_____

_____

_____

_____

Accomplishments/things you did well (in or out of school): _____

_____

_____

_____

_____

Specific things you learned or can do that relate to the job you want:

_____

_____

_____

_____

Post-High School Training

List any training that might relate to the job you want. Include military and on-the-job training, workshops, or informal training (such as from a hobby).

Training/dates/certificates: _____

_____

_____

_____

_____

_____

_____

Specific things you can do as a result: _____

_____

_____

_____

_____

_____

_____

_____

Specific things you learned or can do that relate to the job you want:

_____

_____

_____

_____

_____

_____

_____

_____

WORK AND VOLUNTEER HISTORY WORKSHEET

Use this worksheet to list each major job you have held and the information related to each. Begin with your most recent job first, followed by previous ones.

Include military experience and unpaid work here too. Both are work and are particularly important if you do not have much paid civilian work experience. Create additional sheets to cover all of your significant jobs or unpaid experiences as needed. If you have been promoted, consider handling that as a separate job.

Whenever possible, provide numbers to support what you did: number of people served over one or more years; number of transactions processed; percent sales increase; total inventory value you were responsible for; payroll of the staff you supervised; total budget you were responsible for; and other data. As much as possible, mention results using numbers too.

I have provided several of the worksheets but, if you need more, please feel free to photocopy extras for each of the jobs you need to document.

• •

JOB / VOLUNTEER WORKSHEET

....

Job #1

Name of organization: _____

Address: _____

_____

Employed from: _____ **to:** _____

Job title(s): _____

Supervisor's name: _____

Phone number: (___ **)** _____

Machinery or equipment you used: _____

_____

_____

_____

Data, information, or reports you created or used: _____

_____

_____

_____

People-oriented duties or responsibilities to co-workers, customers, others: _____

_____

_____

_____

_____

_____

Services you provided or goods you produced: _____

_____

_____

_____

_____

_____

Promotions or salary increases, if any: _____

_____

_____

Details on anything you did to help the organization, such as increase productivity, simplify or reorganize job duties, decrease costs, increase profits, improve working conditions, reduce turnover, or other improvements. Quantify results when possible—for example, "Increased order processing by 50 percent, with no increase in staff costs."

_____

_____

_____

_____

_____

_____

Specific things you learned or can do that relate to the job you want:

_____

_____

_____

_____

_____

_____

What would your supervisor say about you? _____

_____

_____

_____

_____

_____

JOB / VOLUNTEER WORKSHEET

....

Job #2

Name of organization: _____

Address: _____

_____

Employed from: _____ to: _____

Job title(s): _____

Supervisor's name: _____

Phone number: ( ) _____

Machinery or equipment you used: _____

_____

_____

_____

Data, information, or reports you created or used: _____

_____

_____

_____

People-oriented duties or responsibilities to co-workers, customers,

others: _____

_____

_____

_____

_____

_____

Services you provided or goods you produced: _____

_____

_____

_____

_____

_____

Promotions or salary increases, if any: _____

_____

_____

Details on anything you did to help the organization, such as increase productivity, simplify or reorganize job duties, decrease costs, increase profits, improve working conditions, reduce turnover, or other improvements. Quantify results when possible—for example, "Increased order processing by 50 percent, with no increase in staff costs."

_____

_____

_____

_____

_____

_____

_____

Specific things you learned or can do that relate to the job you want:

_____

_____

_____

_____

_____

_____

What would your supervisor say about you? _____

_____

_____

_____

_____

_____

JOB / VOLUNTEER WORKSHEET

Job #3

Name of organization: _____

Address: _____

_____

Employed from: _____ **to:** _____

Job title(s): _____

Supervisor's name: _____

Phone number: ( ) _____

Machinery or equipment you used: _____

_____

_____

_____

Data, information, or reports you created or used: _____

_____

_____

_____

People-oriented duties or responsibilities to co-workers, customers, others: _____

_____

_____

_____

_____

_____

Services you provided or goods you produced: _____

_____

_____

_____

_____

_____

Promotions or salary increases, if any: _____

_____

_____

Details on anything you did to help the organization, such as increase productivity, simplify or reorganize job duties, decrease costs, increase profits, improve working conditions, reduce turnover, or other improvements. Quantify results when possible—for example, "Increased order processing by 50 percent, with no increase in staff costs."

_____

_____

_____

_____

_____

_____

Specific things you learned or can do that relate to the job you want:

_____

_____

_____

_____

_____

_____

What would your supervisor say about you? _____

_____

_____

_____

_____

_____

JOB / VOLUNTEER WORKSHEET

··

Job #4

Name of organization: _____

Address: _____

_____

Employed from: _____**to:** _____

Job title(s): _____

Supervisor's name: _____

Phone number: (   ) _____

Machinery or equipment you used: _____

_____

_____

_____

Data, information, or reports you created or used: _____

_____

_____

_____

People-oriented duties or responsibilities to co-workers, customers, others: _____

_____

_____

_____

_____

_____

Services you provided or goods you produced: _____

_____

_____

_____

_____

_____

Promotions or salary increases, if any: _____

_____

_____

Details on anything you did to help the organization, such as increase productivity, simplify or reorganize job duties, decrease costs, increase profits, improve working conditions, reduce turnover, or other improvements. Quantify results when possible—for example, "Increased order processing by 50 percent, with no increase in staff costs."

_____

_____

_____

_____

_____

_____

Specific things you learned or can do that relate to the job you want:

_____

_____

_____

_____

_____

_____

What would your supervisor say about you? _____

_____

_____

_____

_____

_____

_____

KEY ACCOMPLISHMENTS AND SKILLS TO TELL AN EMPLOYER

Here are a few questions that can help you consider which of the things from your history are most important to mention in an interview or include in your resume.

▼▼

1. **What are the most important accomplishments and skills you can tell an employer regarding your education and training?**

   _____

   _____

   _____

   _____

   _____

2. **What are the most important accomplishments and skills you can present to an employer regarding your paid and unpaid work experiences?**

   _____

   _____

   _____

   _____

   _____

   _____

   _____

3. **What are the most important accomplishments and skills you can present to an employer regarding your other life experiences?**

   _____

   _____

   _____

   _____

   _____

   _____

▲▲

The above skills are the ones to emphasize in an interview!

BE CLEAR ABOUT
YOUR JOB OBJECTIVE

Quick Tip

It is important that you have as clear an idea about what you want to do as possible. But whether you do or do not have a clear job objective, this chapter will help show you how to explore career and job alternatives that you might not have considered. It pays to be both well-informed and flexible.

This chapter will help you in a number of ways:

1. It will help you identify jobs that are "best" for you to seek and more clearly identify the range of jobs that you can include in your job search.

2. It will show you how to obtain more information related to jobs that interest you, and to use this information to improve your interview skills.

3. It will assist you in making good career decisions.

One of the worst things you can do in your job search is to look for "any" job. While it is acceptable for you to consider a broad range of jobs, few employers are impressed by someone who doesn't seem to know what he or she wants to do.

A big interview mistake is the failure to present your skills that closely match the job you say you want. Of course, if you are not clear about what sort of job you *do* want, it will be most difficult to present the skills you have to do the job, won't it?

As you may already know, deciding on a job objective can be quite complicated. There are more than 12,000 job titles that are defined by the U.S. Department of Labor and it would be most impractical to try to consider all possible alternatives. But it is likely that you already have some idea of the sorts of jobs that either interest you or that you are most likely to consider. But even if you don't have any idea at all about what you want to do, you need to settle the matter (or at least make it appear as if you have settled it) as you begin your search for a job.

While this book is not designed to provide comprehensive career information, this chapter can help you learn more about the options available to you—and how to use career information sources to improve your interviewing skills, in constructing your resume, and in finding a job that is right for you.

●●●●●●●●●●●●●●●●●●●●●●●●●●●●●●●●●●

CONSIDER JOBS WITHIN CLUSTERS OF RELATED OCCUPATIONS

Most people overlook too many job opportunities. They often do this simply because they don't know about all the occupations that could use a person with their skills, interests, and experience. As I've mentioned, there are more than 12,000 jobs that are defined by the U.S. Department of Labor. This is entirely too large a number for anyone to comprehend in any meaningful way.

Most people simply go about their lives and careers with very little information about the universe of career and job possibilities that might suit them. They often end up in an educational program and, later, find jobs in a haphazard way. That is how it happened for me during my early years and it was probably that way for you. Things simply happened.

But I think that most of us can do better. While I am not suggesting that the process of career planning is a simple one, I do think that there are a few simple things that we can do to help us make better decisions. And, in this chapter, I will present to you a few things that I think can be particularly helpful.

One of those things is to introduce you to several of the ways that labor market experts have organized jobs and information about jobs. Fortunately, the more than 12,000 job titles that exist are not arranged in random order. Someone has spent a lot of time arranging them into clusters of related jobs. Knowing these arrangements can help you in a variety of ways. For example, you might identify possible job targets, consider long-term career plans, write a better resume and, of course, prepare for interviews.

Quick Reference

THE 250 JOBS IN THE OCCUPATIONAL OUTLOOK HANDBOOK (OOH)

I consider the *Occupational Outlook Handbook* to be one of the most helpful books on career information available. I urge you to either buy one or arrange for frequent access to it throughout your job search because it is so useful in a variety of ways.

The *OOH* provides descriptions for about 250 of the most popular jobs in our workforce. While that may not sound like many—compared to the more than 12,000 job titles that exist—these 250 jobs are the ones that about 85 percent of the workforce actually work in. Updated every two years by the U.S. Department of Labor, the *OOH* provides the latest information on salaries, projections for growth, related jobs, skills required, education or training needed, working conditions, and many other details. Each job is described in a readable and interesting format.

SOME WAYS TO USE THE OOH

▼▼

To identify the skills needed in the job you want: You can look up a job that interests you and the *OOH* will tell you the transferable and job-related skills it requires. Assuming that you have these skills, you can then emphasize them in your interviews and resume.

To find skills from previous jobs to support your present objective: Look up *OOH* descriptions for jobs you have had in the past. A careful read will help you identify skills you used there that can be transferred and used in the new job. Even "minor" jobs can be used in this way. For example, if you waited on tables while going to school, you would discover that doing this requires the ability to work under pressure, good communications skills, the ability to deal with customers, work quickly, and many other skills. If, for example, you were now looking for a job as an accountant, you can see how transferable skills used in an apparently unrelated past job (such as waiting on tables) really can be used to support your ability to do another job.

To identify related job targets: Each of the major jobs described in the *OOH* includes a listing of other jobs that are closely related. The listing also includes information on positions that the job might lead to through promotion or experience. And, because the jobs are listed within clusters of similar jobs, you can easily browse descriptions of similar jobs that you may have overlooked. All of this information gives you options to consider in your job search as well as information to include in the job objective section of your resume.

To find out the typical salary range, trends, and other details: While you should *never* (well, almost never) list your salary requirement in a resume or reveal it in a preliminary interview, the *OOH* will help you to know what pay range to expect as well as many other details about the job and trends that are affecting it. But note that your local pay and other details can differ significantly from the national information provided in the *OOH*.

▲▲

Most libraries will have the Occupational Outlook Handbook but you probably won't be able to take it home. There is another book titled America's Top 300 Jobs which provides the very same information and may be available for circulation. You can also order either of these books through most bookstores, something I sincerely recommend based on how often they should be used as a reference tool during your job search and after. Either book costs less than $20 and you can order them by using the order form in the back of this very book.

LIST OF JOBS IN THE OCCUPATIONAL OUTLOOK HANDBOOK

The following is a list of jobs in the current edition of the *OOH*. The jobs are arranged in clusters of related jobs and the listing will give you an idea of other jobs you might want to consider when conducting your job search.

One way to use this list is to check those jobs that you have held in the past as well as those that interest you now. Later, you can look these jobs up in the *OOH* and obtain additional information related to each.

DETAILED TABLE OF OOH OCCUPATIONS BY CLUSTER

EXECUTIVE, ADMINISTRATIVE, AND MANAGERIAL OCCUPATIONS

Accountants and auditors
Administrative services managers
Budget analysts
Construction and building inspectors
Construction contractors and managers
Cost estimators
Education administrators
Employment interviewers
Engineering, science, and data processing managers
Financial managers

Funeral directors
General managers and top executives
Government chief executives and legislators
Health services managers
Hotel managers and assistants
Industrial production managers
Inspectors and compliance officers, except construction
Loan officers and counselors
Management analysts and consultants

Marketing, advertising, and public relations
managers
Personnel, training, and labor relations
specialists and managers

Property and real estate managers
Purchasing agents and managers
Restaurant and food service managers
Underwriters

PROFESSIONAL SPECIALTY OCCUPATIONS

Engineers
Aerospace engineers
Chemical engineers
Civil engineers
Electrical and electronics engineers
Industrial engineers
Mechanical engineers
Metallurgical, ceramic, and materials engineers
Mining engineers
Nuclear engineers
Petroleum engineers
Architects and surveyors
Architects
Landscape architects
Surveyors
**Computer, mathematical, and
operations research occupations**
Actuaries
Computer scientists and systems analysts
Mathematicians
Operations research analysts
Statisticians
Life scientists
Agricultural scientists
Biological scientists
Foresters and conservation scientists
Physical scientists
Chemists
Geologists and geophysicists
Meteorologists
Physicists and astronomers
Lawyers and judges
Social scientists and urban planners
Economists and market research analysts
Psychologists
Sociologists
Urban and regional planners
Social and recreation workers
Human services workers
Social workers
Recreation workers
Religious workers
Protestant ministers

Rabbis
Roman Catholic priests
Teachers, librarians, and counselors
Adult education teachers
Archivists and curators
College and university faculty
Counselors
Librarians
School teachers—kindergarten, elementary,
and secondary
Health diagnosing practitioners
Chiropractors
Dentists
Optometrists
Physicians
Podiatrists
Veterinarians
**Health assessment and treating
occupations**
Dietitians and nutritionists
Occupational therapists
Pharmacists
Physical therapists
Physician assistants
Recreational therapists
Registered nurses
Respiratory therapists
Speech-language pathologists
and audiologists
Communications occupations
Public relations specialists
Radio and television announcers
and newscasters
Reporters and correspondents
Writers and editors
Visual arts occupations
Designers
Photographers and camera operators
Visual artists
Performing arts occupations
Actors, directors, and producers
Dancers and choreographers
Musicians

TECHNICIANS AND RELATED SUPPORT OCCUPATIONS

Health technologists and technicians
Cardiovascular technologists and technicians
Clinical laboratory technologists and
   technicians
Dental hygienists
Dispensing opticians
EEG technologists
Emergency medical technicians
Licensed practical nurses
Medical record technicians
Nuclear medicine technologists
Radiologic technologists

Surgical technicians
Technologists, except health
Aircraft pilots
Air traffic controllers
Broadcast technicians
Computer programmers
Drafters
Engineering technicians
Library technicians
Paralegals
Science technicians

MARKETING AND SALES OCCUPATIONS

Cashiers
Counter and rental clerks
Insurance agents and brokers
Manufacturers' and wholesale
   sales representatives
Real estate agents, brokers, and appraisers

Retail sales workers
Securities and financial service
   sales representatives
Services sales representatives
Travel agents

ADMINISTRATIVE SUPPORT OCCUPATIONS, INCLUDING CLERICAL

Adjusters, investigators, and collectors
Bank tellers
Billing clerks
Bookkeeping, accounting, and
   auditing clerks
Brokerage clerks and statement clerks
Clerical supervisors and managers
Computer and peripheral equipment operators
Credit clerks and authorizers
Dispatchers
File clerks
General office clerks
Hotel and motel clerks
Information clerks
Interviewing and new accounts clerks
Library assistants and bookmobile drivers
Mail clerks and messengers
Material recording, scheduling, dispatching,
   and distributing occupations

Order clerks
Payroll and timekeeping clerks
Personnel clerks
Postal clerks and mail carriers
Receptionists
Record clerks
Reservation and transportation ticket
   agents and travel clerks
Secretaries
Stenographers and court reporters
Stock clerks
Teacher aids
Telephone operators
Traffic, shipping, and receiving clerks
Typists, word processors, and data
   entry keyers

SERVICE OCCUPATIONS

Protective service occupations
Correction officers
Firefighting occupations
Guards
Police, detectives, and special agents
Food and beverage preparation and service occupations
Chefs, cooks, and other kitchen workers
Food and beverage service occupations
Health service occupations
Dental assistants

Medical assistants
Nursing aides and psychiatric aides
Personal services and building and grounds service occupations
Animal caretakers, except farm
Barbers and cosmetologists
Flight attendants
Gardeners and groundskeepers
Homemaker-home health aides
Janitors and cleaners
Private household workers

AGRICULTURE, FORESTRY, FISHING, AND RELATED OCCUPATIONS

Farm operators and managers
Fishers, hunters, and trappers

Forestry and logging occupations

MECHANICS, INSTALLERS, AND REPAIRERS

Aircraft mechanics and engine specialists
Automotive body repairers
Automotive mechanics
Commercial and industrial electronic
   equipment repairers
Communications equipment mechanics
Computer and office machine repairers
Diesel mechanics
Electronic equipment repairers
Electronic home entertainment
   equipment repairers
Elevator installers and repairers
Farm equipment mechanics

General maintenance mechanics
Heating, air-conditioning, and refrigeration
technicians
Home appliance and power tool repairers
Industrial machinery repairers
Line installers and cable splicers
Millwrights
Mobile heavy equipment mechanics
Motorcycle, boat, and small-engine
   mechanics
Musical instrument repairers and tuners
Telephone installers and repairers
Vending machine servicers and repairers

CONSTRUCTION TRADES AND EXTRACTIVE OCCUPATIONS

Bricklayers and stonemasons
Carpenters
Carpet installers
Concrete masons and terrazzo workers
Drywall workers and lathers
Electricians
Glaziers
Insulation workers

Painters and paperhangers
Plasterers
Plumbers and pipefitters
Roofers
Roustabouts
Sheet-metal workers
Structural and reinforcing ironworkers
Tilesetters

PRODUCTION OCCUPATIONS

Assemblers
Precision assemblers
Blue-collar worker supervisors

Food processing occupations
Butcher and meat, poultry, and fish cutters
Inspectors, testers, and graders

METALWORKING AND PLASTICS-WORKING OCCUPATIONS

Boilermakers
Jewelers
Machinists and tool programmers
Metalworking and plastics-working
  machine operators
Numerical-control machine-tool operators
Tool and die makers
Welders, cutters, and welding machine
  operators
Plant and systems operators
Electric power generating plant
operators and power distributors
  and dispatchers
Stationary engineers
Water and wastewater treatment plant
  operators

Printing occupations
Bindery workers
Prepress workers
Printing press operators
**Textile, apparel, and furnishings
occupations**
Apparel workers
Shoe and leather workers and repairers
Textile machinery operators
Upholsterers
Woodworking occupations
Miscellaneous production occupations
Dental laboratory technicians
Ophthalmic laboratory technicians
Painting and coating machine operators
Photographic process workers

TRANSPORTATION AND MATERIAL MOVING OCCUPATIONS

Busdrivers
Material moving equipment operators
Rail transportation occupations

Taxi drivers and chauffeurs
Truckdrivers
Water transportation occupations

HANDLERS, EQUIPMENT CLEANERS, HELPERS, AND LABORERS

JOB OPPORTUNITIES IN THE ARMED FORCES

THE 12,000 JOBS IN THE COMPLETE GUIDE FOR OCCUPATIONAL EXPLORATION (CGOE)

Quick Fact

The *Occupational Outlook Handbook* provides excellent descriptions of the major jobs but does not cover more specialized ones. This can be a limitation if you have experience, education, or interest in a specific area and want to know the variety of jobs that area offers. In some cases, you may also want to know the variety of jobs you might consider in making a career change or in searching for a new job.

❝*All jobs are first organized within just twelve major interest areas.***❞**

ALL JOBS ARE ORGANIZED INTO JUST 12 INTEREST AREAS

Unlike the *OOH*, the *Complete Guide for Occupational Exploration (CGOE)* is a book that does not provide descriptions of jobs. What it does do is arrange virtually every known job—more than 12,000 of them—in a very useful way.

All jobs are first organized within just 12 major interest areas. These areas are then divided into 64 groupings of related jobs and 348 additional subgroups of even more closely related jobs. Each of these groupings and subgroupings are described in an easy-to-understand way, including the types of training, skills required, and many other details. If you are looking for other jobs to consider as job targets, the *CGOE*'s arrangement will allow you to quickly identify groupings of jobs that are most closely related to what you want to do. All along the way, from major interest area to the various subgroupings, helpful information is provided related to each group of jobs. So, even if some of the jobs themselves are not familiar to you, there is enough information provided to help you understand the jobs within that grouping and what they require. In a quick and logical way, you can narrow down the thousands of job possibilities to the dozen or so that most closely match what you want to do and are good at.

The *CGOE*'s 12 major interest areas, along with brief definitions of each, follow. Typically, most of the careers that interest you are within 1 or 2 of these major clusters.

The CGOE's **12 Major Interest Areas**

▲ **1. Artistic:** An interest in creative expression of feelings or ideas.

▲ **2. Scientific:** An interest in discovering, collecting, and analyzing information about the natural world, and in applying scientific research findings to problems in medicine, the life sciences, and the natural sciences.

▲ **3. Plants and Animals:** An interest in working with plants and animals, usually outdoors.

▲ **4. Protective:** An interest in using authority to protect people and property.

▲ **5. Mechanical:** An interest in applying mechanical principles to practical situations by use of machines or hand tools.

▲ **6. Industrial:** An interest in repetitive, concrete, organized activities done in a factory setting.

▲ **7. Business Detail:** An interest in organized, clearly defined activities requiring accuracy and attention to details, primarily in an office setting.

▲ **8. Selling:** An interest in bringing others to a particular point of view by personal persuasion, using sales and promotional techniques.

▲ **9. Accommodating:** An interest in catering to the wishes and needs of others, usually in a one-on-one basis.

▲ **10. Humanitarian:** An interest in helping others with their mental, spiritual, social, physical, or vocational needs.

▲ **11. Leading and Influencing:** An interest in leading and influencing others by using high-level verbal or numerical abilities.

▲ **12. Physical Performing:** An interest in physical activities performed before an audience.

SUBGROUPINGS OF RELATED JOBS

As mentioned earlier, each of the 12 interest areas is further broken down into more specific groupings of related jobs. Each of these subgroups includes information related to that grouping as well as specific job titles that fit into each.

The chart below shows you how the Artistic interest area is broken down into its subgroups. The most specific groupings provide lists of jobs as well as some information regarding each job within the group.

This arrangement makes it easy to locate the types of jobs you want to explore by simply turning to the appropriate section of the *CGOE*. Once there, you can quickly see the specific jobs that are within that grouping and identify other jobs that may be suitable for job targets based on skills you already have.

Look over the sample listing of subgroups for the Artistic interest area that follows. If you are interested in jobs involving artistic skills, this arrangement would allow you to quickly identify major groupings in the *CGOE* that you were most qualified to do or most interested in learning more about.

• •

SUBGROUPINGS WITHIN THE ARTISTIC INTEREST AREA

Literary Arts
Editing
Creative Writing
Critiquing

Visual Arts
Instructing and
   Appraising
Studio Art
Commercial Art

**Performing Arts:
Drama**
Instructing and
   Directing
Performing
Narrating and
   Announcing

**Performing Arts:
Music**
Instructing and
   Directing
Composing and
   Arranging
Vocal Performing
Instrumental
   Performing

**Performing Arts:
Dance**
Instructing and
   Choreography
Performing

Craft Arts
Graphic Arts and
   Related Crafts
Arts and Crafts
Hand Lettering,
   Painting, and
   Decorating

Elemental Arts
Psychic Science
Announcing
Entertaining

Modeling
Personal Appearance

• •

Quick Tip

While the CGOE *is a big book, it is quite easy to use. The subgroupings of related jobs allow you to find jobs of interest quickly. There is also a useful self-assessment section at the beginning.*

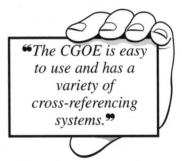

"*The CGOE is easy to use and has a variety of cross-referencing systems.***"**

USING THE CGOE

While the *CGOE* is almost 1,000 pages long, it is very easy to use and will quickly help you identify the many specialized jobs that are related to the skills, education, and experiences you already have. There are also a variety of cross-referencing systems in the *CGOE* that allow you to look up jobs based on education, hobbies and leisure interests, military experience, and many other factors.

ON TO THE DICTIONARY OF OCCUPATIONAL TITLES

While the *CGOE* can be very helpful in exploring career and job alternatives, it does not include descriptions of the more than 12,000 jobs it cross-references (doing so would require the *CGOE* to be almost 2,500 pages long). So, once you locate a job that interests you, the *CGOE* points you to a description for that job in another book, the *Dictionary of Occupational Titles*, also published by our friends at the U.S. Department of Labor. The *DOT* provides brief descriptions for each of the more than 12,000 jobs listed in the *CGOE*, as well as

Quick Tip

Look up the OOH *and/or* DOT *description of a job you will interview for and include details of that job in your resume, cover letter, and interview. You will be much better prepared to target your presentation and give the specific strengths you have that are needed for that job.*

additional cross-referencing systems that you may find useful—including a way to find occupations that are related to a specific industry.

Both the *CGOE* and *DOT* are valuable resources for finding job targets that would be overlooked otherwise. The information they provide can also help you identify skills and other information to include in your interviews, resumes, or cover letters such as the key skills needed in the jobs that interest you.

Quick Tip

The CGOE, DOT, *and* EGOE *are all relatively expensive books to own for personal use, costing about $100 for the set of three. But you can find them at most good libraries and, if they are not there, ask the librarian to order them for you. JIST's Electronic GOE costs more but a lower-priced version for personal use may be released for those who have CD-ROM computer capabilities. They are all published by or available from JIST. You can also use the order form in the back of this book, should you want your own copies.*

THE ENHANCED GUIDE FOR OCCUPATIONAL EXPLORATION

There is one other book that might interest you, titled the *Enhanced Guide for Occupational Exploration* (the *EGOE*, of course). This book uses the same organizational structure as the *CGOE* and includes *DOT* descriptions for about 2,500 jobs. These descriptions cover over 95 percent of the workforce, including all but the most obscure of jobs. Unless you are interested in highly specialized jobs, the *EGOE* will also help you locate a wide variety of jobs that are related to your interests.

NOW YOU CAN GET AT DETAILED DESCRIPTIONS OF MORE THAN 12,000 JOBS VIA COMPUTER

While the books I've just mentioned are very useful, they all have limitations for some uses. For example, you may need to refer to two or three big reference books to get all of the available information on a specific job. Another limitation is that much of the detailed information is provided in coded form that is not easy to understand.

Part of the difficulty of preparing these books is the sheer number of jobs that need to be included. Providing details on all of them requires a massive number of pages. Fortunately, more powerful and less expensive computers with large data storage capabilities now are available to handle this.

A program available on CD-ROM titled *JIST's Electronic Guide for Occupational Exploration*, provides detailed six-page reports on each of the 12,000-plus jobs that are defined by the U.S. Department of Labor. Each report provides a brief description of the job, plus more than 60 details, including training requirements, abilities and skills required, strength needs, work environment measures, and many others—all in easy- to-understand language. A sample copy of one of the reports is provided in chapter 12. To give you some sense of the huge amount of information involved, these reports (equivalent to 75,000 pages) would stretch more than 13 miles if all were printed.

What is particularly important is that the program is very easy to use and very fast. It allows you to look up jobs by interest, occupational grouping, and several other ways. Check with your library to see if it has a copy of the program. If you have a CD-ROM reader on your computer, it may pay to have your own copy of the program.

VALUES, PREFERENCES, AND OTHER MATTERS TO CONSIDER IN DEFINING YOUR JOB OBJECTIVE

Quick Reference

As you probably know, figuring out your career or job objective can be quite complicated. As if choosing from thousands of job titles isn't enough to deal with, there are many other considerations to be made.

I present here a brief review of some of the things that others have found important in making their career plans. While this certainly won't replace a good career planning process, you may find it helpful in considering a variety of issues that relate to deciding on a job objective, preparing for an interview, working on your resume, and making career plans.

DEFINING YOUR IDEAL JOB

If you were to develop a profile of your ideal job, just what would it include? As you probably realize, there is more to this than simply picking out a job title. I have selected a series of questions that you should consider in defining what your ideal job might be. Of course, there is a bit of reality you will have to deal with in doing this (and I have included some of these elements) but dreams can never come true if you don't have them. So, I present the following very important but sometimes overlooked issues for you to consider in planning your job objective.

WHAT SKILLS DO YOU HAVE THAT YOU WANT TO USE IN YOUR NEXT JOB?

Review the skills lists that you worked on in chapter 2 and the key skills you identified at the end of chapter 10. Think about those skills that you enjoy using *and* are good at. Then list the five that you would most like to use in your next job.

1. _____

2. _____

3. _____

4. _____

5. _____

WHAT TYPE OF SPECIAL KNOWLEDGE DO YOU HAVE THAT YOU MIGHT USE IN YOUR NEXT JOB?

Perhaps you know how to fix radios, keep accounting records, or cook food. You don't have to have used these skills in a previous job to include them. Write down the things you have learned from schooling, training, hobbies, family experiences, and other sources. Perhaps one or more of them could make you a very special applicant in the right setting. For example, an accountant who knows a lot about fashion would be a very special candidate if she just happened to be interviewing for a job with an organization that sells clothing.

1. _____

2. _____

3. _____

4. _____

5. _____

WHAT TYPES OF PEOPLE DO YOU PREFER TO WORK WITH?

It is unlikely that you will be happy in any job if you are surrounded by people who you don't like. One way to approach this is to think about characteristics of people who you *would not* want to work with. The opposite characteristics are those that you probably would enjoy.

1. _____
2. _____
3. _____
4. _____
5. _____

WHAT TYPE OF WORK ENVIRONMENT DO YOU PREFER?

Do you want to work inside, outside, in a quiet place, a busy place, a clean place, or have a window with a nice view—or what? For example, I like to have variety in what I do as I am easily bored and so I want a work environment with lots of action and variety (and a window). Once again, you can review what you have disliked about your past work environments to give you clues for what you would most appreciate. Write those things that are most important to have on your next job on the lines below.

1. _____
2. _____
3. _____
4. _____
5. _____

WHERE DO YOU WANT YOUR NEXT JOB TO BE LOCATED—IN WHAT CITY OR REGION?

This could be as simple as finding a job that allows you to live where you are now (because you want to live near your relatives, for example). But, if so, would you prefer to work in a particular area, close to a child care center? If you are able to live or work anywhere, what would your ideal community be like?

1. _____

2. _____

3. _____

4. _____

5. _____

HOW MUCH MONEY DO YOU HOPE TO MAKE IN YOUR NEXT JOB?

Many people will take less money if the job is great in other ways—or to survive. Think about the minimum you would take as well as what you would eventually like to earn. Realistically, your next job will probably be somewhere between your minimum and maximum amount.

1. _____

2. _____

HOW MUCH RESPONSIBILITY ARE YOU WILLING TO ACCEPT?

In most organizations, those who are willing to accept more responsibility are also typically paid more. There *is* typically a relationship between the two. Higher levels of responsibility often require you to supervise others or to make decisions that affect the organization. Some people are willing to accept this responsibility and others, understandably, would prefer not to. Decide how much responsibility you are willing to accept and write that below.

You should also ask yourself if you prefer to work by yourself, be part of a group, or be in charge. If so, at what level? Jot down where you see yourself, in terms of accepting responsibility for others, and in other ways within an organization.

1. _____

2. _____

3. _____

4. _____

5. _____

WHAT THINGS ARE IMPORTANT OR HAVE MEANING TO YOU?

What are your values? I once had a job where the sole reason for the existence of the organization was to make money. Not that this is necessarily wrong, it's just that I wanted to be involved in things that I could believe in. For example, some people work to help others, some to clean up our environment, and others to build things, make machines work, gain power or prestige, care for animals or plants—or something else. I believe that all work is worthwhile if done well, so the issue here is just what sorts of things are important to you. Write these values below.

1. _____

2. _____

3. _____

4. _____

5. _____

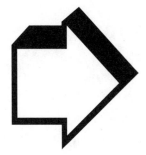

YOUR IDEAL JOB

▼▼▼▼▼▼▼▼▼▼▼▼▼▼▼▼▼▼▼▼▼▼▼▼▼▼▼▼

Use the questions provided previously as a basis for defining your ideal job. Think about each one and select the points that are most important to you. You may want to include other issues that are not covered by the questions but that are particularly important to you. You don't have to be practical here—just dream.

1. _____
2. _____
3. _____
4. _____
5. _____
6. _____
7. _____
8. _____
9. _____
10. _____

WRITE A CLEAR JOB OBJECTIVE STATEMENT—JUST AS YOU NEED TO DO ON A RESUME

Quick Alert

As I have mentioned before, employers are impressed if you are clear about why you want the particular type of job they have to offer. During the interview, you may be asked why you want the job and you need to have a good answer. For many, this can be more difficult to do than it might seem. It assumes, for example, that you have a good idea of the type of jobs that you want. And, even if you are not so certain, you will need to handle this issue in an interview.

One way to clarify your job objective is to write a job objective as if you were writing one for use in your resume. Doing this will force you to spend time researching various career alternatives and to select those that are most acceptable to you. You may end up settling for a broad job objective to cover a variety of jobs that you would qualify for, even if you are not sure that these are the ones that you want in the long term. In some cases, a broad job objective—or even multiple job objectives— will allow you to consider various options while you continue to research alternatives.

The material that follows will help you write a job objective as if you were including this on a resume. I hope you find it helpful in preparing for the interview process. Of course, it will also help you to write your resume.

Quick Tip

If you don't know what type of job you want, concentrate on what you want to do NEXT. That might be working towards a long-term objective such as going back to school or starting your own business. In the meanwhile, you may also need to earn a living, so decide on a short-term job goal that you are qualified for and go after it.

TIPS FOR WRITING A GOOD JOB OBJECTIVE

While the job objective you write should meet your specific needs, here are some things to consider in writing it:

1. **Avoid job titles.** Job titles such as "Secretary" or "Marketing Analyst" can involve very different activities in different organizations. The same job can often have different titles in different organizations and using such a title may very well limit you being considered for such jobs as "Office Manager" or "Marketing Assistant." It is best to use broad categories of jobs rather than specific titles, so that you can be considered for a wide variety of jobs related to

the skills you have. For example, instead of "Secretary" you could say "Responsible Office Management or Clerical Position" if that is what you would really consider—and qualify for.

2. **Define a "bracket of responsibility" to include the possibility of upward mobility.** While you may be willing to accept a variety of jobs related to your skills, you should include those that require higher levels of responsibility and pay. In the example above, it keeps open the option to be considered for an office management position as well as clerical jobs. In effect, you should define a "bracket of responsibility" in your objective that includes the range of jobs that you are willing to accept. This bracket should include the lower range of jobs that you would consider as well as those requiring higher levels of responsibility, up to and including those that you think you could handle. Even if you have not handled those higher levels of responsibility in the past, many employers may consider you for them if you have the skills to support the objective.

3. **Include your most important skills.** What are the most important skills needed for the job you want? Consider including one or more of these as being required in the job that you seek. The implication here is that if you are looking for a job that requires "Organizational Skills," then you have those skills. Of course, your interview (and resume) should support those skills with specific examples.

4. **Include specifics if these are important to you.** If you have substantial experience in a particular industry (such as "Computer Controlled Machine Tools") or have a narrow and specific objective that you *really* want (such as "Art Therapist with the Mentally Handicapped"), then it is OK to state this. But, in so doing, realize that by narrowing your alternatives down you will often not be considered for other jobs for which you might qualify. Still, if that is what you want, it just may be worth pursuing (though I would still encourage you to have a second, more general objective just in case ...).

JOB OBJECTIVE WORKSHEET

Use this worksheet to create a draft of your job objective as it would appear on a resume. It includes a variety of questions and activities that you can use to decide what to include.

1. **What sort of position, title, and area of specialization do you seek?** Write out the type of job you want just as you might explain it to someone you know.

    _____

    _____

    _____

2. **Define your "bracket of responsibility."** Describe the range of jobs that you would accept at a minimum as well as those that you might be able to handle if given the chance.

    _____

    _____

    _____

3. **Name the key skills that you have that are important in this job.** Describe the two or three key skills that are particularly important for success in the job that you seek. Select one or more of these that you are strong in and that you enjoy using and write it (or them) below.

    _____

    _____

    _____

4. **Name any specific areas of expertise or strong interests that you want to utilize in your next job.** If you have substantial interest, experience, or training in a specific area *and* want to include it in your job objective (knowing that it may limit your options), what might it be?

_____

_____

_____

5. **Is there anything else that is important to you?** Is there anything else that you want to include in your job objective? This could include a value that is particularly important to you (such as "A position that allows me to affect families" or "Employment in an aggressive and results-oriented organization"); a preference for the size or type of organization ("A small- to mid-size business"); or some other thing.

_____

_____

_____

Quick Reference

FINALIZING YOUR JOB OBJECTIVE STATEMENT

Look over the following sample job objectives to see how others have written their job objectives. Note that most do not include all the elements that are presented in the Job Objective Worksheet. That is perfectly acceptable. Some are very brief, providing just a job title or category of jobs, while others are quite long and detailed.

Some Sample Job Objectives

▲ Copywriter/Account executive in Advertising or Public Relations Agency.

▲ Program Development, Coordination, and Administration ... especially in a people-oriented organization where there is a need to assure broad cooperative effort through the use of sound planning, strong administration, skills of persuasion to achieve goals.

▲ A responsible position in retail sales.

▲ A middle/upper-level management position with responsibilities including problem solving, planning, organizing, and managing budgets.

▲ Challenging position in programming or related areas that would best utilize expertise in the business environment. This position should have many opportunities for an aggressive, dedicated individual with the leadership abilities needed to advance.

▲ To obtain a position as a financial manager in the Health Care industry, utilizing 16 years of demonstrated success and accomplishment.

▲ To obtain a position as an Elementary School Teacher in which a strong dedication to the total development of children and a high degree of enthusiasm can be fully utilized.

▲ An administrative position in the area of rehabilitation/geriatric health care utilizing my knowledge of clinical, community, and patient services.

▲ Highly skilled Executive Secretary with outstanding professional experience including:

  ✎ Ability to communicate with all levels of management and employees
  ✎ International communication liaison with subsidiary companies
  ✎ Contract negotiation bargaining team member
  ✎ Use of word processing, Windows, Lotus 1-2-3

▲ Seeking a position as a Registered Nurse where I can be most effective in helping other medical personnel assist patients and provide quality health care.

▲ Seeking expanded opportunities where I can use my experience to expand profits.

▲ Obtain a challenging, entry-level position in Broadcast Journalism, with a special interest in reporting, anchoring, and producing with a commercial television station.

▲ Position as a Word Processing Secretary that will utilize my computer knowledge, strong people skills, organizational abilities, and business experience.

Quick Fact

Most employers will be impressed with someone who is very clear about the job they want and why they want it. Few interviews end well unless the interviewer is convinced that you want the job available and have the skills to do it reasonably well.

For this reason, it is essential to have a clear job objective. Then, once you've settled that, go out and get interviews for jobs that closely approximate what you want. In the interview, support your interest in the job by presenting the skills and experiences you have and the advantages you present over others they may be considering. It sounds simple enough—and can be—as long as you are clear about what you want to do and are well organized about finding it.

12

RESEARCH BEFORE THE INTERVIEW—PRINT AND COMPUTER SOURCES

Quick Tip

There is an overwhelming amount of information available on jobs, specific organizations, job seeking, and many related topics. A good library will have hundreds of resource materials available to help you prepare for your interview. Bookstores also have some helpful materials and an increasing number of resources are becoming available via computer software and online services. This chapter will review some of the most important of those resources as well as provide you with advice on how best to use them.

Employers don't have to hesitate when asked what they see as the number one problem with job candidates: a complete lack of preparation. True, a good many people are well prepared to speak about themselves and their accomplishments, but there are two entities involved in a job interview. You must have some knowledge about the other side—the organization and the interviewer—as well.

Unfortunately, gaining that knowledge requires research, and many people resist doing it. As a result, many end up treating job information research as they did their high school term papers—they slap it together and hope for the best, or avoid doing it completely. This lack of preparation often shows in the interview.

This chapter takes the mystery out of research by pointing out where to turn, what to look for, and (unless you're having a particularly bad day) how to have fun doing it.

Quick Tip

Never be afraid to speak up and ask for help, whether you are in a library, online with a computer system, at a recruiter's office, or in a college placement office. You look a lot more foolish when you bumble around than you would if you simply approach the nearest staff person and say, "Could you please help direct me to …?" Librarians in particular are trained to help you and they often welcome a challenging search.

Quick Tip

The industry information you gather will be invaluable to you at the latter stages of the interview process. Knowing that there are only 9,000 available certified property managers and 250,000 real estate firms needing agents, for example, allows you to present yourself as among the top 3 percent in the field—an excellent bargaining chip during the interview and at the salary negotiation table!

THE BASICS: INFORMATION ABOUT THE OCCUPATION, THE INDUSTRY, AND THE ORGANIZATION

In chapter 2, I provided details on the basic resources and techniques for obtaining information about the jobs that most interest you, the industry you are pursuing, and the specific employer. I'll mention some of those resources again in this chapter and add some additional tips and sources of information.

INDUSTRY INFORMATION

The first rule of research is—you aren't going to fool anybody. Many of you think you can skip this section because you've worked in your industry before and have a fairly good grasp of it. But veterans as well as new graduates need to research industry information when preparing for an interview. For instance, do you know how stable your industry is? How many people are in this occupation in the country? In your area? What the average salary range is between entry level and upper level employees in your field? What the biggest challenges are facing your industry in the next five years?

HIGHLY RECOMMENDED INDUSTRY INFORMATION RESOURCES

I mentioned both of the following books back in chapter 2 and want to repeat them here because they are so helpful for getting good information on an industry.

THE U.S. INDUSTRIAL OUTLOOK

This book provides descriptions of 350 industries. Produced by the U. S. Department of Commerce, it will give you an excellent overview of major trends within each industry, the effect of foreign competition, and other details that should be helpful in an interview.

THE CAREER GUIDE TO AMERICA'S TOP INDUSTRIES

These statistics come directly from the U.S. Department of Labor and are of particular value to job seekers. This book provides helpful descriptions of 40 major industries—those providing about 75 percent of all jobs.

The *Career Guide* is easy to read and provides information that can help you present yourself well in an interview. Each description includes an overview of the industry, types of jobs it offers, employment projections, earnings, training required, working conditions, advancement opportunities, industry trends, sources of additional information, and more.

LISTING OF INDUSTRIES IN THE CAREER GUIDE TO AMERICA'S TOP INDUSTRIES

Following is a listing of major industries that are covered in the current edition of the *Career Guide to America's Top Industries*. While most people work in one of these industries, the *U.S. Industrial Outlook* provides information on many other more specialized industries, in addition to those listed here.

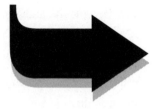

TOP INDUSTRIES IN THE USA

Agriculture, Mining, and Construction
Agricultural services
Construction
Mining and quarrying
Oil and gas extraction

Manufacturing
Aerospace manufacturing
Apparel and other textile products
Chemicals manufacturing, except drugs
Electronics
Food processing
Furniture and fixtures
Motor vehicle and equipment
   manufacturing
Printing and publishing
Steel manufacturing
Textile mill products

Transportation and Communication
Air transportation
Radio and television broadcasting
Telephone communications
Trucking and warehousing

Wholesale and Retail Trade
Department, clothing, and accessory stores
Eating and drinking places
Grocery stores
Motor vehicle dealers
Wholesale trade

Finance and Insurance
Banking
Insurance
Securities and commodities

Services
Advertising
Amusement and recreation services
Child-care services
Computer and data processing services
Educational services
Federal government
Health services
Hotels and other lodging places
Management and public relations services
Motion picture production and distribution
Personnel supply services
Social services
State and local government

Quick Reference

OTHER SOURCES OF INDUSTRY INFORMATION

A good library will have lots of information on industries. Industry trade magazines such as *Advertising Age, Automotive News, Hotel and Motel Management, Modern Healthcare*, and *Supermarket News* are full of articles detailing trends and problems in their particular niche. Grab the last six months' issues and settle down for some interesting reading.

While you have these publications in hand, photocopy and highlight facts that boost your position in that industry, and scribble in the margins some questions you'd like your prospective employer to answer. And always flip to the classifieds section—no use wasting a perfectly good chance to find a job lead!

Next, grab the library's current copy of the *Encyclopedia of Associations*. Don't let its name intimidate you—it is a gold mine of associations listed by categories. There are 63 listings alone for the general "employment" category, including the Career Planning and Adult Development Network, Tradeswomen Inc., and Uglies Unlimited ("dedicated to unattractive individuals who are vexed by discrimination against 'uglies'"). Each entry gives the address, contact name, phone and fax numbers, mission statement, newsletters, and conventions for that group. Pick the ones in your industry category that closely match your situation and give them a call. They will often send you copies of a recent newsletter or journal and provide other information.

Another good general resource is Matthew Lesko's *Info-Power* book published by Information USA, Inc. It lists information sources ranging from the Epidemic Intelligence Service to Displaced Homemakers Job Network to Literature Translators Opportunities. There's a great section on how to research a company, too, that will stand you in good stead down the road.

INFORMATION ABOUT THE OCCUPATION

If you have done the activities in earlier chapters, you should have a good idea of the types of jobs you want as well as your skills and other details. Now your task is to determine how those traits translate into job positions within your field.

For example, let's say you have chosen to work in the history field. You've gathered information on the latest history theories and trends within the field. Now you need to determine if your personal skills and talents would be more conducive to market research, archiving and records management, preparing institutional histories, or teaching, to name a few. How are you going to determine that? Research!

Quick Tip

If you are close to a college campus, take advantage of the placement offices and professors in your industry as well. Don't be shy about asking for their time, as many will be flattered to share their knowledge. In fact, it's not a bad idea to set aside a predetermined amount of time for the discussion. Otherwise, you may find yourself eating dinner with the professor when you walked in shortly before lunch!

Let's begin by reviewing several of the most important and basic sources of career information. While I mentioned these in an earlier chapter, their importance bears repeating.

Quick Reference

HIGHLY RECOMMENDED OCCUPATIONAL INFORMATION RESOURCES

☑ **THE** OCCUPATIONAL OUTLOOK HANDBOOK (OOH)

Updated every two years by the U.S. Department of Labor, I strongly recommend this book. It is essential in preparing for an interview. It provides good information on the 250 or so top jobs in our economy and covers about 85 percent of our workforce.

☑ **THE** COMPLETE GUIDE FOR OCCUPATIONAL EXPLORATION (CGOE)

This book cross-references 12,741 job titles into groupings of related jobs. The system is easy to use and allows you to locate jobs for which you might qualify that you may have previously overlooked. It also provides additional information about each of the job clusters, which may help you in an interview.

☑ **THE** ENHANCED GUIDE FOR OCCUPATIONAL EXPLORATION (EGOE)

Organized like the *CGOE*, this book provides descriptions for 2,500 jobs.

☑ **THE** DICTIONARY OF OCCUPATIONAL TITLES (DOT)

This enormous book is a standard occupational reference that provides brief descriptions for the more than 12,000 jobs that are cross-referenced in the *CGOE*. This book is particularly helpful if you are interviewing for a very specific type of job and you are not that familiar with it.

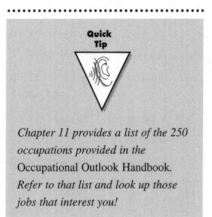

Quick Tip

Chapter 11 provides a list of the 250 occupations provided in the Occupational Outlook Handbook. *Refer to that list and look up those jobs that interest you!*

Quick Reference

SAMPLE JOB REPORTS

I have included occupational descriptions from two sources in this section.

Quick
Reference

I decided to show you actual reports but in a reduced size, so please excuse the smaller-than-normal print size.

The first report comes from the *Occupational Outlook Handbook*. It presents information on Public Relations Specialists and will give you a good idea of what sorts of information to expect on the other 250 jobs described in the *OOH*. The *OOH* reports are very helpful in preparing for an interview because they include skills to emphasize, salary information, and other details that should be of great help to you.

The second report is one of the 12,741 occupational reports available from a software program titled *JIST's Electronic DOT/GOE*. The "DOT" stands for *Dictionary of Occupational Titles* and "GOE" for *Guide for Occupational Exploration*—both are major career references. I selected the description for a job titled Public Relations Representative, which is one of the job titles covered by the more general *OOH* description. The report from the *DOT/GOE* is five pages long and, as you can see, is very different from the *OOH* description. It provides lots of details that may or may not interest you but shows you the incredible amount of detailed information available on occupations.

FIGURE 12-1 Sample *OOH* Description Pg. 1

Communications Occupations

Public Relations Specialists

(D.O.T. 165.017, .167)

Nature of the Work

An organization's reputation, profitability, and even its continued existence can depend on the degree to which its goals and policies are supported by its targeted "publics." Public relations specialists serve as advocates for businesses, governments, universities, hospitals, schools, and other organizations, and strive to build and maintain positive relationships with the public. As managers recognize the growing importance of good public relations to the success of their organizations, they increasingly rely on public relations specialists for advice on strategy and policy.

Public relations specialists handle such functions as media, community, consumer, and governmental relations; political campaigns; interest-group representation; conflict mediation; or employee and investor relations. Public relations is not only "telling the organization's story," however. Understanding the attitudes and concerns of consumers, employees, and various other groups also is a vital part of the job. To improve communications, public relations specialists establish and maintain cooperative relationships with representives of community, consumer, employee, and public interest groups and those in print and broadcast journalism.

Public relations specialists put together information that keeps the general public, interest groups, and stockholders aware of an organization's policies, activities, and accomplishments. Their work keeps management aware of public attitudes and concerns of the many groups and organizations with which it must deal.

Public relations specialists prepare press releases and contact people in the media who might print or broadcast their material. Many radio or television special reports, newspaper stories, and magazine articles start at the desks of public relations specialists. Sometimes the subject is an organization and its policies towards its employees or its role in the community. Often the subject is a public issue, such as health, nutrition, energy, or the environment.

Public relations specialists also arrange and conduct programs for contact between organization representatives and the public. For example, they set up speaking engagements and often prepare the speeches for company officials. These specialists represent employers at community projects; make film, slide, or other visual presentations at meetings and school assemblies; and plan conventions. In addition, they are responsible for preparing annual reports and writing proposals for various projects.

In government, public relations specialists—who may be called press secretaries, information officers, public affairs specialists, or communications specialists—keep the public informed about the activities of government agencies and officials. For example, public affairs specialists in the Department of Energy keep the public informed about the proposed lease of offshore land for oil exploration. A press secretary for a member of Congress keeps constituents aware of their elected representative's accomplishments.

In large organizations, the director of public relations, who is often a vice president, may develop overall plans and policies with other executives. In addition, public relations departments employ public relations specialists to write, do research, prepare materials, maintain contacts, and respond to inquiries.

People who handle publicity for an individual or who direct public relations for a small organization may deal with all aspects of the job. They contact people, plan and do research, and prepare material for distribution. They may also handle advertising or sales promotion work to support marketing.

Public relations specialists maintain positive relationships between their organizations and the public.

Working Conditions

Some public relations specialists work a standard 35- to 40-hour week, but unpaid overtime is common. In addition, schedules often have to be rearranged to meet deadlines, deliver speeches, attend meetings and community activities, and travel out of town. Occasionally they may have to be at the job or on call around the clock, especially if there is an emergency or crisis.

Employment

Public relations specialists held about 98,000 jobs in 1992. About two-thirds worked in services industries—management and public relations firms, educational institutions, membership organizations, hospitals, social service agencies, and advertising agencies, for example. Others worked for a wide range of employers, including manufacturing firms, financial institutions, and government agencies. Some were self-employed.

Public relations specialists are concentrated in large cities where press services and other communications facilities are readily available, and where many businesses and trade associations have their headquarters. Many public relations consulting firms, for example, are in New York, Los Angeles, Chicago, and Washington, DC. There is a trend, however, for public relations jobs to be dispersed throughout the Nation.

Training, Other Qualifications, and Advancement

Although there are no defined standards for entry into a public relations career, a college education combined with public relations experience, usually gained through an internship, is considered excellent preparation for public relations work. The ability to write and speak well is essential. Many beginners have a college major in public relations, journalism, advertising, or communications. Some firms seek college graduates who have worked in electronic or print journalism. Other employers seek applicants with demonstrated communications skills and training or experience in a field related to the firm's business—science, engineering, sales, or finance, for example.

In 1992, well over 200 colleges and about 100 graduate schools offered degree programs or special curricula in public relations, usually in a journalism or communications department. In addition, many other colleges offered at least one course in this field. A commonly used public relations sequence includes the following courses: Public relations principles and techniques; public relations

FIGURE 12-2 Sample *OOH* Description Pg. 2

management and administration, including organizational development; writing, emphasizing news releases, proposals, annual reports, scripts, speeches, and related items; visual communications, including desktop publishing and computer graphics; and research, emphasizing social science research and survey design and implementation. Courses in advertising, journalism, business administration, political science, psychology, sociology, and creative writing also are helpful, as is familiarity with word processing and other computer applications. Specialties are offered in public relations for business, government, or nonprofit organizations.

Many colleges help students gain part-time internships in public relations that provide valuable experience and training. The Armed Forces also can be an excellent place to gain training and experience. Membership in local chapters of the Public Relations Student Society of America or the International Association of Business Communicators provides an opportunity for students to exchange views with public relations specialists and to make professional contacts that may help them find a full-time job in the field. A portfolio of published articles, television or radio programs, slide presentations, and other work is an asset in finding a job. Writing for a school publication or television or radio station provides valuable experience and material for one's portfolio.

Creativity, initiative, good judgment, and the ability to express thoughts clearly and simply are essential. Decision making, problem solving, and research skills are also important.

People who choose public relations as a career need an outgoing personality, self-confidence, an understanding of human psychology, and an enthusiasm for motivating people. They should be competitive, yet flexible and able to function as part of a team.

Some organizations—particularly those with large public relations staffs—have formal training programs for new employees. In smaller organizations, new employees work under the guidance of experienced staff members. Beginners often maintain files of material about company activities, scan newspapers and magazines for appropriate articles to clip, and assemble information for speeches and pamphlets. After gaining experience, they may write news releases, speeches, and articles for publication, or design and carry out public relations programs. Similar to other occupations, public relations specialists in smaller firms generally get all-around experience, whereas those in larger firms tend to be more specialized.

The Public Relations Society of America accredits public relations specialists who have at least 5 years of experience in the field and have passed a comprehensive 6- hour examination (5 hours written, 1 hour oral). The International Association of Business Communicators also has an accreditation program for professionals in the communications field, including public relations specialists. Those who meet all the requirements of the program earn the designation, Accredited Business Communicator. Candidates must have at least 5 years of experience in a communication field and pass a written and oral examination. They also must submit a portfolio of work samples demonstrating involvement in a range of communication projects and a thorough understanding of communication planning. Employers consider professional recognition through accreditation a sign of competence in this field, and it may be especially helpful in a competitive job market.

Promotion to supervisory jobs may come as public relations specialists show they can handle more demanding managerial assignments. In public relations firms, a beginner may be hired as a research assistant or account assistant and be promoted to account executive, account supervisor, vice president, and eventually senior vice president. A similar career path is followed in corporate public relations, although the titles may differ. Some experienced public relations specialists start their own consulting firms. (For more information on public relations managers, see the *Handbook* statement on marketing, advertising, and public relations managers.)

Job Outlook

Keen competition for public relations jobs will likely continue among recent college graduates with a degree in communications—journalism, public relations, advertising, or a related field—as the number of applicants is expected to exceed the number of job openings. People without the appropriate educational background or work experience will face the toughest obstacles in finding a public relations job.

Employment of public relations specialists is expected to increase about as fast as the average for all occupations through the year 2005. Recognition of the need for good public relations in an increasingly competitive business environment should spur demand for public relations specialists in organizations of all sizes. However, corporate restructuring and downsizing, in an effort to cut costs, could limit employment growth. Employment in public relations firms should grow as firms hire contractors to provide public relations services rather than support full-time staff. The vast majority of job opportunities should result from the need to replace public relations specialists who leave the occupation to take another job, retire, or for other reasons.

Earnings

Median annual earnings for salaried public relations specialists who usually worked full time were about $32,000 in 1992. The middle 50 percent earned between $24,000 and $51,000 annually; the lowest 10 percent earned less than $17,000; and the top 10 percent earned more than $62,000.

A College Placement Council salary survey indicated new college graduates entering the public relations field were offered average starting salaries of about $21,000 in 1993.

According to a 1992 salary survey by the *Public Relations Journal*, the median entry level salary of public relations account executives was almost $21,000 a year. Median annual salaries of all public relations account executives ranged from $28,000 in public relations firms to about $36,000 in corporations. Manufacturers, utilities, and scientific and technical firms were among the highest paying employers; museums and miscellaneous nonprofit organizations, religious and charitable organizations, and advertising agencies were among the lowest paying employers. The survey indicated an annual median salary for all respondents, including managers, of about $44,000. Some highly successful public relations workers earn considerably more.

In the Federal Government, persons with a bachelor's degree generally started at $22,700 a year in 1993; those with a master's degree generally started at $27,800 a year. Public affairs specialists in the Federal Government in nonsupervisory, supervisory, and managerial positions averaged about $45,400 a year in 1993.

Related Occupations

Public relations specialists create favorable attitudes among various organizations, special interest groups, and the public through effective communication. Other workers with similar jobs include fundraisers, lobbyists, promotion managers, advertising managers, and police officers involved in community relations.

Sources of Additional Information

A comprehensive directory of schools offering degree programs or a sequence of study in public relations, and a brochure on careers in public relations, are available for $10 and $2, respectively, from:
☞ Public Relations Society of America, Inc., 33 Irving Place, New York, NY 10003-2376.

Current information on the public relations field, salaries, and other items is available from:
☞ *PR Reporter*, P.O. Box 600, Exeter, NH 03833.

Career information on public relations in hospitals/health care is available from:
☞ The American Society for Health Care Marketing and Public Relations, American Hospital Association, 840 North Lake Shore Dr., Chicago, IL 60611.

SOME COMMENTS ON THE REPORT THAT FOLLOWS

Until very recently, it was very difficult to obtain the detailed information provided in the sample *JEDOT/GOE* report that follows. Much of the data was collected by the U.S. Department of Labor but was either not published or was available only via specialized sources. But inexpensive computers now make it possible to store and retrieve substantial data available on thousands of occupations. The software that produced the report that follows is the first one to make this information readily available to a wide group of users. Although the amount of data it provides may be "over kill" for most people, at least it is finally available.

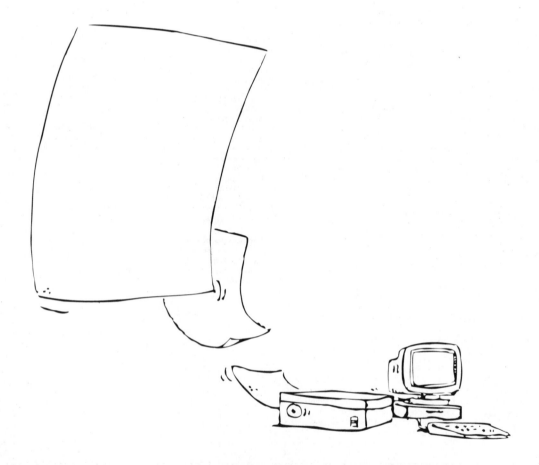

FIGURE 12-3 Sample *JEDOT/GOE* Occupational Report Pg. 1

PUBLIC-RELATIONS REPRESENTATIVE
PROFESSIONAL AND KINDRED OCCUPATIONS

Plans and conducts public relations program designed to create and maintain favorable public image for employer or client: Plans and directs development and communication of information designed to keep public informed of employer's programs, accomplishments, or point of view. Arranges for public relations efforts in order to meet needs, objectives, and policies of individual, special interest group, business concern, nonprofit organization, or governmental agency, serving as in-house staff member or as outside consultant. Prepares and distributes fact sheets, news releases, photographs, scripts, motion pictures, or tape recordings to media representatives and other persons who may be interested in learning about or publicizing employer's activities or message. Purchases advertising space and time as required. Arranges for and conducts public-contact programs designed to meet employer's objectives, utilizing knowledge of changing attitudes and opinions of consumers, clients, employees, or other interest groups. Promotes goodwill through such publicity efforts as speeches, exhibits, films, tours, and question/answer sessions. Represents employer during community projects and at public, social, and business gatherings. May research data, create ideas, write copy, lay out artwork, contact media representatives, or represent employer directly before general public. May develop special projects such as campaign fund raisers or public awareness about political issues. May direct activities of subordinates. May confer with production and support personnel to coordinate production of television advertisements and on-air promotions. May prepare press releases and fact sheets, and compose letters, using computer. May disseminate facts and information about organization's activities or governmental agency's programs to general public and be known as Public Information Officer (profess. & kin.).

INTERESTS (GOE code Nos.) 11.09.03
The first two digits represent one of 12 Major Interest Groups. The middle two digits identify one of the Work Groups within the chosen Major Interest Group, and the last two digits specify a Subgroup within the chosen WorkGroup.

11.09.03   LEADING-INFLUENCING
11.09.03   PROMOTION
11.09.03   PUBLIC RELATIONS

DOT NUMBER.............. .... 165.167-014
The DOT Code number (Dictionary of Occupational Titles) identifies three types of information -- occupational information, the worker traits, and the statistical codes. The first three digits provide information on the occupational categories; the second three digits are the source of the Worker Functions -- the Data-People-Things ratings, and the last three digits serve to give an unique identification of the specific job title in an occupational group.

Occupational Category 165.167-014
165.167-014   ADDITIONAL PROFESSIONAL, TECHNICAL, AND MANAGERIAL OCCUPATIONS
165.167-014   Occupations in Administrative Specializations
165.167-014   Public Relations Management Occupations

Data, People, Things 165.167-014
The middle three digits of the DOT occupational code are the Worker Functions ratings of the tasks performed in the occupation. Every job requires a worker functioning to some degree in relation to data, to people, and to things. A separate digit expresses the worker's relationship to each of these three groups:

Data	People	Things
(4th Digit)	(5th Digit)	(6th Digit)
0 Synthesizing	0 Mentoring	0 Setting Up
1 Coordinating	1 Negotiating	1 Precision Working
2 Analyzing	2 Instructing	2 Operating-Controlling
3 Compiling	3 Supervising	3 Driving-Operating
4 Computing	4 Diverting	4 Manipulating
5 Copying	5 Persuading	5 Tending
6 Comparing	6 Speaking-Signaling	6 Feeding-Off Bearing
	7 Serving	7 Handling
	8 Taking Instruction-Helping	

Data - 1 (Hi = 0, Lo = 6) 165.167-014
Coordinating: Organizing things. Planning projects. Deciding in which order things must be done. Checking to be sure the steps are done on time and correctly.
People - 6 (Hi = 0, Lo = 8) 165.167-014

FIGURE 12-4 Sample *JEDOT/GOE* Occupational Report Pg. 2

Speaking, Signaling: Talking or making motions so people can understand you and getting an answer from them. Telling people what to do in a way that they understand.
Things - 7 (Hi = 0, Lo = 7) 165.167-014
Handling: Moving or carrying things.

Unique Job Identification 165.167-014
The last three digits in the DOT number differentiate 014 from all others in the 165 Occupational Classification.

TRAINING 5457
For the purpose of rating jobs, Training Time is defined as the amount of General Educational Development (GED) and Specific Vocational Preparation (SVP) required of a worker to acquire the knowledge and abilities necessary for average performance in a particular job-worker situation. In the data display, the first three numbers refer to the GED divisions of Reasoning, Math, and Language, and the last number reflects the SVP code. There are six levels in each of the three GED positions, and nine levels for SVP. In each case, the higher the number, the higher the requirement.

GED 5457
Reasoning Development: - 5 (Hi = 6, Lo = 1) 5457
Defining problems, collecting data, and drawing conclusions about all kinds of problems.
Mathematical Development: - 4 (Hi = 6, Lo = 1) 5457
Algebra: Deal with systems of real numbers; linear, quadratic, rational, exponential, logarithmic, angle and circular functions, and inverse functions; related algebraic solution of equations and inequalities; limits and continuity; and probability and statistical inference. Geometry: Deductive axiomatic geometry, plane and solid, and rectangular coordinates. Shop Math: Practical application of fractions, percentages, ratio and proportion, measurement, logarithms, practical algebra, geometric construction, and essentials of trigonometry.
Language Development: - 5 (Hi = 6, Lo = 1) 5457
Reading: Read literature, book and play reviews, scientific and technical journals, abstracts, financial reports, and legal documents. Writing: Write novels, plays, editorials, journals, speeches, manuals, critiques, poetry, and songs. Speaking: Conversant in the theory, principles, and methods of effective and persuasive speaking, voice and diction, phonetics, and discussion and debate.

SVP 5457
Specific Vocational Preparation - 7 (Hi = 9, Lo = 1) 5457
Over 2 years up to and including 4 years.

APTITUDE 11333344454
Each of eleven aptitudes is rated from (1) to (5), with (1) being the highest, and (5) being the lowest.
General Learning Ability: - 1 (Hi = 1, Lo = 5) 11333344454
Must be in the top 10 percent of the population in the ability to "catch on" or understand instructions and underlying principles; the ability to reason and make judgments. Closely related to doing well in school.
Verbal Aptitude: 1 (Hi = 1, Lo = 5) 11333344454
Must be in the top 10 percent of the population in the ability to understand the meaning of words and to use them effectively. The ability to understand relationships between words and to understand the meaning of whole sentences and paragraphs.
Numerical Aptitude: 3 (Hi = 1, Lo = 5) 11333344454
Must be in the middle third of the population in the ability to perform arithmetic operations quickly and accurately.
Spatial Aptitude: 3 (Hi = 1, Lo = 5).................................. 11333344454
Must be in the middle third of the population in the ability to think visually of geometric forms and to comprehend the two-dimensional representation of three-dimensional objects. The ability to recognize the relationships resulting from the movement of objects in space.
Form Perception: 3 (Hi = 1, Lo = 5) 11333344454
Must be in the middle third of the population in the ability to perceive pertinent detail in objects or in pictorial or graphic material. Ability to make visual comparisons and discriminations and see slight differences in shapes and shading of figures and widths and lengths of lines.
Clerical Perception: 3 (Hi = 1, Lo = 5)............................... 11333344454
Must be in the middle third of the population in the ability to perceive detail in verbal or tabular material. Ability to observe differences in copy, to proofread words and numbers, and to avoid perceptual errors in arithmetic computation. A measure of speed of perception is required in many industrial jobs even when the job does not have verbal or numerical content.
Motor Coordination: 4 (Hi = 1, Lo = 5) 11333344454
Can be in the lower third of the population, excluding the bottom 10 percent, in the ability to coordinate eyes and hands or fingers rapidly and accurately in making precise movements with speed. Ability to make

Copyright 1995, JIST Works, Inc., 720 N. Park Ave., Indianapolis, IN 46202

FIGURE 12-5   Sample *JEDOT/GOE* Occupational Report Pg. 3

movement response accurately and swiftly.
Finger Dexterity: 4 (Hi = 1, Lo = 5) 11333344454
Can be in the lowest third of the population, excluding the bottom 10 percent, in the ability to move fingers, and manipulate small objects with fingers, rapidly or accurately.
Manual Dexterity: 4 (Hi = 1, Lo = 5) 11333344454
Can be in the lowest third of the population, excluding the bottom 10 percent, in the ability to move hands easily and skillfully. Ability to work with hands in placing and turning motions.
Eye-Hand-Foot Coordination: 5 (Hi = 1, Lo = 5) 11333344454
Can be in the bottom 10 percent of the population in the ability to move the hand and foot coordinately with each other in accordance with visual stimuli.
Color Discrimination: 4 (Hi = 1, Lo = 5) 11333344454
Can be in the lowest third of the population, excluding the bottom 10 percent, in the ability to match or discriminate between colors in terms of hue, saturation, and brilliance. Ability to identify a particular color or color combination from memory and be able to perceive harmonious or contrasting color combinations.

PHYSICAL REQUIREMENTS .... SNNNNNNFFFNFFNFNNOON
Twenty physical demand factors are rated, the first being strength. Strengths are rated S for Sedentary Work, L for Light Work, M for Medium Work, H for Heavy Work, and V for Very Heavy Work. The other 19 factors are rated N for No Requirements Specified, O for Occasionally, F for Frequently, and C for Continuously. When no requirement (N) is specified, this only means that no information on this characteristic was provided -- some work environments <u>may</u> require this in some conditions.

Sedentary Work: S .... SNNNNNNFFFNFFNFNNOON
 Exerting up to 10 pounds of force up to 1/3 of the time and/or
a negligible amount of force from 1/3 to 2/3 of the time to lift, carry, push, pull, or otherwise move objects, including the human body.
Involves sitting most of the time, but may involve walking or standing for brief periods of time.
Climbing: N .... SNNNNNNFFFNFFNFNNOON
No requirements specified.
Balancing: N .... SNNNNNNFFFNFFNFNNOON
No requirements specified.
Stooping: N .... SNNNNNNFFFNFFNFNNOON
No requirements specified.
Kneeling: N .... SNNNNNNFFFNFFNFNNOON
No requirements specified.
Crouching: N .... SNNNNNNFFFNFFNFNNOON
No requirements specified.
Crawling: N .... SNNNNNNFFFNFFNFNNOON
No requirements specified.
Reaching: F .... SNNNNNNFFFNFFNFNNOON
Extending hand(s) and arm(s) in any direction from 1/3 to 2/3 of the time.
Handling: F .... SNNNNNNFFFNFFNFNNOON
Seizing, holding, grasping, turning or otherwise working with hand or hands from 1/3 to 2/3 of the time. Fingers are involved only to the extent they are an extension of the hand, such as to turn a switch, shift automobile gears.
Fingering: F .... SNNNNNNFFFNFFNFNNOON
Picking, pinching, or otherwise working primarily with fingers from 1/3 to 2/3 of the time (rather than with the whole hand or arm as in handling).
Feeling: N .... SNNNNNNFFFNFFNFNNOON
No requirements specified.
Talking: F .... SNNNNNNFFFNFFNFNNOON
Expressing or exchanging ideas by means of the spoken word to impart oral information to clients or to the public and to convey detailed spoken instructions to other workers accurately, loudly, or quickly; from 1/3 to 2/3 of the time.
Hearing: F .... SNNNNNNFFFNFFNFNNOON
Must perceive the nature of sounds by ear from 1/3 to 2/3 of the time.
Tasting/Smelling: N .... SNNNNNNFFFNFFNFNNOON
No requirements specified.
Near Acuity: F .... SNNNNNNFFFNFFNFNNOON
Requires clarity of vision at 20 inches or less from 1/3 to 2/3 of the time.
Far Acuity: N .... SNNNNNNFFFNFFNFNNOON
No requirements specified.
Depth Perception: N .... SNNNNNNFFFNFFNFNNOON
No requirements specified.
Accommodation: O .... SNNNNNNFFFNFFNFNNOON

Copyright 1995, JIST Works, Inc., 720 N. Park Ave., Indianapolis, IN 46202

FIGURE 12-6 Sample *JEDOT/GOE* Occupational Report Pg. 4

Adjustment of lens of eye to bring an object into sharp focus. This factor is required when doing near point work at varying distances from the eye; up to 1/3 of the time.
Color Vision: O .... SNNNNNNFFFNFFNFNNOON
The ability to identify and distinguish colors is required up to 1/3 of the time.
Field of Vision: N .... SNNNNNNFFFNFFNFNNOO**N**
No requirements specified.

ENVIRONMENT................. .... NNNN3NNNNNNNNN
All environmental condition factors, except Noise Intensity Level, are coded with a letter that represents the presence and frequency of the condition in the work situation. **N** means Not Present, **O** means Occasionally Present, **F** means Frequently Present, and **C** means Continuously Present. Note that some jobs may include some environments noted as "Not Present." Always check with an employer about the requirements for a specific job.

Exposure to Weather: N.... .... **N**NNN3NNNNNNNNN
Not Present.
Extreme Cold: N N**N**NN3NNNNNNNNN
Not Present.
Extreme Heat: N NN**N**N3NNNNNNNNN
Not Present.
Wet and/or Humid: N........ .... NNN**N**3NNNNNNNNN
Not Present.
Noise Intensity Levels are symbolized by **1** = Very Quiet, **2** = Quiet, **3** = Moderate, **4** = Loud, and **5** = Very Loud.
Noise Intensity Level: 3 .... NNNN**3**NNNNNNNNN
Moderate
Vibration: N NNNN3**N**NNNNNNNN
Not Present.
Atmospheric Conditions: N NNNN3N**N**NNNNNNNN
Not Present.
Proximity to moving mechanical parts: N......................... NNNN3NN**N**NNNNNN
Not Present.
Exposure to electrical shock: N NNNN3NNN**N**NNNNN
Not Present.
Working in high, exposed places: N NNNN3NNNN**N**NNNN
Not Present.
Exposure to radiation: N NNNN3NNNNN**N**NNN
Not Present.
Working with explosives: N NNNN3NNNNNN**N**NN
Not Present.
Exposure to toxic or caustic chemicals: N NNNN3NNNNNNN**N**N
Not Present.
Other environmental conditions: N NNNN3NNNNNNNN**N**
Not Present.

TEMPERAMENTS .... D,I,V,P,
Each temperament factor is identified by one of eleven alphabetic characters. The applicable character is shown with the description of the temperament factor below.

A = Working ALONE or Apart in Physical Isolation from Others.
D = DIRECTING, Controlling or Planning Activities of Others.
E = EXPRESSING Personal Feelings.
I = INFLUENCING People in their Opinions, Attitudes, and Judgments.
J = Making JUDGMENTS and Decisions.
P = Dealing with PEOPLE.
R = Performing REPETITIVE or Short-Cycle Work.
S = Performing Effectively under STRESS.
T = Attaining Precise Set Limits, TOLERANCES, and Standards.
U = Working UNDER Specific Instructions.
V = Performing a VARIETY of Duties.

D DIRECTING, Controlling or Planning Activities of Others: Involves accepting responsibility for formulating plans, designs, practices, policies, methods, regulations, and procedures for operations or projects: negotiating with individuals or groups for agreements or contracts; and supervising subordinate workers to implement plans and control activities.

Copyright 1995, JIST Works, Inc., 720 N. Park Ave., Indianapolis, IN 46202

FIGURE 12-7 Sample *JEDOT/GOE* Occupational Report Pg. 5

I INFLUENCING people in their opinions, attitudes, and judgments: Involves writing, demonstrating, or speaking to persuade and motivate people to change their attitudes or opinions, participate in a particular activity, or purchase a specific commodity or service.
V Performing a VARIETY of duties: Involves frequent changes of tasks involving different aptitudes, technologies, techniques, procedures, working conditions, physical demands, or degrees of attentiveness without loss of efficiency or composure.
P Dealing with PEOPLE: Involves interpersonal relationships in job situations beyond receiving work instructions.

WORK FIELDS 261
Work Fields are categories of technologies that reflect how work gets done and what gets done as a result of the work activities of the job; the purpose of a job. The 96 work fields range from the specific to the general and are organized into homogeneous groups, based on related technologies or objectives, such as the movement of materials, the fabrication of products, the use of data, and the provision of services. The Work Field 261 is defined as:
WRITING
Creating, expressing, or depicting one's own ideas in various media.

MATERIALS, PRODUCTS,
SUBJECT MATTER, SERVICES 896
Materials, Products, Subject Matter, and Services refers to the objects or outcomes of Work Field activities. Examples include bread, botany, logs, and records. The Department of Labor has identified 386 such categories. The definition for the MPSMS 896 is:
ADVERTISING AND PUBLIC RELATIONS SERVICES
This group includes insurance and real estate services and clerical, accounting, general administration, financial, advertising, photofinishing, and similar business services of general nature rendered by various clerical workers, accountants, auditors, personnel officers, plant managers, bank officials, insurance and real estate agents, stockbrokers, public relations representatives, photofinishers, divers, sign painters, and related workers. Specialized business services, such as transportation, communication, public utility, merchandising, medical, legal, government, etc., are classified in their respective service groups.

SOC
Standard Occupational Classification: 3320
The SOC is the basis for the occupational arrangement used in the National Industry-Occupation Employment Matrix, which is the source of data on current and projected employment used to compile information for the Occupational Outlook Handbook.
In that arrangement, this job will be found under:
  PUBLIC RELATIONS SPECIALISTS AND PUBLICITY WRITERS

CIP
Classification of Instructional Programs: 080299
Instructional programs for training or advancement in this job will normally be found under the classification/s of:
  BUSINESS AND PERSONAL SERVICES MARKETING OPERATIONS, OTHER

OES
Occupational Employment Statistics: 34008
When a census is conducted to count the citizens in the United States, one of the questions on the census form asks for the occupation of each citizen. The data reported on this form is cataloged into about 500 categories by the Office of Employment Statistics. There is no accurate way to know how many people work in each of the thousands of occupations in the Dictionary of Occupational Titles. We only know, with reasonable accuracy, how many people work in each of the 500 OES categories.
You can use the OES number or the OES classification to find information about the size of the category and salaries in government reports. These reports should be available from the branch of your state government which provides employment services to residents of your state.
The title attached to the OES number 34008 is:
  PUBLIC RELATIONS SPECIALISTS AND PUBLICITY WRITERS

Copyright 1995, JIST Works, Inc., 720 N. Park Ave., Indianapolis, IN 46202

Quick Reference

OTHER SOURCES OF OCCUPATIONAL INFORMATION—PEOPLE

The good news is you've already picked up a substantial portion of this information during your industry research; it's almost impossible to separate the two areas at times. The better news is that you can now take a break from the library and rely on more person-to-person techniques to shape what you have already learned.

So, pick up the telephone and contact people that work in the industry. Ask for their advice on where your skills could be best applied. Be sure to talk with people who work at a variety of levels, from association leaders to practitioners to technicians in satellite industries. For instance, if you are interested in office management, get in touch with members of a local professional association that most closely relates to your interest, an office supplies firm, a temporary firm that specializes in placing office personnel, or actual office managers.

Bring up anything you are curious about. For example, ask the office manager how often his or her position is needed in smaller businesses versus larger ones, what are the long-term advantages and disadvantages of full-time work as opposed to temporary assignments, how other members of a staff often treat this position, characteristics of successful office managers, etc. Continually compare this information to your situation.

Quick Tip

Don't neglect to send a brief, sincere thank-you note to each person you talk to in this process. Because a job search is never completely linear, it's always possible one of these contacts could evolve into a job interview, so you want to position yourself to take the early advantage.

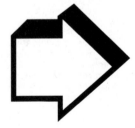

Quick Case Study

....

I was recently told of a situation that illustrates how thank-you notes can work. A local magazine publisher had met with a freelance writer who had contacted her to explore business writing in general. Three days after the conversation, the writer's portfolio and a thank-you note arrived in the mail. That afternoon, the publisher's editor resigned, so she immediately called the writer to schedule an interview. The publisher told me she did this for two reasons: 1) the writer had impressed her with her professionalism, and 2) the writer's phone number was right in front of her. That's exactly how informal contacts can pay off.

INFORMATION ABOUT THE INTERVIEWER

Quick Fact

By now, you have established a working relationship with your local librarians and a smooth phone presence when getting in touch with the right people. Both traits will serve you well in the next phase: researching the specific company and interviewer. Here you want to focus on company missions, ethics, areas of recent growth, and weak spots.

According to librarian Mary-Ellen Mort in Oakland, California, the best sources for information on local organizations are local newspaper articles, local directories, and area trade journals. Some libraries have clipping files of articles on area companies, CEOs, and industries. Ask your new library friends for ranked lists of local companies in your field. Depending on the library's size, you may even lay your hands on annual reports and various promotional literature, too. If the library doesn't carry copies of these materials, request them from the organization itself.

If the organization is a small, privately owned company, this type of information may not be available at all. In that case, explore comparable companies and apply what you find. And don't forget—it's never a mistake to pick up the phone and talk with the organization's suppliers, customers, and current employees.

But now that you've gathered all this raw data, how do you apply it to the interview? Here are some questions your research should answer.

Quick Tip

Offer to drop by and pick up the organization's material in person rather than have it mailed to you. This fosters several positives: 1) It allows you to meet with the receptionist and make a positive impression with an insider (good news travels fast, especially when it concerns a future employee); 2) It strengthens an impression that you are well-organized and very interested; 3) It forces you to travel the route in advance and scout out potentially slowing traffic patterns, confusing addresses, and so forth.

Organization Research Questions

1. Who are the prospective employers and what do they do?
2. What has the organization done in the last three years?
3. Where is the organization headed? What new products or services are on the horizon?
4. What/who is the competition? Where is this organization at an advantage or disadvantage?
5. What are the success factors?
6. How can the job you are pursuing contribute to the organization's success?

Granted, translating columns of numbers and sales slogans into tangible answers to these questions takes some thoughtful application on your part. However, don't let it scare you into not even trying. For starters, pick up a copy of Lelia K. Kight's *Getting the Lowdown on Employers and a Leg Up on the Job Market* for some down-to-earth, instructive steps in interpreting annual reports. And, as with the industry journals, be sure to read the CEO's message at the beginning. This carefully crafted editorial sets the tone for the year past and its direction in the years ahead.

Ultimately, when it comes to finding out information about your specific interviewer, you may have to rely on the telephone once again. Politely and unobtrusively ask current employees about this person's style of work, how he or she spends the day, what types of behaviors earn a frown from this person, and so forth. The information you can dig up could be invaluable.

COMPUTER ONLINE SERVICES

Another place you can turn for information of all kinds is perhaps the most exciting advancement in the career industry—computer online services and bulletin boards.

Quick Case Study

A mining engineer by training and education, Stan was between assignments and looking for a temporary position. An agency sent his resume to the head of an engineering department at an oil refinery headquartered in San Francisco, and although Stan didn't have any experience in this area, he was invited west for a job interview. As it turned out, the person interviewing him was the brother of a high school acquaintance he had known years earlier in central Florida. Had he been previously aware of this, he could have gotten some inside information from his old acquaintance and established this personal relationship with his interviewer prior to boarding the airplane.

The debate over the advantages and disadvantages of Prodigy, CompuServe, America Online, and Internet could fill another book—suffice it to say that all have incredible networking capabilities. Post your occupational question here and you'll get replies from different levels and experiences across the country.

Much of what you want to know about an industry or organization may be available through a bulletin board system—and the number of bulletin board systems increases daily. And while the databases and articles are valuable, the assistance doesn't stop there. Executives, employees, and fellow job seekers freely share information, leads, and advice on a 24-hour basis—and it's all literally at your fingertips (no searching through library shelves!).

Quick Case Study

Already the business world is full of job seekers who have landed positions through bulletin board systems. Take, for instance, Terry Carroll, a law student at Santa Clara University in California. According to *U.S. News and World Report*, the former computer designer caught the eye of two lawyers by responding to queries posted on CompuServe's legal forum. They promptly invited him to assist them on cases. Then when Carroll lost his computer job and decided to take up law full-time, he put the word out via electronic mail. Within 24 hours he had made six contacts and heard about six more job openings.

A PARTIAL LISTING OF ONLINE CAREER RESOURCES

Quick Reference

Don't underestimate the fun of this newest job search tool. Candidates who skip the research stage because it's "too boring" will find themselves fascinated by the interactive, immediate-gratification format of bulletin board systems.

While there is a tremendous amount of data and interactive advice available from the major online services, I've listed some of the career-specific services available from America Online's Career Center. This is a special service set up to provide resources for career planning and job seeking. These services are impressive and always expanding.

THE CAREER RESOURCE LIBRARY

The Career Resource Library can be of value if you or someone you know requires assistance with any of the following career development tasks:

- selecting a career direction or goal
- conducting an effective job search
- selecting a vocational/technical program of study and institution
- selecting a college and major
- obtaining financial assistance to attend school or college
- finding work with your state or the federal government
- analyzing the future of a particular career field or industry
- researching potential employers
- starting and operating a small business
- working from home
- understanding your personality style and make-up
- enhancing your personal and social development
- dealing with job discrimination
- career planning after retirement

The information available via this library includes information from diverse sources and in many formats including:

- audio cassettes

- ✍ books
- ✍ CD-ROM and computer software programs
- ✍ conferences
- ✍ films
- ✍ magazines
- ✍ newsletters
- ✍ newspapers
- ✍ online databases
- ✍ phone and fax services
- ✍ professional associations
- ✍ professional services
- ✍ videotapes
- ✍ workshops and seminars

You can even order career books and materials via this career center. Many JIST books (including this one) are available there via our online catalog, and we have a variety of career information available there as well. You can even download the latest JIST catalog in its entirety from the Career Resource Library and send orders via e-mail.

COMPANY PROFILES—HOOVER'S HANDBOOKS

The Company Profiles—Hoover's Handbooks database includes portfolios of more than 900 of the largest, most influential, and fastest growing public and private companies in the United States and the world. The Reference Press (Austin, Texas) creates and manages this database. Each profile includes:

- ✍ overview of operations and strategy
- ✍ founders' names and company history
- ✍ names, ages, and salaries of key officers
- ✍ headquarters address, telephone number, and fax number
- ✍ locations of operations

Quick Reference

✍ lists of divisions, subsidiaries, products, services, and brand names

✍ names of key competitors

The Reference Press provides an alphabetical list of all companies in the database, so you can scroll through this or go directly to a company in which you are interested. You may also search for companies located in a particular state, region, or country. And if you don't know which company you are looking for, type in one or more search words. For instance, if you are interested in locating companies that make submarines, you can search for this word and discover that General Dynamics and Teneco are the two largest submarine makers in the country.

EMPLOYER CONTACTS

Employer Contacts is a collection of information on more than 5,000 American employers, supplied by Demand Research Corp. (Chicago, Illinois). This service assists you in finding potential employers that match your occupational interests and goals.

Demand Research Corp. specializes in compiling and distributing information on every U.S. public company listed on the NYSE, the AMEX, and the NASDAQ National Market System. Each listing here includes:

✍ the company's name, address, phone, and fax numbers

✍ ticker symbol

✍ exchange affiliation

✍ full name of the chief executive officer

✍ full name of the chief financial officer

✍ primary industry classification

CAREER GUIDANCE SERVICES

For some lucky folks, their skills and interests point to one definite career direction. For the other 99 percent of us, figuring out how to translate our talents into job positions can be an agonizing process. The online Career Center offers three unique areas to help you set your feet in the right direction.

Quick
Fact

CAREER FOCUS 2000

The Career Focus 2000 service consists of a series of four "workbook" exercises that you may download and complete at your leisure. CF 2000 is designed to guide you in selecting a career direction in line with your personality, and in developing a plan for reaching your career goal. It is appropriate for anyone who is undecided about a career direction or unsure about how to reach a career goal.

The heart of the CF 2000 is an interest inventory. This inventory allows you to sample 225 work activities and then compare your strongest interests to approximately 1,000 occupations as a means of finding occupations that match your interests.

CAREER ANALYSIS SERVICE

This is a very comprehensive, computer-assisted analysis service designed to identify occupations that match your interests, abilities, and work preferences. This service is appropriate for individuals who desire a more thorough analysis of career options than what is possible with the Career Focus 2000 program.

A questionnaire allows you to indicate your preferences for various work activities and situations. You then e-mail your answers back to the Career Center, where a professional career counselor enters your answers into an occupational database produced by the U.S. Department of Labor. The counselor compares your preferences to more than 10,000 occupations. Within 48 hours, you receive a listing of occupations (by job title) that best match your interests, abilities, and work preferences.

There is a one-time charge of $39.95 to use the Career Analysis Service.

CAREER COUNSELING

Here you may meet privately with an experienced, professional career counselor online—in real time—to discuss your career needs and problems. Counseling is available on an appointment basis, and there is no additional fee for this service other than the normal America Online fees.

These are just a few of the many services available via computer, and more will become available in the future. If you know how to get to these services, they can be worth your time!

13

DRESS AND GROOMING TIPS AND OTHER LAST-MINUTE PREPARATIONS THAT WIN THE INTERVIEW

Quick Tip

You've thoroughly researched the organization and practiced your answers until they are smooth and highly informative. But you're not completely ready for the interview yet—the night before, you need to gather the right support materials to complement your presentation. This chapter gives you tips on what to bring to the interview, how to dress and groom, and other details.

PACK YOUR BRIEFCASE LIKE A PROFESSIONAL

American Express isn't the only thing you don't want to leave home without. You want to pack for the interview with the same care as you would for a vacation or overnight trip—even more care in fact because there will be no hotel service to bring you a forgotten resume, and no corner drugstore that sells extra copies of references.

Organize your briefcase or portfolio the night before, so you don't forget an important item in the last-minute rush. Be sure to include the following.

- **Resume:** Never assume the interviewer already has a copy of your resume. In fact, bring several copies in case you are asked to speak with more than one person during your visit.

- **References:** Again, bring several copies of your references in case you need to hand out extra copies. Yes, the interviewer could photocopy the list, but do you really want a black-and-white smudged version in someone's hand as opposed

Quick Tip

Organization and neatness are the keys to success at this stage. You want to be able to find anything in your briefcase immediately, and that material should be neat and uncreased. Think of it as opening your desk drawer in front of the boss.

Quick Tip

It's not necessary to whip out a $100 Mont Blanc pen or an engraved fountain pen to impress an interviewer. However, do pass over the ones with chewed caps, leaky ink, or advertising printed down the side. Likewise, leave the red, purple, and multicolored inks at home—go with your basic, business black or blue. If necessary, invest in a new pen at an office supply store—it will cost you less than $1.

to your neatly prepared version? It's also a great idea to bring along a "cheat sheet" of dates and addresses that allow you to fill out a standard application quickly— tear out the worksheets in chapter 10 to help with those easy-to-forget details. Sure, it's doubtful anyone would actually call or write to your elementary school principal, but it scores points in your favor to be ready with that information— especially when most applicants merely write in the city in which it's located and leave it at that.

☞ **Organization background materials:** Hey, this is not a pop quiz! The interviewer is not going to test your memory of what you've read about the company as much as find out if your talents match their needs. By all means, take along copies of reports and articles. There's a good chance the interviewer may not be aware of that information, and having it on hand to refer to keeps you from appearing to guess at statistics, figures, and goals.

☞ **Note pad and pen:** According to educator and lecturer Carol Price, who teaches communications seminars with Career Track, a person does well to tackle almost any situation with a pad and pen in hand. "Ask the interviewer's permission to take notes so that you can walk away smarter than when you came in,"

Price suggests. "If you walk in empty-handed, what you're implying is 'I don't care what you're going to say.'"

- **Proof of past accomplishments:** The other thing you must have in hand, according to Price, is a folder that says "I do good work." Basically, it is evidence that the company isn't thinking of hiring someone who talks a good game and puts on a great interview face but never performs. In creative fields, this often is referred to as a portfolio—a collection of articles, layouts, advertisements, etc., that illustrate your best work. However, even those whose jobs require more traditional tasks such as typing, answering phones, consulting with customers, or sales can build a portfolio, says Price. (In fact, even the creative folks should add some of her suggestions to their work to round out the picture.)

To create such a "good deed" file, begin this Friday by writing down five things you—not necessarily your boss—believe you did well this week, even if they are routine tasks. Then put that list away and continue this trend for an entire month. At the end of the month, narrow the four or five lists down to 10 accomplishments that stand out. At the end of the year, review the 120 and cull that down to 25. Formalize the language that describes those 25 achievements, and print them out in an organized manner on your resume along with your references. According to Price, "When someone asks, 'What can you bring to this organization?' not only are you going to say, 'I'm good with people,' which is what everyone says, but you're going to hand that person proof."

> **"***Women and men who fit the definition of attractive may have an edge in an interviews.***"**

DRESS PROFESSIONALLY

Quick Fact

According to a National Bureau of Economic Research report released this year, attractive people may have an edge in interviews and may be better employees due to increased self-confidence. Furthermore, women and men who fit the societal definition of attractiveness earn an average of 10 percent more than their counterparts.

And therein lies the secret: Society's definition of attractive includes quality clothes; an appropriate, neat hair style; and properly applied makeup for women; along with your physical appearance. If you are less than satisfied with your face and body shape, don't despair: Two out of three ain't bad. In an interview, it's extremely good.

IMAGE TIPS FOR MEN FROM A PROFESSIONAL

According to interviewers, a suit is the outfit of choice for most office, professional, and management jobs. If this makes sense in your situation, here are some suggestions from Anne Marie Sabeth's specific clothing guidelines, as presented in her book *Business Etiquette in Brief.*

▼▼

SUIT CUTS: Most organizations with rigid cultures encourage male employees to wear single-breasted, as opposed to double-breasted, suits. The reason is that the American (or single-breasted) jacket provides a more classic look, while the European (or double-breasted) jacket gives a more trendy or fashion-forward image. And a double-breasted suit on a man who stands less than six feet tall can make him look like a character from a bad gangster movie. Choose the style that best fits the atmosphere you gathered from your research. If in doubt, go with single-breasted!

When wearing a double-breasted suit, button all the buttons when standing or walking. If your single-breasted jacket has two buttons, button the top one. If it has three, button the center one when walking or standing.

FABRICS: One hundred-percent wool blends (especially wool gabardine) are always good choices. When purchasing a suit, scrunch the material to be sure it doesn't wrinkle—this assures you will look as crisp leaving the interviewer's office as you did when you arrived. You don't want your last, lingering impression to be wrinkled.

SHIRTS: Long-sleeved shirts are the rule in business—never wear a short-sleeved shirt to interview for any management or office job. White shirts portray the most formal look, while light blue shirts give a more casual appearance. A button-down collar makes a suit jacket or sport coat appear less formal, so go with the choice that makes the most sense for your situation.

TIES: Width is what counts with ties. Because tie width varies over time, look in a good men's clothing store and get the latest "in" width. The tip of the tie should touch the top of a man's belt buckle. As for fabrics, always wear a silk or silk-like tie; the knitted versions are dated and the polyester ones simply look cheap. A more daring pattern is often acceptable in business these days, so a geometric design or floral pattern is fine. However, stay away from Looney Tunes and Disney cartoons as they may not portray an image of seriousness.

SUSPENDERS: If you choose to wear suspenders, select a pair that buttons rather than clips on. Otherwise, the potential for disaster goes without saying.

BELTS, SOCKS, AND SHOES: Black and cordovan are always fashion-wise color investments for belts and shoes. Tassel loafers are accepted with suits in some business cultures, but wing-tips portray a more conservative look. Choose the appropriate style to match the rest of your ensemble. Socks should reach mid-calf to avoid showing leg.

POCKET SQUARES: An optional accessory, pocket squares generally aren't appropriate until after 5 P.M., unless you are in a more creative environment such as advertising. If you have an all-day interview followed by a social evening ahead of you, a pocket square is an excellent way to convert the suit to match the cocktail atmosphere. Be sure the one you select complements your tie. However, you *do not* want the fabrics to match, so beware of retailers who sell matching ties and pocket scarves! It's a trap for the fashionably backward.

JEWELRY: Yes, society accepts earrings for men these days but only in a more casual setting than a job interview. Stick to a wedding band, class ring, or other nongaudy ring on the ring finger and a watch with a basic black leather or metal band.

Quick Fact

IF A SUIT IS NOT APPROPRIATE

A suit is appropriate for many office jobs but is not for many others. For instance, if you are applying for a construction job or pool lifeguard, wearing a suit could actually hurt your chances of landing the position. In cases where the job involves more physical labor, consider the business casual look. Unfortunately, too many people have misinterpreted this term to mean "sloppy." Business casual is actually defined as a crisp pair of slacks with a matching sports shirt and well-maintained footwear. Depending on the position, a sport coat and tie may be appropriate.

Quick Tip

When is it appropriate for men to remove their jackets? According to Sabeth, only when the person who has arranged the meeting (in this case, the interviewer) invites others to do so. Make sure yours is comfortable—you could be wearing it for hours.

IMAGE TIPS FOR WOMEN FROM A PROFESSIONAL

In her book *Business Etiquette in Brief*, Anne Marie Sabeth also provides suggestions for women. Sabeth suggests that, while you may have spent thousands of dollars and a lot of work and energy to earn a degree, your appearance remains one of the main factors that will encourage others to want to work with and for you.

☑ **SUITS:** Although tailored dresses with shoulder pads (giving the illusion of more height) are quite acceptable today, the classic suit still portrays the most authority. You can't go wrong if you select a high-quality suit in navy, gray, taupe, or black tones. As for skirt lengths, that depends on the industry you choose and the company's attitude. For an interview, play it safe: Skirts should be no shorter than slightly above the knee and fall no lower than just below mid-calf. Miniskirts have no place in a professional environment unless you will be working in retail.

☑ **FABRICS:** Follow the men's cue and give any fabric you select the scrunch test. You'll discover linen suits look great, but they don't pass this test. Pass over them when selecting for an interview.

☑ **BLOUSES:** The color of your blouse has a definite impact on your overall look. As with suits, solid colors are the wisest investments. For this particular occasion, choose tones to benefit the particular suit you have selected. For example, if wearing a light-colored suit, add an authoritative look with a dark or brightly colored blouse.

☑ **HOSIERY:** Image consultants have found that women who wear hosiery in their own skin tone portray a more conservative image than those who wear darker or colored stockings. However, in retail, colored hosiery may be perfectly acceptable. The only option you don't have is to go without hose at all, no matter how tan your legs may be.

☑ **SHOES:** The classic pump generally works best in business. Heels should measure one to two inches, depending on the height of the woman. By investing in leather rather than synthetic materials, you convey a more distinguished image. Recommended colors: navy, black, cordovan, and taupe.

☑ **HANDBAGS/BRIEFCASES/PORTFOLIOS:** It's always best to invest in leather accessories. The same colors apply here as with shoes. "I'm always asked whether it's appropriate to carry both a purse and a briefcase," Sabeth writes. "My answer is 'yes,' as long as the purse is a shoulder bag that is compact in appearance. Also, it should contain only necessary items (wallet, hair brush, basic cosmetics). If you have it packed full and it accidentally drops open, your life history could be revealed."

☑ **JEWELRY:** When selecting jewelry, apply the "Rule of 13." After you dress in the morning, do a quick count of your accessories. Include the ornate buttons on your suit, the buckles on your shoes, your eyeglasses, scarf, and jewelry. If the count is less than 13, you're probably well balanced in appearance. If you tally more than 13, play it safe and remove unnecessary pieces. The never-never-nevers in the interview situation: dangling earrings, double-pierced ears (or noses), dark-tinted eyeglasses, and perfume that can be detected by someone more than an arm's length away.

IF FORMAL BUSINESS DRESS IS NOT APPROPRIATE

Quick Alert

While most office, professional, and managerial jobs require formal business attire, you may be looking for a job where that just would not be appropriate. Use your judgment. In most cases, it is better to overdress a bit rather than not be dressed well enough. As with men, overdressing for a certain jobs such as driving a delivery truck will not help you.

ONE FINAL DRESS AND GROOMING TIP

I've said it before, and I'll say it again …

MIKE FARR'S INTERVIEW DRESS AND GROOMING RULE

> *Dress and groom like the interviewer is likely*
> *to be dressed—only neater.*

You can usually figure out how the person who will interview you is likely to dress by observing others in similar positions. In general, it is pretty safe to dress in a way that the interviewer would find acceptable. But better yet, dress and groom one notch higher than he or she does for safety's sake.

HOW TO ANSWER PROBLEM INTERVIEW QUESTIONS AND HANDLE UNUSUAL INTERVIEW SITUATIONS

Introduction

Chapter 4 reviewed the basics of how to answer problem interview questions. Chapter 5 then showed you how to use those basic techniques to answer 10 key interview questions. I suggested then that having good answers to those 10 basic interview questions—and mastering the techniques for answering problem questions in general—would prepare you for most difficult or awkward questions you might face. Since I won't cover those 10 questions in detail in this section, it is important that you review those chapters before you read on.

Because of the importance of the basic interview techniques, I will review them in the first chapter of this section. I have also provided additional information on answering a wide variety of interview questions that were not covered earlier. The focus of this section is to prepare you to answer a variety of general and specific problem questions. I've defined a problem question as one whose straight reply could be damaging to your chances of getting the job. For instance, to be brutally honest when the interviewer asks, "What don't you like about your present job?" you might answer, "My boss is a jerk." While that might be an honest

answer, it is unlikely to present you as a good candidate for a new job.

If I've not covered the specific problem question that most concerns you, I have at least tried to provide you with a process for approaching it. I do hope this information helps you.

Chapters in This Section

Chapter 14: How to Answer Problem Interview Questions— A Review

Reviews the content covered in chapters 4 and 5 but adds information not provided in those. This is very important material, so I hope you don't mind a more thorough review of it.

Chapter 15: Answers to Specific Problem Questions

While there are thousands of potential interview questions that might be asked of you, I anticipate those that are most likely to cause problems. This is not a chapter to read from beginning to end. Instead, I suggest you browse it to find questions that relate to you and, I hope, find a way to respond positively.

Chapter 16: Nontraditional Interview Approaches

Describes a variety of unconventional interview situations you may face, such as being interviewed over breakfast or via video.

Also a variety of "creative" approaches for getting interviews. This chapter covers some of these and helps you prepare for the unexpected.

Chapter 17: Pre-employment Testing

Tests are being used more and more to provide additional information to enable employers to make good hiring decisions. This chapter tells you what to expect and gives you some tips for taking these tests.

14

How to Answer Problem Interview Questions— a Review

Quick Tip

This chapter provides a quick review of the basic techniques that I recommend in answering most problem questions. Those techniques are presented in more detail in chapters 4 and 5. For the best possible comprehension of this section, you'll need to read them if you have not already done so.

As mentioned in Section 1, about 80 percent of all people who get interviews do not, according to employer surveys, do a good job in answering one or more interview questions. This is a very big problem in the job search and has kept many, many good people from getting jobs that they are perfectly capable of handling. However, they didn't get those jobs because they failed to convince the employer that they had the needed skills and other characteristics to do the job.

So, at issue here is not your ability to *do* the job, it is your need to improve your ability to communicate clearly that you *can* do the job. This chapter will review the basic techniques to answer most interview questions. This is a very important topic, particularly if you already know that you have a "problem" that will be an issue for an employer.

TO BE CONSIDERED, YOU MUST MEET AN EMPLOYER'S EXPECTATIONS

Quick Fact

Employers are people, just like you, and they want to make a good decision in hiring someone. Think about it—hiring the wrong person will cause them much extra work and grief. If the person does not perform well, they will have to spend extra time supervising that person. If the employee does not stay very long, the employer will lose lots of training time and have to hire and train all over again. And if the person they hire does not work out and has to be replaced, this creates a situation that most employers desperately want to avoid—firing someone.

"*How well you do in an interview will often be the key factor that an employer will consider.***"**

So employers are very much motivated to hire a "good" person. They want someone who has the skills to do the job and usually base this on the applicant's past work experience and education. These "credentials" are very important in considering one person over another and, if you don't meet the minimum criteria, often you just won't be considered.

Assuming that you have done your homework (as presented in Section 2 of this book) and know your skills and the types of jobs that you are best suited for, then you are seeking jobs for which you do have the necessary skills and, at least, the minimum credentials. This being the case, how well you perform in the interview will often be the key factor in an employer giving you a chance over someone else who has better credentials. You see, it is not always the best person who gets the job, it is often the one who has the best communication skills.

THE THREE EMPLOYER EXPECTATIONS

These were presented in Section 1 but are repeated here, because they are an important element in understanding what an employer will be looking for during an interview.

The Three Major Employer Expectations

▲ **1. Appearance**—Do you look like the type of person who will succeed on the job?

▲ **2. Dependability**—Can you be depended on to be reliable and to do a good job for a reasonable length of time?

▲ **3. Credentials**—Do you have the necessary training, experience, skills, and credentials that indicate you are able to do the job well?

Notice that I put credentials third? This is because I assume that you have the minimal credentials to be considered for the job in question. Appearance is first, because if you do create a negative impression (as about 40 percent of all job seekers do) you are unlikely to be considered at all. That leaves expectation number 2 as the one that most employers will focus on during the interview.

THE 10 MOST FREQUENTLY ASKED PROBLEM QUESTIONS

Quick Reference

Way back in chapter 5, I provided detailed answers to 10 interview questions. I have carefully selected those 10 questions because I feel that they are representative of the types of questions that most often create problems for people in an interview. Often, the actual question will not be phrased in the same way, but the employer is usually asking one of those questions in a different form. That is why I proposed in chapter 5 that, if you can provide a good and honest response to each of the following 10 questions, you will be better prepared to answer most other interview questions.

Since I provided detailed answers in chapter 5 to each of the questions that follow, I won't repeat them here. The list may help you recollect them, though.

10 Most Frequently Asked Problem Questions

1. Why don't you tell me about yourself?
2. Why should I hire you?
3. What are your major strengths?
4. What are your major weaknesses?
5. What sort of pay do you expect to receive?
6. How does your previous experience relate to the jobs we have here?
7. What are your plans for the future?
8. What will your former employers (or teachers, if you are a recent student) say about you?
9. Why are you looking for this sort of position and why here?
10. Why don't you tell me about your personal situation?

A QUICK REVIEW OF THE THREE-STEP PROCESS

Quick Reference

In answering any interview question, it is essential that you understand what the employer really wants to know. In some cases, this will be quite obvious and you can answer directly. Questions regarding credentials and job-related skills often have no hidden agenda and can be answered in a forthright manner—though some answers are clearly better than others.

But the big problem for most job seekers is that many interview questions are not what they seem to be at all. Some questions, like "Why don't you tell me about yourself?" don't seem to have a direct answer. And others, such as "Do you come from this area?" often have hidden agendas (in this case, the employer is probably trying to find out if you are likely to remain in this area due to family or other ties).

To help you answer these less-than-direct questions, I have developed a simple technique that you can use to answer most interview questions.

Quick Reference

THE THREE-STEP PROCESS FOR ANSWERING INTERVIEW QUESTIONS

☑ Step #1: Understand What Is Really Being Asked

Most questions relate to Employer Expectation #2 regarding your adaptive skills and personality. This includes such questions as: Can we depend on you?; Are you easy to get along with?; Are you a good worker? The question may also relate to Employer Expectation #3, namely, do you have the experience and training to do the job if we hire you?

☑ Step #2: Answer the Question Briefly, in a Nondamaging Way

A good response to a question should acknowledge the facts and present them as an advantage, not a disadvantage.

☑ Step #3: Answer the Real Question by Presenting Your Related Skills

Once you understand the employer's real concern, you can answer the hidden question by presenting the skills you have that relate to the job.

REVIEW OF THE "PROVE IT" TECHNIQUE

Once you understand what an employer is really asking, the third step

---

The "Prove It" Technique

▲ **1. Present a Concrete Example:** People relate to and remember stories. Saying you have a skill is not nearly as powerful as describing a situation where you used that skill. The story should include enough details to make sense of the who, what, where, when, and why.

▲ **2. Quantify:** Whenever possible, numbers should be used to provide a basis for what was done. For example, the number of customers served or the amount of cash handled.

▲ **3. Emphasize Results:** It is important to provide some data regarding the positive results you obtained. For example, sales increased by 3 percent over the previous year or profits went up 50 percent. Use numbers to quantify your results.

▲ **4. Link It Up:** While the connection between your story and doing the job well may seem obvious to you, make sure it is clear to the employer. A simple statement is often enough to accomplish this.

Quick Reference

of the Three-Step Process suggests that you answer the real question being asked. I suggest that you use the following technique to do this most effectively:

The activities in Section 2 of this book helped you identify key statements and accomplishments to use in the "Prove It" technique. Together, the Three-Step Process and "Prove It" techniques form the basic approach to answering problem questions, and it is most important that you understand and use these techniques to improve your interviewing skills.

Quick Tip

Technically, this is a free country and interviewers can ask whatever they wish. Dumb questions, questions in poor taste, and personal questions can all be asked. It's what employers do that can get them in trouble with the law. It is illegal to hire or not hire someone based on certain criteria. It is also very difficult to prove that someone actually does that.

As a job seeker, the more important issue might be whether or not you want the job. If you refuse to answer a certain question, fine. But also realize the question was probably intended to find out whether you will be a good employee. That is a legitimate concern for an employer and you have the responsibility, if you want the job, to let them know you will be a good choice.

There are situations (thankfully, very rare) where an interviewer's questions are offensive. If that is the case, you can easily conclude that you will not work for such a person. Ever. You just might, in this sort of situation, tell that employer just what you think. Or you might report the firm to the authorities. Yes, this would be a situation where a thank-you note would not be required.

LEGAL AND ILLEGAL QUESTIONS

You haven't been thrown to the sharks completely when you walk into an interview. Thanks to a variety of federal and local laws, there are a host of ways to phrase a question that are off-limits to interviewers. Notice I said "phrase" a question—the illegality is not in what they want to know as much as how they go about discovering that information.

Title VII of the Civil Rights Act (enacted in 1964 and still very much in effect) makes discrimination on the basis of race, sex, religion, or national origin illegal in hiring discussions. The more recent Americans With Disabilities Act requires that an employer provide an equal opportunity for an individual with a disability to participate in the job application process and to be considered for a job. Both of these major laws present real problems for employers who can be proven to illegally discriminate against protected groups in their hiring. For example, consider the legal problems that the following questions might present:

· ·

Some Questions That Could Create Problems for an Employer

- ☞ Are you married, divorced, separated, or single? (Sets up potential grounds for sex discrimination.)
- ☞ How old are you? (Whoops! Age discrimination lawsuits looming!)
- ☞ Do you go to church regularly/What is your religious preference? (Likely to discriminate because they don't agree with your beliefs?)
- ☞ Have you ever changed your name? (Related to marital status.)
- ☞ Where were you born? Where was your nearest relative born? (National origin.)
- ☞ Do you have many debts?
- ☞ Do you own or rent your home?
- ☞ What social or political organizations do you belong to?
- ☞ What does your spouse think about your career?
- ☞ Are you living with anyone?
- ☞ Are you practicing birth control?
- ☞ Were you ever arrested?
- ☞ How much insurance do you have?
- ☞ How much do you weigh/how tall are you?
- ☞ Do you have any physical or mental handicaps?
- ☞ Have you ever been treated by a psychiatrist or psychologist?
- ☞ How many days were you absent from work because of illness last year?

· ·

Quick Case Study

▲ In 1992, Delta Airlines found out firsthand how financially damaging discriminatory questions can be. Former Pan American flight attendants that were added to Delta's payroll when the two companies merged filed complaints with the New York State Division of Human Rights. More than 100 women alleged that, during job interviews, they were asked to answer questions that included "How old are you?" "What is your marital status?" "If not married, why not?" "Are you taking birth control pills?" and "Have you ever had any tissue removed from your body?" The extensive bad press alone was enough to harm Delta's reputation with customers at a time when airlines needed every dime to stay in business.

Quick Tip

What should you do if you are asked what you think is an illegal question? I suggest answering the first one without comment, because odds are good it was an unintentional slip on the interviewer's part. Should you get hit with second and third "violations," you might inform the interviewer (if you choose to do so) that these questions are illegal and you don't wish to answer them. Then ask the interviewer to explain why and how the questions apply to the position you are discussing. It should be easy to decide, based on that information, if you want to volunteer answers or subtly invite the next line of questions.

Quick Reference

There are situations where a specific job might require an answer to some questions that might appear to be illegal for other jobs. For example, a firefighter would need to be in good physical condition and health-related questions are acceptable. But, in general, interview questions should focus only on your ability to do the job. If a question doesn't seem right to you, it probably isn't.

AND NOW, A WORD ON BEHALF OF OUR EMPLOYERS

Yes, it's easy to understand why the flight attendants at Delta were up in arms over the questions they were subjected to. After all, there's rarely anything more personal than the type of birth control you are using and it is humiliating to be asked to place your private life at the interviewer's feet.

But at the same time, employers of all sizes are sued for all sorts of things. Most of them land in hot water for incidents that stem from nothing more than miscommunication. The termination of a single employee now can arguably violate dozens of statutes. "It is very infrequent that someone sues just for discrimination anymore," Elizabeth du Fresne, a lawyer in Miami told *Inc.* magazine recently. "They also sue for battery, for intentional infliction of emotional distress, for negligent hiring or negligent retention. All of these have unlimited compensatory and punitive damages. And they can be brought against companies and individuals alike, so a manager's personal assets are now on the line."

Quick Fact

According to the U.S. Equal Employment Opportunity Commission (EEOC), in a recent year some 270,000 allegations were filed with the commission and its 82 state and local counterparts. *Inc.* magazine reports that complainants numbered just over 150,000—some had lodged more than one charge. The number of complaints has been rising sharply—up about 30 percent in just two years and 2,200 percent in the past two decades.

Many people now sue simply for being terminated, even though the employer did nothing wrong. But it can cost employers between $5,000 and $20,000 just to defend themselves through the charge-filing stage, where claims are brought before the EEOC or a state agency. Defending these suits also costs time and results in substantial loss of revenue even when there is no valid basis for a complaint. As a result, many employers are becoming increasingly careful when they hire, screening people far more thoroughly so that they are less likely to have to terminate someone later. Other employers are simply hiring fewer people.

Naturally, with lawsuit possibilities of great concern, employers want to know as much about a candidate's situation, personality, motivations, and potential as possible before they take a risk and hire someone that won't work out—and might sue them for it.

Quick Tip

Many times, when an interviewer asks an illegal question, he or she is trying to gauge the integrity of your character. Here are some questions interviewers have developed to handle this challenge legally:

"Describe a past hardship and how you handled it."

"How are you doing on goals you've set for yourself?"

"Have you ever helped a friend through a tough problem and what did you learn?"

"What are your dreams for the future?" (Notice the more personal, open attitude of this question versus "What are your goals for the future?")

"Do people come to you for advice?"

"How many hours a week are you willing to work to succeed?"

> **"**Being prepared for open-ended interview questions may better your chances of getting the job.**"**

SMART INTERVIEWERS USE OPEN-ENDED QUESTIONS TO AVOID PROBLEMS—AND STILL GET THE INFORMATION THEY WANT

Employers want to get the information they need to make a safe, profitable decision. You, the candidate, want some privacy and a fair chance to be considered based on your merits. Open-ended interview questions generally achieve both goals.

For instance, instead of asking "Are you living with anyone?" interviewers can phrase the question as "Do you foresee any situations that would prevent you from traveling or relocating?" This allows you to decide what information about your private life applies to the job at hand. Of course, if you are not prepared for such a question, you can provide information that might damage your chances.

So, you see, employers will often want to know details of your personal situation for legitimate reasons: they want to be sure that you can be depended on to stay on the job and work hard. That, if you remember, is Employer Expectation # 2 and is of great concern to most employers. Your task in the interview is to provide information indicating that, yes, you can be counted on to do the job. Often, if you don't get that idea across, you simply will not be considered.

15

ANSWERS TO SPECIFIC PROBLEM QUESTIONS

Quick Tip

This chapter is divided into two sections. The first deals with issues that most people experience and are often legitimate issues for an employer to explore. This includes things such as gaps in your employment history or being fired from a previous job. The second section presents issues that many believe are inappropriate areas for an employer to consider when making a decision to hire, such as age, race, and gender.

Many of the questions may not relate to you at all. For example, if you are young and just entering the workforce, you won't be interested in answering questions directed to those who are "old." So the way to use this chapter is to review only those issues or questions that relate to your situation and skip over those that don't.

The basic techniques for answering most problem interview questions have already been covered (in chapters 5 and 14), and I've given examples of "good" answers to 10 of the most frequently asked questions (in chapter 5). We won't go over that territory again here. What I will do is give you tips for handling a variety of specific questions that may or may not relate to you.

Many of the issues that are covered in this chapter are those that most workers experience. They are not sins and you will find that, if you learn to handle them well, they will not become a major problem in being considered for a job.

Most of these questions are also more likely to be an issue in a traditional interview. You may remember that I defined a traditional interview (way back in chapter 3) as one where there is a job opening and you are just one of several candidates for the position. Traditional interviews are not a lot of fun for most people, but preparing for the types of concerns an employer is likely to raise will improve your ability to handle less formal meetings as well.

One good thing about the traditional interview is that you can accurately guess—and prepare for—the questions most likely to be asked. In fact, that's one of the biggest complaints human resource personnel have about this style. They, too, can predict what type of answers applicants will give to their routine questions. Yet, because it is the most straightforward way of getting information, this interviewing approach lives on at organizations of all sizes across the country.

Even mentioning that some of the things in this chapter might be regarded as "problems" by an employer will make some people angry. For example, some would object to any mention that someone over 50 might experience discrimination in the labor market—although anyone over 50 knows that their age makes it harder to get a good job. Others will resent that employers would even consider such things as race, religion, native origin, child care, and other "politically sensitive" matters in evaluating people for employment. But some do, albeit unfairly.

Employers, as I have said before, are simply people. They want to be assured that, yes, you will stay on the job for a reasonable length of time and do well. Sometimes, you just need to get this message across. You also have to realize that very, very few interviewers have had any formal interview training. They are merely trying to do their best and may, in the process, bumble a bit. They may ask questions that, technically, they should not. But you should consider forgiving them in advance for this, if their intent is simply to find out if you are likely to be reliable. That is a legitimate concern on their part and you will often have to help them find out that, in your case, their concerns are unwarranted.

In that context, I suggest you consider your situation in advance and be able to present to the employer that, in your case, being "overqualified," or having children, or being over 50, or whatever your situation, is simply not a problem at all, but an advantage.

So, at the risk of offending someone, I have included information in this chapter that is a bit sensitive. But I think that you, as a job seeker, need to accept reality and look for ways to overcome problems. It can be done. It is true that some employers are unfair. Some do consider things in making hiring decisions that should not be a factor. In the interview, learn to be candid and present your problems as potential advantages. But do note that, in most cases, you should try to answer the question using the Three-Step Approach that I reviewed in the previous chapter.

Quick Case Study

You can never be sure what will concern an employer. Like all people, some will have concerns that just will not make sense to you. Some will make assumptions that may or may not be true. For example, I once had a boss who did not believe in hiring managers who had college degrees. He believed that those without degrees were often just as good or better—and would be happy being paid less money. I'm not at all sure he was right, but I do know that few managers with college degrees were on his staff. As you might guess, he did not have a degree himself, and I suspect his real concern was to avoid hiring someone who had better credentials than he did.

TYPICAL PROBLEM AREAS

Following are brief reviews of some of the problem areas you are most likely to run into.

Quick Fact

GAPS IN WORK HISTORY

Many people have gaps in their work history. If you have a legitimate reason for major gaps, such as going to school or having a child, tell the interviewer in a matter-of-fact tone. By all means, don't apologize or act cagey about it. You could, however, add details about an alternative, related activity you did during that period that would strengthen your qualifications for the job at hand. This reinforces that you aren't out-of-touch with what that employer needs—you merely chose not to actively practice it for a while.

During the conversation, it may help to refer to dates in years rather than months. For example, if asked when you worked in the restaurant business, reply, "from '92 to '93" rather than "from November 1992 to June 1993." Of course, if pressed, give the exact dates without hesitation.

BEING OUT OF WORK

Some of the most accomplished people I know have been out of work at one time or another, and one out of five people in the work force experiences some unemployment each year. It's really not a sin and many bosses have experienced it themselves, as have I.

The traditional resume technique is to write "19xx to Present" when referring to your most recent job, which makes it look as if you are still employed. If you use this trick, however, realize that it puts you in an uncomfortable position right off the bat. One of the first things you will have to do in the interview is explain that this is not actually the case.

Again, the best way to handle this problem is to add details about consulting or temporary work you have done in the meantime. This approach paints you as too busy to update your resume, rather than simply deceitful. While "too busy" isn't exactly commendable, it gets you out of the out-and-out liar category. What's more, experienced interviewers have seen this approach dozens of times and usually regard it as harmless.

Quick
Fact

BEING FIRED

If you have been fired at some point in your history, analyze the reason(s) before you make the appointment with the interviewer. This way, you are prepared to put the situation in the most thoughtful, upbeat light possible.

In most cases, people are fired for reasons that don't have to do with performance. Usually, they are fired as a result of interpersonal conflicts. If this is your situation, it does not automatically indicate that you will have the same problem with a different employer—a fact you can get across by being as cooperative and pleasant with the interviewer as possible. Simply state that there was a personality conflict, describe it in general terms ("My supervisor was the type of person who valued speed over quality, and the differences led to my dismissal"), and drop it. Never go into great detail, spouting off who said what to whom. It may all be true, but instead of winning sympathy, you'll earn suspicion about your part in creating the problem.

GET AN ALTERNATE REFERENCE

While you may have had conflict with a previous boss, there are often others at your previous place of employment who thought well of you. If so, it is often wise to get written recommendations from them in advance. You should also contact those people to find out how they might help if asked to provide a reference.

Quick Case Study

· ·

Julie Sturgeon, who contributed to this manuscript, provided the following situation from her own experience:

I once was driven away from a company because my supervisor displayed what I considered sexist remarks and attitude. One year later I finally landed an interview for my dream job. But when the interviewer asked if she could contact that hated supervisor, I hemmed, hawed, stalled, and practically tap-danced on top of the question. I finally blurted out that I didn't think that person was still with the company.

Naturally, this stumbling put my interviewer on alert. When I refused to crack and give the supervisor's name, she asked permission to contact the owner of that former company, a man she knew well. Relieved to be done with the topic, I agreed.

After I was hired, she called me into her office and relayed that the owner (who turned out to be an investor in the start-up company I'd just joined) gave her all the details of my former boss' bullying personality. He even told her that he had no doubt I'd still be with his company if I hadn't been driven away by poor management. That remark sealed my job offer, and I won points for being unwilling to air the bloody details. However, I was lucky. An admission that there was a personality problem and an offer to contact someone else in the company would have been a much smarter—and less risky—move.

HONESTY IS OFTEN THE BEST POLICY

Quick Reminder

Among the worst ways to answer the "Why were you fired?" question: Lie about it. For instance, I once spoke with a young man who told me in the interview that he left his previous position due to an atmosphere of personal abuse. He apparently either forgot about this lie, or became so relaxed he figured I wouldn't care, because he whipped out an award he won and pointed out the date. "See, I just wanted you to know that I earned this award on the 14th and by the 30th they let me go. It couldn't have been my fault," he blurted out. I immediately crossed his name off the list of possibilities.

The next gentleman I met with said he didn't know why he was fired; his employer refused to give an explanation. His story was that he came to work one day, his boss walked into the room, told him he was fired and to go home, and walked out. More digging revealed he was paid 40 percent more than other employees and the company was having financial troubles—he thought that might have something to do with it. Still, he remained so cagey about the issue, I eventually recommended someone else for the position, despite his strong credentials. To this day, I find his story about the circumstances surrounding his termination suspect.

JOB HISTORY UNRELATED TO YOUR CURRENT JOB OBJECTIVE/CHANGING CAREERS

Chances are this isn't as important an issue as you may assume. Sure, the interviewer is curious and wants to get to know you better, but if it were a real barrier, you wouldn't have been invited for an interview in the first place. Stick to a planned schedule of emphasizing your skills and how they relate to the job you are discussing. For instance, a teacher who wants to become a real estate sales agent could point to her hobby of investing in and fixing up old houses. She could cite superior communication skills and an ability to motivate students in the classroom. Stay focused on your objective and this line of questioning won't even register a blip on the "uh-oh" scale.

SOME SPECIFIC "STICKY QUESTIONS"

Following are several questions you may run into. Be prepared!

✎ What can you tell me about yourself?

I've mentioned this question before, and repeat it now because it is probably the number one question on the popularity scale, and it almost always kicks off the interview. Again, don't be tempted to go back to childhood and talk about your hard-working parents, your dog, and whatnot. Describe yourself in terms of what the interviewer wants to hear: your work ethic, your skills that apply to this job, your educational background, etc.

✎ What is your greatest strength?

Overall, this is such a positive question, few people have a problem coming up with an answer. Where they trip up is in not supporting that answer. So if you want to emphasize your people skills, for instance, back it up with a short example of how that translates in the workplace. Then brace yourself for its counter question:

✎ **What is your greatest weakness?**

I talked about this question back in chapter 5, and mention it here to remind you to choose something that isn't overtly negative. Being a workaholic or a perfectionist or too critical of your own work isn't necessarily a strike against you.

Quick Tip

The following tip from America Online's Career Center, hosted by Jim Gonyea, may work for you (although it's not for everyone).

Q: The most difficult question I have ever been asked in an interview is "What is your greatest weakness?" One piece of advice that I received was to make the weakness sound like a potential strength. I tried this in an interview but the interviewer saw right through it and replied, "Isn't that a strength?" Do you have any thoughts on this weakness question that seems to always be asked?

A: Obviously, this difficult question is designed to see how you answer the question, not so much what your answer is. (Like, who's going to reveal some major weakness that will kill all chances of employment! Plus, the person asking the question knows he or she is going to get some pre-made answer.)

The response that works best for me: "Hmmmm, a good question but in all honesty, I do not believe I have any major weaknesses that would affect my job performance. I consider myself to be professional and have dedicated myself to top performance. I am more concerned about my strengths and work value and how I can be of help to this organization. Perhaps we could talk more about that."

✎ **What would you like to accomplish during the next ten (or five) years?**

Talk about what you want to do for that employer, not for yourself. "I'd like to cut production costs by at least 5 percent and find ways to streamline the layout procedure so that we can add publications without adding staff," is a much better answer than "I'd like to be making 25 percent more in salary and own my own magazine."

✎ **How long have you been looking for another job?**

Never give an actual time frame! Casually reply, "Time isn't a factor because I'm searching for the position that best matches my skills and goals."

✎ **What type of person would you hire for this position?**

Flashback: You're casting your ballot for class president and mark the box for your opponent out of modesty. You lost then and you'll lose now if you don't

Quick Tip

Note that all of Section 5 is devoted to helping you answer questions related to salary.

Quick Tip

Be prepared to explain why you left all the jobs listed on your resume. To help you form an acceptable response to the "Why did you leave?" question, use the acronym CLAMPS:

C = Challenge. You weren't able to grow professionally in that position.

L = Location. The commute was unreasonably long.

A = Advancement. There was nowhere to go. You had the talent, but there were too many people ahead of you.

M = Money. You were underpaid for your skills and contributions.

P = Prestige. You wanted to be with a better organization.

S = Security. The organization was not financially stable.

choose yourself! "I'd hire someone who, beyond a shadow of a doubt, has the skills and people experience to handle this job. I would definitely hire myself."

✎ Are you willing to take a pay cut from your present position?

You aren't willing to discuss salary yet, so politely say so. "I feel we are still in the process of getting to know one another—I'd feel more comfortable talking about salary once we agree on employment" (or something to that effect).

✎ Why do you want to work for our organization?/Why should we hire you?

These questions, which are really one and the same, are at the heart of every question in any interview. Appropriate responses are covered in some detail in chapter 5.

✎ Why do you want to leave your present job?

Note: Do not, under any circumstances, give into complaints about the atmosphere at your current position!

Acceptable answers include this being a step in your career plans and wanting a better job location. "After introducing a more nutritious menu plan to the day care center and establishing a fun yet informative healthy lifestyle program for the after-school crowd, I've reached the top of the ladder at this smaller firm. I want the opportunity to use my expertise and continue to grow in a larger organization."

✎ How do you normally handle criticism?

Aah, an easy question if you take it on the chin well. But, because most of us aren't that admirable, we have to put a twist on this common question. "Obviously, criticism comes from not doing the job properly, and I'm eager to correct any mistakes or misunderstandings the minute they arise. I'm grateful to the person who cares enough to help me out in that respect."

✎ How do others view your work?

Just who are "others"? Colleagues, supervisors, clients, subordinates—the ability to see yourself from all perspectives is a plus in this situation. "The people I manage know that I will set the example before I ask them to make sacrifice of time or convenience. My colleagues understand that I am sympathetic to how our departments must work together for the common good. My supervisors are impressed with my dedication and realize that if I promise something, I will deliver it. And clients view the product that my department produces as a symbol of quality."

✎ How do you feel about working overtime and on weekends?

Even if this prospect does not appeal to you, this question can be answered so that your response does not harm you. "I have no problem devoting evening hours and Saturdays to getting a special project done. I also believe that a balanced life leads to a fresh, energetic employee who is less likely to burnout, so I try to pace myself for a consistent, dependable job performance over the long term, too."

✎ What do you do for fun in your spare time?

This question has a dual motivation. First, the interviewer is confirming your response to the "Will you work overtime?" question. If you replied yes to that question but then outline a lifestyle that involves weekends at a cabin, evenings at the gym, and commitments to various nonprofit and community events, it's unlikely you'll cancel those plans to work overtime. On the other hand, this is also an opportunity for the interviewer to confirm those things he or she can't legally ask, such as if you have a family, if you attend church, etc. "My in-laws have a cabin by a nearby lake and the children enjoy going there on weekends. I accompany them when I can, but sometimes projects prevent that. Of course, the grandparents welcome those times so they can spend one-on-one time with Jim and Sally."

✎ Describe your typical day.

Naturally, leave out the fact that you aren't a morning person or you start winding down at 4:30 P.M. to hit the parking lot by 5 P.M. This is your opportunity to advertise how well you can organize yourself and conceptualize long-term projects. "I keep a calendar on my desk with appointment times recorded on the left side and tasks to accomplish that day on the right. I allot time each day to stay in touch with other departments and to return any missed phone calls promptly. Overall, my entire day is focused on providing customers with a top-notch product."

Quick Tip

Interviewers also like to pose the "What do you like best/least about your present job?" set of questions as well. As previously advised, continue to look at your current job's opportunities rather than specific tasks. "I don't like to type my own memos," is honest but short-sighted.

✎ What do you like most about your present boss?

For most candidates, it's not to hard to find something nice to say in response to this question. Do frame your answer on the type of supervision your boss provides and not necessarily on a personality type. "I appreciate the regular feedback," is a more useful response than "I enjoy the fact that he/she always has an upbeat attitude," even though both are certainly positive answers.

✎ What do you like least about your present boss?

You knew this was coming based on the previous question. Again, stick to management principles and skip the personality conflicts.

ANSWERING QUESTIONS IN AN UNORGANIZED INTERVIEW

Quick Reference

The unorganized interview is just that: the line of questioning is often random and you find yourself wondering where it's all leading. Most of the time this haphazard, sloppy style signals an inexperienced interviewer. In that case, the person is apt to fall victim to the "halo effect," an assumption that implies you have all the good traits that person has simply because he or she likes you. (Experienced interviewers are trained and constantly reminded not to make this leap.) Take advantage of the situation by mirroring the interviewer closely; if possible, draw him or her into a more personal conversation.

"The unorganized/ unstructured interview may be a ploy to get you to let your guard down."

Of course, even peculiar questions have a reason behind them if placed in the hands of a professional interviewer. So beware: The unorganized/unstructured interview may be a ploy to see what you say when you relax and let your guard down—don't toss caution overboard. It can be a tactic to get you out of the practiced answer rut and let your personality do the talking.

Here's a sampling of the off-the-wall questions interviewers have thrown out for discussion. Remember, there's no right or wrong answer, only a need to show that you can have fun, think on your feet, and relate to people.

● "Creatively speaking, how old will you be in 10 years?" If you blink and add 10 to your present age, you missed the boat. Try "Younger than I am now" or "Still younger than my mother."

Quick
Reference

- If you were a car, which one would you be and what year did you appear? Joyce Cohen, president of Career Directions in Fairfield, Connecticut, suggests answers such as a '57 Thunderbird ("because it's a classic"), a Porsche ("it's a high-performer") or a DeLorean ("it dared to be different").

- If you were an idea, what would you be?

- At your retirement party, what will you be most honored for?

- What are you disappointed that I didn't ask you?

- Let's assume that reincarnation is a fact. If you could return in another life as anything, what would you choose to be?

- Which sport that you've never participated in would you like to learn and why?

- If you had one wish, what would it be?

- You just won the state lottery worth $20 million. How are you going to spend it?

- If you were a color, which would you be? Why?

Cohen brings up a crucial point about these Barbara Walters-style questions: What do you look like while your brain's gears are turning? If you appear pained, defensive, or thrown off-guard, red flags may start flying. Some people wrinkle their noses, frown, or look irritated. Others smile, chuckle, and seem stimulated by the question. It's obvious which group makes the better impression, so practice fielding some of these wacky questions from a friend before going into any interview.

SENSITIVE QUESTIONS HAVING TO DO WITH YOUR PERSONAL SITUATION OR STATUS

There are a variety of laws and regulations that require employers to consider each applicant on his or her ability to do a job rather than such personal attributes as race, religion, age, handicap, and other things. Most employers are wise enough to avoid making decisions based on things that should not matter and they will try to hire someone who convinces them that they can do the job well.

Quick Tip

"Turtling"—A Basic Technique for Turning a Negative into a Positive

Like a turtle on its back, a problem is a problem only if you leave it that way. By turning it over ("turtling" is what I have termed it), you can often turn a perceived disadvantage into an advantage. For example:

Too Old: "I am a very stable worker requiring very little training. I have been dependable all my life and I am at a point in my career where I don't plan on changing jobs. I still have ten years of working until I plan on retiring. How long has the average young person stayed here?"

Too Young: "I don't have any bad work habits to break, so I can be quickly trained to do things the way you'd prefer. I plan on working hard to get established. I'll also work for less money than a more experienced worker."

You can use the turtling technique on most problem questions to turn what some may see as a negative into, in your case, a positive.

So, a good interview discusses your strengths without lying about them. It also assures the interviewer that you are not a stereotype—but in order to prevent misconceptions you must know what they are and subtly address them.

For this reason, even if your "problem" does not come up in the interview—because the law forbids the question or the interviewer is too uncomfortable to ask—it may be to your advantage to bring it up and deal with it. This is particularly so if you think that an employer might wonder about the issue or that it might hurt you if you don't answer it. However you handle the interview, the ultimate question you have to answer is "Why should I hire you?"—so provide a good answer, even if the question is not asked quite so clearly.

TOO OLD

According to a 1993 survey cosponsored by the Research Committee of the Society for Human Resource Management (SHRM) and the Commerce Clearing House, when employers face an older person across the interviewing desk, they are afraid the person won't be able to adjust to changes in the business environment. Among the specific concerns and comments:

- Older employees have created the greatest challenges for us. Employees hired 15 or more years ago may not have the education or technical skills to move forward.

- Attempts to increase accountability and employ more team-oriented strategies have met with resistance.
- Older workers have not adapted to drastic changes in procedures and technology.

Quick Fact

The biggest problem with the "too old" category is figuring out if you truly belong in it. The over-65 growth rate in our country is slowing, and the biggest group taking over the job market is the aging Baby Boomers— those between the ages of 35 and 54. In fact, according to a Small Business Administration report, workers in the 45 to 54 age range are expected to increase by an amazing 72.2 percent by the year 2000. And the Hudson Group reports: Everyone who will be working in the year 2000 has already been born, and two-thirds of them are at work today. So what is "too old"?

"Older workers often have things going for them that younger workers do not."

Don't let these negative preconceptions discourage you—there are plenty of ways to combat them effectively during the job interview. For starters, understand that the flood of younger workers is slowing to a trickle, so employers eventually will have no option but to fight over the qualified older workers.

To push the interviewer along that path, present your wealth of experience and maturity as an advantage rather than a disadvantage. Older workers often have some things going for them that younger workers do not. Emphasize your loyalty to previous employers, and highlight accomplishments that occurred over a period of time. If you encounter hesitation after the first interview, meet the fear head-on with a question such as "Are you concerned about compensation?" or "If I could reduce your costs significantly, would you be willing to keep me in consideration?"

Quick Fact

If you have more than 15 years of work experience, draw upon your more recent work for examples of work habits and successes. Select activities that best support your ability to do the job you are now seeking and put the emphasis on them. You don't automatically have to provide many details on your work history from earlier times—unless it is clearly to your advantage.

To avoid sounding "too old," mention something topical (like the fact that you own a notebook computer, would welcome the refreshing opportunity to operate in a self-directed team situation, or that you have enrolled in a technology course related to the job). Your background research on the organization should reveal a host of ways to plug your up-to-date knowledge and current worthiness.

"Never forget that you may be competing with a younger person for the position."

However, don't assume that you've done enough preparation by organizing this type of information before the interview. It's equally vital to practice vocalizing your responses. As Georgetown University professor Arthur Bell points out in his book, *Extraviewing*, older applicants were taught to write more (and better) and to speak less in school. In this case, it's perfectly natural that you would take more time to consider a question such as "Tell me how you like to be managed." But never forget that you may be competing with a younger person for the position—someone who may be trained to handle discussion in a more rapid manner. Bell cautions that, held against that standard, many interviewers interpret the tendency to pause and think as a sign of incomprehension or, worse, approaching senility.

Be aware of your voice tone as you deliver this information, too. Avoid

Quick Tip

If you've made it a point to brag that you don't know anything about computers, start changing right now. "This is not and will not be an era in which a manager enters, re-enters, or stays in the corporate structure without going back to skills that only his or her secretary had to know 20 years ago," reminds Milan Moravec of Walnut Creek, California-based Moravec and Associates consultants. Don't let fear of failure stand in your way: Today's computer users don't have to know about programming or computer languages, and the software is extremely easy to use.

sounding too formal. However, many times the interviewer will be younger than you and may find it difficult to relate to you informally. A condescending attitude towards a younger interviewer won't get you anywhere but to the front door. Make a conscious effort to treat the interviewer as a professional equal and you'll automatically dispel the misconception that you can't change with the times.

TOO YOUNG

Youth may be a sought-after quality in prime-time television commercials, but that perspective doesn't always hold in the interviewer's office. Unfortunately, young persons before you have burned many organizations through immaturity and underdeveloped work ethics. True, flexibility in the workplace is a current buzzword, but oftentimes young people have a hard time grasping the fact that an office isn't the equivalent of a school term. Chances are the interviewer is secretly praying you won't ask about vacations, two-week Christmas breaks, and Wednesday afternoons off to join a new aerobics class.

Quick Fact

Young people need to present their youth as an asset rather than a liability. For example, perhaps you are willing to work for less money, accept less desirable tasks, work longer or less convenient hours, or do other things that a more experienced worker might not. If so, say so.

Emphasize the time and dedication you put into school projects, and activities you gave up to reach your goals. Above all, conduct yourself with maturity, show some genuine enthusiasm and energy, and you'll leave the interviewer with the impression you need a chance, not a guidance counselor.

Quick Tip

From America Online's Career Center, hosted by Jim Gonyea.

Q: The interview question that really threw me is the one about where I see myself five years from now. I am a 62-year-old female in an extremely tight job market. I cannot plan my destiny as I might have at age 21 in the '50s. In the interviewer's eyes, I may have only a couple of years of "life" left. What should be my response?

A: Regardless of whether you plan to work in five years or not, don't give the impression that you're ready to retire any day now. If they ask you what your plans are in five years, offer what you might like to do occupationally. You're not required by law to comply with your plans, just to state them.

If you are turned down in favor of a more experienced worker, don't despair. Despite the major layoffs that continue to besiege American companies, 72 percent of executives polled in a national survey conducted by Accountemps fear there will be a shortage of skilled labor between now and the year 2000. Keep hammering away at your particular skills, your trainability, and your available years of dedication—and some employer will be happy to snag you.

OVERQUALIFIED/TOO MUCH EXPERIENCE

It doesn't seem to make sense that you could have too much experience, but some employers may think so. They may fear you will not be satisfied with the job that is available and that, after awhile, you will leave for a better one. So, what they really need is some assurance of why this would not be the case for you. If, in fact, you are looking for a job with higher pay—and if you communicate this in some way during the interview—it is quite likely that the company will not offer you a job for fear that you will soon leave.

This may not be far from the truth. After a period of unemployment, most people become more willing to settle for less than they had hoped for. If you are willing to accept jobs where you may be defined as overqualified, consider not including some of your educational or work-related credentials on your resume—though I do not necessarily recommend doing this. Be prepared to explain, in the interview, why you *do* want this particular job and how your wealth of experience is a positive and not a negative.

Quick Reference

You've worked hard and long to get to the peak of your career, only to have interviewers shy away because your resume is *too* strong. Employers are afraid, of course, that you will become bored by the job duties and take the next job offer that comes your way. It's a legitimate fear, and one you should resolve in your own mind before you push for the position. Is there a chance you could feel stifled, unsatisfied with this position? Yes, being unemployed or underemployed is an unpleasant situation, but settling for an unsatisfying position brings its heartaches, too. If you do want to continue pursuing the job for whatever reason, go out of your way to assure the interviewer that you aren't a job gypsy. Maintain high enthusiasm for the organization's future, and present ways you could grow in this position. Suggest how you could assist other departments, solve long-term problems, build profit, and use your experience to help out in other ways.

Remember, the interviewer is also mentally calculating salary requirements during this time. Unfortunately, the very secrecy surrounding the figure has him or her worried that the interview time will be ultimately wasted. Your goal is to raise your desirability to the point where the organization is willing to chip in the extra money it thinks it takes to get you.

Decide ahead of time which benefits you are willing to negotiate, too, and drop a few hints in that direction if possible. See chapters 18 and 19 for specific tactics to handle the money discussion.

NEW GRADUATE/NOT ENOUGH EXPERIENCE

Sometimes a degree isn't what it's cracked up to be. Every spring newspapers across the country blast headlines about how difficult it is for today's graduates to find a job in their areas of study. To discourage you even further, these reporters always manage to dig up some biology major who has worked for minimum wage behind a fast food counter for the last five years.

Before you start believing the bad press too much, keep in mind that such articles only show one side of the story. Yes, it is difficult to find a position with a skinny resume. But a well-rounded one is not guaranteed to magically unlock doors either. To balance the doom-and-gloom reports, mentally arm yourself with these balancing projections:

- The current Lindquist-Endicott Report from Northwestern University reports that small- to mid-sized companies tend to be the most active recruiters and large companies are doing less hiring. For your part, companies outside the FORTUNE 500 ranks can be more open to letting you take on new projects and directions. Take a secretarial position to get in the door of a smaller firm and you are less likely to be railroaded into that line of work for years.

- Students are recognizing that they must take control of their careers and make their own decisions. More than 8 out of 10 (83 percent) students surveyed in a recent Right Associate's Career Expectations and Attitudes Comparison cited their own interests and skills as the major influence on their career choice. Other traditional influences—family pressure, anticipated salary, and luck/chance—have dropped significantly in popularity. When you interview for a position that matches your personality and talents, your natural enthusiasm for that job goes a long way in impressing interviewers.

- Labor Secretary Robert Reich has noted that "employers have more incentive to train," because the young labor force is much smaller than it was during the Baby Boomer years. About 17 percent of all workers now get formal, on-the-job skills training, up from 11 percent 10 years ago. Computer literacy is the key—and young people are more computer-smart than their elders were.

Quick Tip

Good news! Entry-level jobs are no longer the comedown they once were. Nationally syndicated career columnist Jane Bryant Quinn started out at Newsweek magazine sorting each day's mail—"which required me only to remember the alphabet," she recalls. A majority of today's "lower-level" jobs call for more knowledge, judgment, and autonomy than that—and they can lead to bigger things.

So if you fall into the "not enough experience" category, emphasize the adaptive skills you identified in chapter 9 that would tend to overcome a lack of experience.

Again, consider expressing a willingness to accept difficult or less desirable conditions as one way to break into a field and gain experience. For example, indicating that you are willing to work weekends and evenings or are able to travel or relocate may appeal to an employer and open up some possibilities.

Quick Case Study

▲ Howard W. Scott Jr., president of Dunhill Personnel Systems, likes to tell the story of his first job search back in 1959. The broadcast major from Northwestern University ran into walls at almost every turn. Finally, a station manager in Roswell, New Mexico, offered Scott a position at $50 a week. "But I have a degree from Northwestern!", he cried. To which the station manager replied, "I know—otherwise it would have been $40 a week." And that's the one thing about interviewing that hasn't changed since our parents' days: The same sacrifices are necessary to break into nearly any field.

▲ Don't overlook acceptable experiences such as volunteer work, family responsibilities, education, training, or anything else that you might present as a legitimate activity that supports your ability to do the work you feel you can do.

Quick Tip

From America Online's Career Center, hosted by Jim Gonyea.

Q: I have 24 years of experience in the computer and electronics fields and have attended college part-time. I completed over 90 semester units, but don't have a degree. For the last seven years, I have been teaching in the industry for a private company, so I know the business pretty well. Of course some companies won't even talk to you if you don't have a degree, even if it's in an obscure, irrelevant subject. I've even thought of "buying" a degree from a diploma mill, but I really don't like the idea. It would take me at least two years to finish a degree part-time though. Any ideas on how to beat this roadblock?

A: Unfortunately, for some employers who demand a degree as part of the qualifications package, there is no substitute. While you should continue to stress your experience, skills, knowledge, and current coursework, for some employers the lack of the degree will exclude you from their employment.

This is a simple fact of life. Perhaps, if you are so close to the degree, you should seriously consider completing it. Then you will have the advantages the degree can bring for the rest of your life. A bargain, I believe!

☿ ISSUES RELATED TO BEING A WOMAN

As the cigarette commercial used to drone: "You've come a long way, baby." But although the numbers of women in the work force have increased rapidly, employers still imagine problems. According to the comments expressed in a recent survey conducted by the Society of Human Resource Management: "Working women with children have difficulties finding adequate child care in our area. Time off and absenteeism are big issues for our working mothers." "Gaining coworker acceptance of women in nontraditional roles is a serious problem. Many of our executives are uncertain how to manage women." "We have more women managers, but few women officers and only one percent on the board of directors. The glass ceiling is a reality."

Interestingly enough, women employers are often just as concerned as male employers are about a woman's family status. In both cases, they assume that a woman may, for example, have child-related problems and want to be certain that this will not become a work-related problem.

☑ FAMILY STATUS AND CHILDREN

THE CHILD CARE ISSUE

Arthur Bell points out that approximately 90 percent of all working women are in their child-bearing years; fully 80 percent of that number can be expected to have one or more

Quick Tip

Don't make the mistake of assuming that just because a woman interviews you, it isn't necessary to bring up the child care issue. Even though she may be in the same boat herself, empathy rarely plays a role in landing you a position in today's tough job market. I've personally discussed candidates with female colleagues who mentioned that child care could pose a huge attendance problem with some of the potential applicants. An interviewer's main focus is hiring someone who can do the job—regardless of whether they are a man or woman.

children. More than half (54 percent) of all working mothers now care for one or more children under age 5. The stress, not to mention the financial hardships of paying for full-time child care can create potential disruptions for women in the workplace. Bell refers to a *Harvard Business Review* study documenting that "on average, working mothers put in an 84-hour work week between their homes and their jobs; working fathers put in 72 hours, and married people with no children put in 50." Those numbers are staggering: a mother essentially holds down two full-time jobs plus overtime. And that's not taking into account the fact that elder care generally falls on the shoulders of women in our country, too. So, your number one task is to assure the interviewer that, although you don't intend to abandon your children, you do intend to devote the necessary time to the job.

Again, it's simply a matter of turning the situation into a positive. Why not present your resourceful nature by giving an example of how you secured reliable child care? Or illustrate your management skills by describing how you handled work responsibilities when your child was ill and you needed to be at home. Be prepared to back up your loyalty claims with actual numbers of days missed from previous jobs.

☑ GAINING EQUALITY

It seems almost laughable that with the number of women in today's workplace, some interviewers would still be uncertain how to manage women. Yet sensational headlines of sexual harassment and discrimination have trickled down to all levels of an organization.

According to Carol Price, an educator and lecturer with Career Track who specializes in teaching women power presentations, it's best to begin establishing your equal status the second you walk in the room. "Once you do that, I really believe gender issues go away," she says.

OK, so how do you "establish equal status" without appearing like a militant on a mission—another image that frightens employers? Simply look like you belong at the interview. "That means my head is held up, my shoulders are back, I walk in without hesitation and I put my hand out," says Price. The handshake in particular is crucial. "A handshake was originally devised to prove we were weaponless. In a job interview, that translates to 'you and I are equal in value' when my hands goes out," Price says.

Quick Tip

The best handshake for a woman is the firm, web-to-web version. This means the web between your thumb and forefinger is touching the other person's web. This virtually eliminates the fingertip handshake, which Price maintains is a subtle signal for a man to protect you. "And we certainly don't want any part of being protected in a job interview!", she laughs.

During the interview itself, do not complain—or even mention—the lack of opportunity for women at your current or last job as the reason you are seeking new employment. In fact, don't bring up the fact that there may be questions about your sex's competency at all. Assume you are accepted and you will be, Price advises. "I don't live in an ivory tower," she adds. "I know there are jerks out there that won't see you as worthwhile if you have ovaries. But the bottom line, at minimum, is that they set up an appointment with you. At worst, they have to see you for quota purposes. At best, they are interested in your skills. So if you go in with the attitude 'He won't think I'm as good as Bill simply because I'm female,' you act that way. You start believing your own press and then you're in serious danger."

In a book titled *Managing a Diverse Work Force*, the author (John P. Fernandez) asked people to respond to a series of statements regarding women in the workplace. They were asked to either agree or disagree with each of the following statements:

1. The increasing employment of women has led to the breakdown of the American family.

2. Many women obtained their current position only because they are women.

3. Pluralism will force us to lower our hiring and promotion standards.

4. Many women use their gender as an alibi for difficulties they have on the job.

5. Many women are not really serious about professional careers.

6. Many women are too emotional to be competent employees.

The results: Thirty-five percent of the women surveyed and 27 percent of the men did not agree with any of these statements; 46 percent of the women and 45 percent of the men agreed with one to two statements; 16 percent of the women and 22 percent of the men agreed with three to four of the questions; and 3 percent of the women and 7 percent of the men agreed with five to six of the statements.

ISSUES RELATED TO BEING A MAN

While it is seldom brought up, there are certain biases that tend to be held against men, just because of their gender. Men are expected to have steady employment and not take time off for raising a family. Those who do not aspire to higher status can be quickly branded as losers. And, just as for women, you will find few males in certain occupations dominated by women, such as grade school teacher, clerical worker, and nurse. While some would argue that is because these jobs pay poorly and have low status, that is clearly not always the case.

In the recent past, many men have been frustrated in their inability to move up in pay and stature. A big reason is the large number of baby boomers who are competing for the limited number of management jobs—and the greater number of educated and qualified women in the workforce who want the same things. Perhaps unexpectedly, the competition has become tough.

Even so, there are few situations where being a man will work against you, particularly if you have a good work history. For example, how many men get questions about their plans to have or care for children?

SEXUAL PREFERENCE

Quick Fact

You may be astounded to find this category in this chapter. However, these days unmarried men and women can create suspicion as to their sexual preference in some interviewers' minds.

The fears are twofold. The first is that their departments will become a stage for airing social concerns to the detriment of producing products or services. The Society of Human Resource Management reveals that its respondents said, "We have not encountered any pressures from gay/lesbian groups directly. However, employees continue to voice their concerns about having to work with these groups and the potential risk—real or perceived—that they pose," and "In our traditional conservative culture, managers have deeply ingrained biases and fears of gay and lesbian employees."

And with health-care costs a serious issue in most companies, the potential cost for employees at greater risk to become HIV-positive plays a factor. True, homosexuals are not the only group infected, and most interviewers readily acknowledge that. But while I have advocated attacking stereotypes head-on in the other categories, here I advise you adopt the military's "don't ask, don't tell" policy. The risks of divulging such personal information are too great to broach this subject in an interview.

MILITARY CAREER

The military has long had a reputation among the youth of this country as an excellent job-training ground. Indeed, this is correct in many cases—the law enforcement field usually welcomes this experience with open arms. However, military service can work against you if you aren't aware of the misperceptions interviewers may form before you ever walk into their offices. Number one, some people perceive military personnel as dangerously aggressive. Hollywood has fostered this stereotype by painting pictures of a wild-eyed, angry killing machine roaming the jungles. Recent media reports of increased cases of spouse and child abuse in

Quick
Fact

military families have added to the perception. "But they don't take into account that the population is generally younger, newly married, concentrated, and away from home," says Bob Stein, director of transition supports and services at the Department of Defense. "If you took a similar population in the private sector, the numbers might be the same." So, make a conscious effort to counteract the stereotype by remaining calm and pleasant at all times during the interview.

The second common misperception is that military personnel are too likely to follow orders rather than be creative. In some jobs this is not necessarily a problem. However, even factory positions are evolving into self-directed teams that require creative input from each member of the team. Be sure to mention ideas you have for growing within your position and interacting with others to overcome this liability.

Third, the sheer number of people exiting the military every year causes concern with some interviewers. "People assume there are hundreds of thousands of persons being fired," Stein confirms. "That's not the case at all. Because we are such a large organization, for the past 10 years we've averaged 354,000 separations a year. It includes everything from retirees to bedwetters …

"But the impression you get from reading some media is that all these people received a pink slip in the mail and were told to be gone by Thursday afternoon at 2 P.M.," he adds. Be sure to bring up why you left the military to put the interviewer's mind at rest that it had nothing to do with the private concept of being "fired." As one Air Force colonel expresses it, "If I were in business, I'd look at the military cuts as a godsend. People just don't understand what today's military is like. We're talking about the cream of the crop." So convey that to the interviewer in no uncertain terms!

Stanley Hyman, a 69-year-old counselor in Crystal City, Virginia, who teaches interviewing skills to military personnel suggests not using military badges of honor such as service-academy rings and anchor tie clips when dressing for the interview. "Wear a watch with hands," he also recommends. "You don't need one that tells time on the moon. And a watch that beeps during an interview is death," Hyman told *U.S. News & World Report*. As for the language you use, avoid the excessive jargon that is common in military life.

Do emphasize that your experience in the military marks you as a leader, and has taught you discipline, responsibility, and dependability.

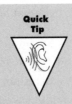

Quick Tip

Lean on your local military transition office for assistance! There are 330 such offices available around the world to help with virtually every aspect of the job search—a boon for those who've been in the military for years and have not looked for a job in some time.

MINORITIES

The good news is a majority of interviewers are aware that they shouldn't care about another person's race, religion, or skin color—and most do not. The bad news is the issue continues to impact the business environment and its needs. Take a look at what employers said in a recent survey conducted by the Society of Human Resource Managers:

- "Finding African-Americans with education and experience for advancement in our industry is difficult."

- "African-American workers interpret managerial actions as having a racial bias. Managers find it very challenging to convey constructive criticism and direction without being accused of bias."

- "Asians have encountered language and cultural difficulties. Some are not willing to disagree with the boss, which hinders continuous improvement."

On the upside, the survey also reveals that the last decade has introduced more African-Americans, Hispanics, and Asians into the employee populations of many organizations that participated in the study. This increase is expected to continue due to the shrinking numbers of young people, the rapid pace of industrial change, and the ever-rising skill requirements of the emerging economy. These trends make the task of fully utilizing minority workers' skills particularly urgent between now and 2000.

My advice to women holds true for minorities as well. Assume you are equal. Shake hands firmly and look the interviewer in the eye. Then present the skills and abilities you have to do the job.

Quick Tip

From America Online's Career Center, hosted by Jim Gonyea.

Q: What do you think are interviewers' impressions of applicants that speak Street talk? Are there any statistics on this? Do you have any references or advice for the Street talk-speaking applicant?

A: While I have no statistics on the subject of employer reactions to job seekers who speak Street talk, I can state that most employers desire applicants who can communicate (in writing and orally) in regular English.

Employers are constantly complaining that job seekers have poor English skills. If your English is good, then being able to speak Street talk may or may not be a value (depending upon the employer's customer base). If Street talk is the only English you speak well, then my guess would be your employment options will be less than what they could be.

RECENT GRADUATE

If you have recently graduated, you probably are competing against those with similar levels of education *and* more work experience. If you don't have a lot of work experience related to the job you want, you will obviously want to emphasize your recent education or training. This might include specific mention of courses you took and other activities that most directly relate to the job you now seek.

New graduates need to look at their school work as the equivalent of work experience. Indeed, it *is* work in that it required self-discipline, the completion of a variety of tasks, and other activities that are similar to those required in many jobs. You also may have learned a variety of things that are directly related to doing the job you want. You should present these during the interview in the same way you might present work experiences.

If you can, you should also play up the fact that you are familiar with the latest trends and techniques in your field and can apply these skills right away. And, since you are experienced in studying and learning new things, you will be better able to quickly learn the new job.

NO DEGREE OR LESS EDUCATION THAN TYPICALLY REQUIRED

If you want a job that is often filled by someone with more education, you must emphasize the experience and skills you have to do the job, as well as provide assurance that your lack of degree will not be a hindrance. You can simply avoid mentioning that you do not have a degree.

Note that I do not suggest that you misrepresent yourself here by overstating your qualifications or claiming a degree you do not have. That would result later in your being fired and is clearly not a good idea. But again, there is no law that says you need to mention your weaknesses.

RECENTLY MOVED

Employers may sometimes be concerned that someone who has recently moved to an area may soon leave. If you are new to the area, make sure that the employer knows you are here to stay. Provide a simple statement that presents you as a stable member of the community rather than someone with a more transient lifestyle.

HAVE A DISABILITY

Biases against those with disabilities is real enough that the government has passed laws to prevent unfair discrimination—the Americans With Disabilities Act. But no one will ever successfully pass a law against stereotypes. That's the true barrier you are up against in the interview no matter how many government agencies exist to back up your eligibility.

Quick Fact

According to a Society of Human Resource Management survey, many respondents indicated that accommodating employees with disabilities presents difficulties for their organizations. Among the specific comments: "We are a small organization and accommodation of physical requirements for disabled workers and time off for illness and medical treatment cause disruption to work and schedules." "Some disabled workers are looked upon with disdain by their managers and peers. We have to overcome these attitudes."

I assume you will not seek a job that you can't or should not do. That, of course, would be foolish. So that means you are seeking a job that you are capable of doing, right? And, that being the case, you don't have a disability related to doing this job at all. But, as I said, the employer will still use his or her judgment in hiring the best person for the job, and that means people with disabilities have to compete for jobs along with everyone else. That is fair, so you need to present to an employer a convincing argument for why the company should hire you over someone else.

Most importantly, don't assume that the person chatting with you understands the technical details of your handicap. I see nothing wrong in casually mentioning how you have worked around your disability in other positions.

Just remember to remain matter-of-fact in your explanation—avoid a defensive tone at all costs—and you will not only put the interviewer at ease but also assure him or her that your future colleagues will admire your abilities and attitude, too.

Quick Case Study

I once worked a temporary job taking inventory at a department store. My partner that first day was a young woman who had an artificial arm. My first reaction was an inner groan: I assumed she wouldn't be able to write, so I automatically would have to keep the tally sheets. Furthermore, with only one "real" hand, she would be too slow in reaching for and reading the tags. Fortunately, she had the confidence to smile, introduce herself, and proceed to tell me how the artificial arm worked. It took less than two minutes to put my doubts to rest and less than five to prove I had been a clod (thank goodness I had kept my prejudices to myself). The two of us teamed up the entire week and received much praise for our quick work.

NEGATIVE REFERENCES

Most employers will not contact your previous employers unless you are being seriously considered as a candidate for the job. If you fear that one of your previous employers may not give you a positive reference, here are some things you can do:

1. List someone other than your former supervisor as a reference, someone who knew your work there and who will put in a good word for you.

2. Discuss the issue in advance with your previous employer and negotiate what they will say. Even if not good, at least you know what they are likely to say and can prepare potential employers in advance.

3. Get a written letter of reference. In many cases, employers will not give references over the phone (or negative references at all) for fear of being sued. Presenting a letter in advance assures that you know what is said about your performance.

CRIMINAL RECORD

Quick Alert

It should be obvious that a resume or application should not include negative information about yourself. So if you have ever been "in trouble" with the law, you would certainly not mention it there. Newer laws even limit an employer from including such general questions on an application as "Have you ever been arrested?" and limit formal inquiries to "Have you ever been convicted of a felony?".

In this country, we are technically innocent until proven guilty, and that is why employers are no longer allowed to consider an arrest record in a hiring decision. Being arrested and being guilty are two different things. Arrests for minor offenses are also not supposed to be considered in a hiring decision. The argument has been that minorities tend to be more likely to have arrest records and consideration of arrest records in a hiring decision is, therefore, discriminatory.

A felony conviction is a different matter. These crimes are more serious and current employment laws do allow an employer to ask for and get this information—and to use it in making certain hiring decisions. For example, few employers would hire an accountant who had been convicted of stealing money from a previous employer. Certain types of arrest records, such as those for child molesting, are also allowed to be considered by an employer in making certain hiring decisions. For example, few would place a person with this kind of record in charge of childrens' programs.

If you have an arrest or conviction record that an employer has a legal right to inquire about, my advice is to avoid looking for jobs where your record would be a big negative. The accountant in the example above should consider changing careers. Even if the applicant did get a job by concealing his or her criminal history, that person could be fired at any time in the future. Instead, I might suggest they consider selling accounting software, starting their own business, or getting into a completely different career unrelated to accounting.

As always, your interview should emphasize what you can do rather than what you can't. If you chose your career direction wisely and present a convincing argument that you can do the job well, many employers will, ultimately, overlook previous mistakes. As you prove yourself and gain good work experience, your distant past becomes less important.

90 MORE PRACTICE QUESTIONS

Here is a list of questions most often asked by recruiters who interview new graduates at college campuses. While some of the questions may not apply to your situation, they will give you a good idea of the types of questions a trained interviewer might ask. Look over the list and identify any that you will need practice in answering. Then, practice!

1. What are your future vocational [career] plans?

2. In what school [work] activities have you participated? Why? Which did you enjoy the most?

3. How do you spend your spare time? What are your hobbies?

4. In what type of position are you most interested?

5. Why do you think you might like to work for our company?

6. What jobs have you held? How were they obtained?

7. What courses [job duties/positions] did you like best? Least? Why?

8. Why did you choose your particular field?

9. What percentage of your school expenses did you earn? How?

10. How did you spend your vacations while in school?

11. What do you know about our company?

12. Do you feel that you have received good general training?

13. What qualifications do you have that make you feel you will be successful in your field?

14. What extracurricular offices have you held?

15. What are your ideas on salary?

16. How do you feel about your family?

17. How interested are you in sports?

18. If you were starting school all over again …?

19. Can you forget your education and start from scratch?

20. Do you prefer any specific geographic location? Why?

21. Do you have a girl (boy) friend? Is it serious?

22. How much money do you hope to earn at age ____?

23. Why did you decide to go to the school you attended?

24. How did you rank in your graduating class in high school? Other schools?

25. Do you think that your extracurricular activities were worth the time you devoted to them? Why?

26. What do you think determines a person's progress in a good company?

27. What personal characteristics are necessary for success in your chosen field?

28. Why do you think you would like this particular type of job?

29. What is your father's occupation?

30. Tell my about your home life during the time you were growing up.

31. Are you looking for a permanent or temporary job?

32. Do you prefer working with others or by yourself?

33. Who are your best friends?

34. What kind of boss do you prefer?

35. Are you primarily interested in making money?

36. Can you take instructions without feeling upset?

37. Tell me a story!

38. Do you live with your parents? Which of your parents has had the most profound influence on you?

39. How did previous employers treat you?

40. What have you learned from some of the jobs you have held?

41. Can you get recommendations from previous employers?

42. What interests you about our product or service?

43. What was your record in the military service?

44. Have you ever changed your major field of interest? Why?

45. When did you choose your major?

46. How did your grades after military service compare with those previously earned?

47. Do you feel you have done the best work of which you are capable?

48. How did you happen to go to post-secondary school?

49. What do you know about opportunities in the field in which you are trained?

50. How long do you expect to work?

51. Have you ever had any difficulty getting along with fellow students and faculty? Fellow workers?

52. Which of your school years was most difficult?

53. What is the source of your spending money?

54. Do you own any life insurance?

55. Have you saved any money?

56. Do you have any debts?

57. How old were you when you became self-supporting?

58. Did you enjoy school?

59. Do you like routine work?

60. Do you like regular work?

61. What size city do you prefer?

62. When did you first contribute to family income?

63. Define cooperation.

64. Will you fight to get ahead?

65. Do you demand attention?

66. Do you have an analytical mind?

67. Are you eager to please?

68. What do you do to keep in good physical condition?

69. How do you usually spend Sunday?

70. Have you had any serious illness or injury?

71. Are you willing to go where the company sends you?

72. What job in our company would you choose if you were entirely free to do so?

73. Is it an effort for you to be tolerant of persons with a background and interests different from your own?

74. What types of books have you read?

75. Have you plans for further education?

76. What types of people seem to rub you the wrong way?

77. Do you enjoy sports as a participant? As an observer?

78. Have you ever tutored another student?

79. What are your own special abilities?

80. What job in our company do you want to work toward?

81. Would you prefer a large or a small company? Why?

82. What is your idea of how the industry operates today?

83. Do you like to travel?

84. What kind of work interests you?

85. What are the disadvantages of your chosen field?

86. Do you think employers should consider grades? Why or why not?

87. Are you interested in research?

88. If married, how often do you entertain at home?

89. What have you done that shows initiative and willingness to work?

90. Wouldn't you feel better off in another company?

PRACTICE, PRACTICE, PRACTICE

Quick Reminder

It is not enough to read and think about problem questions. As I have said before in this book, interviewing is an art of conversation and interaction. In order to get better at answering problem questions, you do need to think about responses in advance. This is particularly true for those problem questions that you fear will hurt you if you are asked them in an interview.

You need to practice your interviewing skills *out loud*. If possible, get someone to act as an interviewer and have them throw problem questions at you. Use the Three-Step Approach presented in chapter 4 to answer most questions and your interviewing skills will surely improve.

16

NONTRADITIONAL INTERVIEW APPROACHES

Quick Tip

Much of the information in this chapter has been assembled from a variety of expert sources (other than mine). It includes the tricks employers use to give themselves an edge in the interview. It pays to know what you may be up against if you run into a trained interviewer. This chapter also provides you with a variety of techniques for getting and handling interviews using non-traditional methods.

I noted early on that we need to have a new definition of an interview, one that differs from the traditional definition. There never has been one type of interview and smart job seekers have always tried nontraditional approaches. This chapter presents a variety of nontraditional techniques. You may also tangle with an interviewer who is trained to manipulate you and who will use techniques designed to unsettle you or to elicit negative information that you would not normally have shared. But some of the tips in this chapter will help place you on equal footing in these relatively rare situations.

NONTRADITIONAL TECHNIQUES FOR GETTING INTERVIEWS

There's one sad fact about job interviewing we all must face: Interviewers don't devote their days to searching for us. If you want job offers, you must go to the interviewers and convince them that spending 1 hour of their time with you will more than offset the other tasks they could accomplish during that 60 minutes. This section takes a look at some of the more creative ways to land interviews that have worked for some job seekers.

Quick Fact

Yes, the old mail-a-cover-letter-and-resume approach is still going strong in the business world, much to the delight of the U.S. Post Office. But its popularity has nothing to do with its effectiveness—in fact, it ranks among the worst ways to land a job. According to a *National Business Employment Weekly* survey of 1,500 successful job seekers, only 2 percent landed positions through unsolicited mailings. By locating an in-person contact, you have much more control of your interviewing destiny than if you merely send along some paperwork.

Throughout this section you will encounter some rather off-the-wall ways to land an interview. And I certainly encourage you to dream up some on your own as well. But how do you know if your plan is too outlandish and doomed to make you unhirable? Certainly any creative plan is bound to cause some rolled eyeballs among interviewers, so you had better expect some rejections from the beginning. It simply goes with the territory. However, I recommend scrapping your plan if it in any way offends people, could physically or mentally harm someone, or brings into question your maturity and ability to handle a professional position.

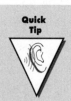

Quick Tip

While you can simply drop in on a prospective employer unannounced, it is usually preferable to first arrange for an interview by phone. This is especially true for employers that are of particular interest to you.

YOU FIRST HAVE TO GET TO THE RIGHT PERSON

Before you can implement any of the techniques in this chapter, you must have a plan ready for those times when you meet with resistance. Your first assignment is always to identify the proper person to contact. If you remember from earlier chapters, that person is the person who is most likely to hire or supervise you. If the organization is large enough to have a separate personnel department, that would *not* be your target (unless, of course, you wanted to work in that department).

▼▼▼

Tips for Getting the Right Name and Overcoming Resistance

Here are some suggestions for using the phone to get the name of the target person:

Act ignorant. Pretend you are a client or a candidate who has forgotten the person's name and say: "Hi. This is terribly embarrassing, but I forgot the name of the person who supervises the _____ department. Can you help me?"

If you do manage to get through to the contact person, but he or she resists your overtures, try these techniques:

They say: I'm really busy—I don't have any time to talk to you.

You say: I understand that. Let me just ask you a quick question then. Would you mind looking over my resume and telling me who I should send it to?

They say: I have no time to meet with you.

You say: I understand that you're busy. So and so told me you would be, but she insisted that my job search would be pointless if I didn't get to talk to you even for a few minutes. I don't want to interrupt your day. Could I take 10 minutes tomorrow morning or after 5:30 this evening? You have my word I'll watch the time.

They say: There aren't any jobs. We'll file your resume and call you if there's an opening.

You say: Thank you. But I've been watching how you're shaping the department and I have some ideas you would be interested in. Could we meet briefly?

▲▲▲

Quick Tip

There are three truths you need to know about landing an interview. Number one, the job hunter does all the work—always. Don't expect anyone not related by blood or marriage to "call you if they hear of any openings." It's your responsibility to keep checking back with all contacts.

Second, contacts and networking get the quickest and best results. Want ads account for only 15 percent of the jobs organizations are trying to fill at any one time. Search firms and employment agencies account for another 10 percent or so. That leaves at least 75 percent of the available positions for you to sniff out yourself.

And third, it takes 200 to 300 telephone calls or contacts to turn up 10 live job leads. However, this is an average; you can't count on precisely five leads from 100 to 150 calls. You must make as many calls as possible to locate the underground job market.

Quick Case Study

Talking to unknown persons on the phone can be intimidating. But you also have to take into consideration how they will react to you. For example, never use a speaker phone. Doing so will create a negative impression and you risk ticking off the person you have called and ruining the contact before it's made.

Take, for instance, etiquette expert Ann Marie Sabeth's experience. As a favor for a placement firm in her hometown of Cincinnati, she agreed to meet and advise executives who recently had been laid off. In May 1994, a gentleman called her at 7:30 A.M. to arrange a time to meet—using a speaker phone throughout the entire conversation. "I was so turned off by that, I told him June 25 was the earliest I could see him!" Sabeth says. "It was something he wanted right away but there was no way I was going to work with someone that rude."

Ditto this advice for car and cellular phones.

THE INFORMATION INTERVIEW

The information interview has become widely used (and abused) since the mid-1970s. Richard Bolles popularized it in his book *What Color Is Your Parachute?* In essence, it is to be used by job seekers who have not yet decided exactly what they want to do—or where. To correctly use the technique, you must first define your ideal job in terms of skills required, size and type of organization, salary level, interests, what sort of co-workers appeal to you, and other preferences. The next step is to gather information on just where a job of this sort might exist and what it might be called.

Quick Tip

From Thomas Canden's The Job Hunter's Final Exam: *(True or False?)*

A guaranteed way to generate employment interviews is to run an advertisement describing skills, experience, and salary.

False. In 30 years of experience, I've never met anyone who got a job that way. If answering a blind ad is a long shot, running a blind ad yourself is an even longer shot, and certainly a more expensive one.

Granted, running an ad is a different approach. But so is wearing a sandwich board stating "I want a job" and parading up and down Main Street. Most readers will only wonder why the person isn't using more conventional techniques and assume that something must be wrong if he or she has to advertise.

If you do your homework before using this method, and if you are truly honest and sincere about seeking information but not a job, then the technique is both effective and fun. Unfortunately, this technique has been misused. People who really want a job have used this method as a trick to get in to see someone. ("I'm not looking for a job but am conducting a survey …") That is dishonest and most employers resent being tricked. Many employers are now wary about anyone, even the sincere ones, asking to see them for any reason. Bolles laments this and points out that some trainers and career counselors who should know better have encouraged this dishonesty. He does add, however, that the technique is still useful, particularly outside of larger cities and with smaller organizations.

The information interview's other exciting twist: It is the only interview where you are in charge of the questions and the organization is put on the spot to answer. Make your questions count.

BECOME A CONSULTANT

You'd be surprised at how many job offers consultants receive during the normal course of their contacts. The reason, of course, is that consultants often prove their worth on these short-term projects. Talk about backing up your statements with proof—consulting is the ultimate demonstration. And for your job search purposes, some employers are more ready to allot time for a consultant, who is seen as a fellow professional, than a job applicant. They also are likely to refer you to colleagues with enthusiasm, since having discovered you is a reflection of their good judgment.

**Quick
Tip**

There is one slight drawback to the consulting angle: You must have an impressive track record in that area. If you don't, try offering to work for the company for one or two weeks at no salary. This "intern" approach affords you the same opportunity to prove yourself that the consultant enjoys.

And yes, it does work. I personally know a man who waltzed into a weekly business newspaper with this very proposition. Thinking she had nothing to lose, the publisher gave him an empty desk and a few story leads. Today, he is the editor of that paper.

Best of all, consulting pulls in a few extra paychecks—a definite morale booster during anyone's job search. Who knows? You may find that consulting beats a full-time job.

VALENTINES, TELEGRAMS, AND OTHER UNUSUAL ATTENTION-GETTING TACTICS

Let's be perfectly straight with each other from the beginning: Not every employer is going to appreciate or even like the tactics I'm about to suggest. Some of the more flamboyant strategies need aggressive, hard-to-offend people to carry them off. If you are anything less than hard-boiled, skip them. Whatever technique you select here (or create on your own) must reflect your personality, or you've gone to a lot of trouble and expense for nothing. You are blatantly selling yourself in these instances, so make sure the message is something you can deliver in the interviewer's office.

Here are some of the more creative, unusual ideas Burdette E. Bostwick outlines in his book, *111 Techniques and Strategies for Getting the Job Interview*:

**Quick
Reference**

☑ START A NEWSLETTER

A computer, printer, and simple layout software can put you in the newsletter business in a matter of hours. More to the point, the newsletter gives you a direct "in" with the offices of a prospective employer. If you write, produce, and distribute your newsletter intelligently, you'll find friends among executives who could be of value to you.

Whatever your field, be sure your newsletter has value to the executives on your list. Otherwise, it's merely another piece of junk mail that lies unopened for a few days before it's swept into the trash can. Focus on

Quick
Reference

new concepts, interpretations, and regulations. Most executives don't have time to read everything that comes across their desks, so they would appreciate summaries of top happenings in the industry.

Also, invest some time (and cash, if necessary) into having talented graphic designers and editors glance over your newsletters, at least for the first few issues. Remember, the newsletter represents you in the same way as your resume, so you don't want to muck up your chances with misspellings; poor grammar; or a cluttered, inappropriate layout.

☑ HOLIDAY GREETINGS

Bostwick tells of an artist seeking a job with an advertising agency who sent the agency president a personally developed valentine. She was invited to an interview and offered a job. Spend some time developing ways to tie your industry into any holiday on the calendar, including the interviewer's birthday or company anniversary date.

For example, office administrator Tamara Castleman discovered that the new boss she hoped to work for just had a baby daughter. She purchased an ordinary Hallmark card that joked about the late nights and stress of a new baby and added her own message below the inside verse: "A top notch assistant could uncomplicate your life and leave you with more time to spend with the new one. Let's discuss what I can do to help you." She got the interview.

Don't limit yourself to cards, either. Depending on your budget, you may find it practical to send bouquets ("to brighten your staff's day during these stressful deadlines"), food baskets, engraved wine bottles, and so forth. I'd suggest you shy away from silly marketing toys that people soon toss. The generosity and team spirit you display by sending a gift that gives pleasure to everyone in the office will go a long way toward ensuring your popularity.

☑ DRIVE A TAXI

Follow the marketing genius of one job hunter moonlighting as a cab driver. According to *Advertising Age*, this innovative person created a sign that read "This taxi is being driven by an unemployed advertising copywriter." He then kept a portfolio of his work and a stack of resumes in the vehicle. The campaign spawned several freelance assignments before yielding a job three months after he posted the sign.

Look around for a part-time job that offers you the same independence and visibility. There's a side bonus with this tactic: You'll earn a paycheck as you search.

☑ SUPPORT A POLITICAL CANDIDATE

Bostwick claims that millions of people gain jobs through political connections, where loyalty and party support are highly regarded. In fact, sometimes you don't even have to appear at a workplace—simply knowing the right person is an effective way of getting the interview.

"The 'Work-without-pay' strategy is a powerful lure for gun-shy employers."

☑ WORK WITHOUT PAY

Don't dismiss the work-without-pay solution. The self-confidence this strategy promotes is a powerful lure for employers gun-shy about making a mistake. Bostwick uses Preston Smith's case as an example: Smith was fired from a hand tool company due to a personality conflict. Undaunted, he went to a former customer and asked if he could work for him, without salary, to see if he could come up with any new ideas. The deal: If he did produce anything profitable, Smith would receive a commission. You know the rest of the story—the man produced several top-selling ideas and was eventually hired (and promoted).

This tactic is particularly helpful if the company expresses interest but can't quite get past the personality conflict that caused your dismissal or is concerned that you aren't qualified.

Quick Tip

Do use some discretion with the work-for-free angle. Don't offer this solution right off the bat—some unscrupulous companies that may intend to hire you anyway will use this generous offer to save a couple of bucks. Secondly, set a time limit on the free trial offer that you believe matches the reason the company is resisting. For instance, if the problem is competency, 10 to 12 days should set the record straight. If it's a question of personality, you may need to consider donating 2 to 3 weeks; human interactions are complicated and less time may not satisfy the issue.

☑ SHOULD I ARRIVE UNANNOUNCED?

Many times you'll hear or read a tale of someone who landed a job by driving straight from Orlando to Omaha, thus impressing the interviewer with his or her dedication. Unfortunately, for every success story there are thousands of others who lost any hope of being considered for a job because their unannounced presence interrupted the executive's day. Play it safe—try everything else before you resort to this often irritating tactic.

HOW TO SHINE IN UNUSUAL INTERVIEW SITUATIONS

Quick Reference

Just as the types and intensity of interview questions have changed in the past few decades, so, too, have the conditions surrounding an interview. If you envision only an executive sitting behind a desk while you sit opposite him or her in a chair and answer questions for an hour, you could be in for a rude—and fatal—awakening.

More interviewers are taking the opportunity to get away from an office setting to give them a fresher perspective on you and the position for which you are applying. Also, rather than solely relying on verbal questions, many organizations are using more in-depth, quantitative measurements to help them make their selections.

Truly prepared candidates gear up for computer pop quizzes, Hollywood-style tryouts, and group "discussions." Here are some pointers to help you not only survive but add pizzazz to your presentation when dealing with nontraditional settings and requests.

Quick
Reference

THE "LET'S DO LUNCH" INTERVIEW

Discussing a job over a pasta salad has become more commonplace. For instance, some large company interviewers routinely set up appointments at the airport or a nearby hotel during visits (or even layovers) to various cities. Believe me, it is far easier to present your job strengths from a semiprivate table in a restaurant than in a crowded lobby or terminal with curious travelers eavesdropping on your conversation!

Even local employers may suggest the interview take place at a restaurant to give the interviewer a chance to view you in a different light. "You can bet your bottom dollar if I were hiring you, I'd take you out to eat to see how you interact with other people," says Anne Marie Sabeth, founder of At Ease etiquette service and author of *Business Etiquette in Brief.* "Do you talk more or listen more? Are you more interested in the meal than me? Do you offer me the rolls before digging into the basket yourself?

"These little things seem petty, but I can guarantee you that today, Corporate America is finally getting smart—they want the best. There's no room for those little things that are offensive to people," she adds.

Quick
Tip

The number one mistake you can make when invited to lunch or dinner after an interview: assume the interview is over. Even though the conversation is more relaxed and no longer centered on how you would handle the job position per se, the other person is still evaluating your responses. Don't let down your guard and abandon your best behavior.

☑ MORE MEAL TIME TIPS

When dining during an interview, treat everyone in the restaurant with equal respect and utmost courtesy. Unfortunately, some job applicants believe that in order to prove they are aggressive and in control, they should order the wait staff about. With more employers today emphasizing self-directed teams, total quality management, and flat-line organizational charts, a bossy attitude may only net you a rejection letter.

When selecting from the menu, remember that you will be expected to continue a conversation during the meal, so don't assume this is time to strap on the feedbag. You want

Quick
Reference

to be mindful of three things: how easy the entree is to eat, the quantity, and the cost. In the latter category, it is always a good idea to mirror the price range your host chooses. Ordering the catch of the day while the interviewer eats a club sandwich blatantly says, "I play fast and loose with other people's money."

Don't order alcohol, even if the interviewer indulges. You can only win by ordering a soda or tea: Refraining keeps your head at its clearest and it shows you can exercise self-discipline—a valuable trait during times when employers are making every effort to cap health-care, workers' compensation, and employee assistance program costs.

Watch your posture carefully during the meal. Some hints etiquette expert Charlotte Ford recommends are:

1. Rest your hands in your lap when you are not eating or, if it makes you more comfortable, rest your forearms on the edge of the table. Don't rest your upper arms on the table, though, or you will tend to sprawl. You may also rest your elbows on the table between courses.

2. When you eat, bring the food to your mouth, don't bend to meet it halfway between your plate and your chair. Again, keep the elbow of an idle arm off the table while you are eating—it sets up a conversation barrier when all your host can see of you is your arm.

3. Drink when your mouth is empty and after you have wiped your lips with your napkin, so as not to leave food on the glass. When drinking iced tea, place the long-handled spoon in the saucer before drinking. If there is no saucer, hold the spoon handle against the side of the glass while you drink.

☑ SPECIFIC TIPS FOR SPECIFIC FOODS

Which foods are easy to eat? Nearly everything on the menu, if you know and are comfortable with the proper etiquette. Rely on these tips for handling more traditional restaurant fare, from *Etiquette: Charlotte Ford's Guide to Modern Manners.*

Cheese: When served as part of a fresh fruit entree, cut the cheese and eat it with a fork.

**Quick
Reference**

Fish: When a small fish is served to you whole, first cut off the head and the tail, then slit the fish from one end to the other lengthwise and lift the fillet away and up from the backbone. Put the tip of your knife under one end of the bone and with the knife and fork, gently lift out the entire skeleton. Place the bones on the side of your plate or on your butter plate. Eat the fish with knife and fork or only with a fork. If you find a bone in your mouth, take it out with your thumb and forefinger.

Olives, Celery, Pickles: When olives, celery, or pickles are served as a garnish, lift them from the dish with your fingers. Take small bites around the pit of a large olive. Put small olives into your mouth and drop the pits into your partially closed fist. Celery, olives, and pickles in salads are eaten with a fork.

Potatoes: Eat French fries with a fork if you are at the table. Cut the fries with the side of your fork into manageable pieces; don't nibble at them from the end of your fork. When eating them with other finger foods, such as hamburgers, eat French fries with your fingers.

Spaghetti: Ask the wait staff to bring you a spoon with your spaghetti. Then hold the spoon in your left hand, twirl the spaghetti into a nest in the spoon and carefully lift the forkful to your mouth.

VIDEO INTERVIEWS: SMILE, YOU'RE ON CAMERA

Employers no longer have to rely on a face-to-face meeting to interview you. Video conferencing, the latest buzzword in meetings and seminars, is making inroads in the interviewing process as well.

Video conferencing is, for all practical purposes, the same picture phone seen on *The Jetsons* cartoon a few decades ago. Images and audio are transferred via phone lines to television screens, and in some cases, computer screens.

Quick Case Study

▲ Companies such as Nike, Ford, General Motors, and WordPerfect have begun using this system for some interviews, but videoconferencing isn't limited to FORTUNE 500 companies. "We get customers so small, they pay by personal check," assures Lynn Yannalfo, videoconferencing services coordinator at Management Resources, a company that handles the process for interviewers. Expect that list of employers to grow: Management Resources, after launching the service in 1993, now handles 50 interviews a month, and that rate is climbing. Costs for this service run around $250 for the first half hour and $50 for each additional 15-minute increment. That's a much cheaper bill than buying an airline ticket and putting you up in a hotel overnight.

▲ According to Lynn Yannalfo of Management Resources, employers rely on videoconferencing more to hire mid- to upper-level sales executives than entry level positions. But no matter which position you are discussing in front of the cameras, do not walk into the studios assuming the session is merely a preliminary chat before the "real" interview. "We initially thought videoconferencing would be used for screening processes," Yannalfo confesses. "But we've had a lot of situations where the employer will make an offer right there on the video and the candidate accepts—and the two have never met face-to-face."

▲ Of course, you stand to gain from a videoconferencing interview as well. For starters, you can easily schedule an interview with an employer based in another city over lunch break—a far better use of your time than taking 48 hours away from either your present job or job search to meet that employer in the conventional way. Also, If you are currently employed, interviewing this way is easier to keep secret from colleagues.

▲ You might even suggest a video interview to a distant employer who seems reluctant to schedule an interview with you because they are not yet convinced that your skills are worth the airfare. In this case, videoconferencing is a cost-effective alternative.

Quick Reference

SECRETS TO A GOOD VIDEO PERFORMANCE

The biggest shock to candidates interviewing with this process is the inherent time delay. Yannalfo compares it to the old ship-to-shore calls; however, the pause for videoconferencing is about half a second as compared to two or three full seconds. Still, for a population used to instantaneous communication, any time delay requires an adjustment.

Furthermore, silence is one of the most uncomfortable situations for most people to handle. They rush to fill the void with sound—a major mistake in this instance. You'll wind up stepping all over the interviewer's ques-

**Quick
Reference**

tions and interrupting his or her follow-up comments. So, definitely practice pausing before an answer to be sure the interviewer has indeed completed his or her thought.

Videoconferencing's picture quality also throws a majority of candidates. "A lot of people think they are going to see the person on television like you see the anchor on the 6:00 P.M. news," Yannalfo confirms. It's simply not that good yet, especially when one of the parties moves around.

Management Resources recommends you sit as quietly as possible. Certainly don't freeze stiff as a statue, but it is a good idea to forgo gestures such as waving your arms, throwing your palms up, ticking off points on your fingers, etc. Remember, even though there is a camera present, this is still an interview, not a performance.

Also, select solid colors when you choose your outfit for the event. The busier the picture, the more work the equipment has to do to transmit all that data across the phone lines. Anything that slows down the system detracts from the purpose at hand: proving to the interviewer you are the best candidate for the job.

**Quick
Fact**

HANDLING IN-HOUSE TAPING

Some employers now record interviews and set up a tripod and video camera right in the interviewer's office. They stand to gain a lot from even an amateur recording:

✔ The playback button allows them to zero in on specific answers where the interviewer may not have taken specific notes (or the interviewer can omit note-taking altogether).

✔ They may compare different candidates' answers on the same questions.

✔ They can watch the tapes whenever and wherever they want.

✔ They can evaluate all interviewees the same day.

✔ They can send the tapes to managers at another location.

The tape provides complete, inexpensive documentation of interviewing practices.

In fact, even the Equal Employment Opportunity Commission has given the videotaped version of an interview its stamp of approval, because an employer can now quickly prove whether it interviewed a diverse group of people, if the questions were within legal limits, and so forth.

"Videotape yourself privately to check for annoying verbal habits."

However, videotaped interviews offer little advantage to you, the candidate. Unfortunately, although the interviewer may miss verbal habits such as starting each sentence with "Well," or saying "OK" 22 times, these mannerisms stick out like a sore thumb when replayed countless times on tape. Not to mention that poor answers, ill-conceived attempts to dodge questions, nervous gestures, and the like don't have a chance to fade. They live on in full color every time he or she pushes the VCR play button.

Furthermore, as Walt Slaughter, president/owner of an outplacement consulting firm in Tennessee points out, the videotaped interview "presupposes that job candidates think and project themselves equally well in front of the camera." That may be true in a perfect world, but on the job hunt, that isn't the case.

But there are things you can do to prepare for a videotaped interview. Videotaped interviewing lends itself well to a structured format, so if you can familiarize yourself in advance with the set-up, you will be ahead of the game. It's always a good idea to videotape yourself privately to check for annoying verbal habits. Above all, don't let the mechanics of the camera sidetrack you from focusing on your task: answering the questions and establishing a relationship with the interviewer!

**Quick
Tip**

*Beware of search firms that want to
videotape interviews to pass out to
potential employers. Some such firms
present one good candidate and several who are unqualified in order to
quickly "sell" a particular person.
It's also possible they'll want to
coach you on certain questions, a
practice future employers could view
as unethical. If the company gets
"caught" by such standards, you may
go down with it. Investigate the situation thoroughly before consenting.*

OTHER NONTRADITIONAL VIDEO INTERVIEW USES

The use of video is not restricted just to traditional interview settings. Colgate-Palmolive
has found success asking potential employees
to physically demonstrate how they would
handle job and management situations.
Turnover in jobs using this technique has
averaged 5 to 10 percent, compared with an
estimated 20 to 25 percent for the rest of the
company. And the numbers get even better:
Two thirds of those hired four years ago have
been promoted—more than three times the
estimated promotion rate at the company's
other plants, *U.S. News and World Report*
has chronicled.

Quick Case Studies

These "real-life" scenarios can take on many forms. One Colgate candidate was
asked to get employees to wear hard hats in a dangerous area of a factory.
Interviewees for the collections division at Geico Insurance are observed while they
pick up a phone and actually explain to the caller that the company will not be
paying for certain claims. At pharmaceuticals manufacturer Purdue Frederick
Company, sales reps vying for promotions watch video tapes of actors interviewing
for fictional sales positions. The real job candidates need to decide why their fictional counterparts should or should not be hired.

There's little you can do to actually rehearse for such surprise video scenarios, but, again, preparation will help. Playacting usually crops up at a second or third interview, and this is where paying attention to the company atmosphere and philosophies that you picked up in earlier meetings will pay off. Add to that the well-honed confidence you've acquired from knowing your strengths and weaknesses and you should be able to sail through the videotaping with relative ease.

COMPUTER TESTING

Yes, this is the age of the computer, but ease of use is not the main reason employers may ask you to sit down and take a multiple-choice screening test at the keyboard. Employers gain because as industrial psychologist Greg Lousig-Nont puts it, "A one-on-one interview is fine for determining whether a candidate is personable, but nice people don't necessarily move the goods." Several studies have shown that humans will be more honest with a computer than with another human.

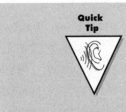

Computer screening may rear its head via telephone contacts, too. For instance, job seekers in Pic 'n Pay shoe stores dial an 800 number and answer a 100-question interview via phone mail.

Arthur Bell describes some almost unbelievable study results in his book, *Extraviewing*. Dr. John Griest at the University of Wisconsin got the ball rolling when his computer-delivered questions prompted a suicidal patient not only to confess his mental state but also that he currently had a gun in his possession! Researchers Dennis Nagoa and Christopher Martin then discovered students will confess their true grade averages and SAT scores to a computer. Duke University documented that people would admit to drinking significantly higher amounts of alcohol when a computer asked them about it than when a person made the same inquiry. In the business field, corporate users report that job applicants display similar candor with the computer. In fact, one retailer discovered that approximately 15 percent of its applicants actually tell a computer that, if hired, they intend to quit that job in less than a year.

Quick Fact

Sound fantastic? The explanation is even more surprising: Some people believe that the computer somehow "knows" the right answer and will catch them in a lie. Others simply relax when dealing with the computer's technical, nonjudgmental approach. For whatever reasons you may feel compelled to present yourself in a bad light, stifle the urge. The computer has no mythical powers, and this *is* a screening interview and your answers carry the same weight as if you had delivered them face-to-face.

However, some programs are set up to provide more data than just monitoring your a, b, or c responses to the questions. Some also time how long you paused before answering, record when you changed your mind and canceled an answer in favor of another, and compile contradictory responses between similar questions.

Needless to say, computer interviewing is not extremely popular among job candidates. Those seeking higher responsibility positions tend to be insulted by the lack of personal attention. However, computer-delivered screening tests are perhaps the most unbiased shot you have at getting in to discuss the position with those who have hiring authority. Computers cannot react to your age, gender, race, height, weight, attractiveness, accent, etc. If you treat your answers to the typed interview with the same respect as you would verbal ones, you have the advantage over those who let the computer psych them out.

PANEL AND GROUP DISCUSSIONS

You may be asked to talk with more than one person at a time because it saves time. It also allows all staff involved in the hiring decision to see you under the same circumstances. And finally, if the group of questioners are

---

Quick Tip

Because of the computer's amazing power to draw out the truth, employers tend to use them to ask the more delicate and personal questions—even when you are face-to-face with another human. That's because the philosophy works in reverse: Interviewers are more likely to vocalize the tough questions they would otherwise skip if the computer weren't there prodding them. So if your interviewer starts glancing at his or her computer screen for the next question, immediately brace yourself to counter a series of personal questions.

your future coworkers, it gives the people most affected by your presence a chance to see how well you fit in.

Your best approach is to treat each interviewer with an equal amount of respect. Look the person who is speaking in the eye during the question, but direct your reply to the entire group. While you may relate to one person in the group better than the others, interact with each person in the group. This is not to say, however, that identifying the leader of the group isn't important—it's imperative when it comes to selecting the most advantageous place at the table to sit.

Group interviews often take place around a table in a conference room. Here are some tips to present yourself best in this situation:

Quick Tip

If you are given a choice, take the seat closest to the group's leader. If you are in doubt who that person is, Seattle-based management consultant Mike Woodruff offers this hint: The leader usually chooses an even-numbered seat—the one farthest from the door is the natural spot for running the meeting.

✔ Keep briefcases and purses on the floor, not on the tabletop or on spare chairs. This prevents you from seeming spread out and messy.

✔ The table isn't a screen, so keep your feet on the floor. If you must cross them, do so at the ankles. Otherwise, you appear inattentive and altogether too casual.

✔ Keep your arms above the table and your hands in view.

✔ Don't cross your arms in front of you, even to lean on them—it communicates hostility.

✔ Sit straight and don't slouch. You will look alert and interested.

INTERVIEW TECHNIQUES EMPLOYERS USE TO PSYCH YOU OUT

☑ WHY WOULD THEY WANT TO TRICK YOU?

Employers today are all too aware of the costs associated with hiring the wrong person, so they want to be sure they hire the best candidate.

And that can include "tricking" you into admitting background weaknesses, questionable ethics, and personal secrets that indicate you cannot handle the job. While some techniques appear quite innocent, their effects can be deadly if you are unaware of what is happening.

Keep in mind, though, that turnabout is fair play. You can prepare for these devious interviewers by knowing what to do when subjected to scrutiny. As always, though, I do not encourage you to lie but to know in advance that your task in an interview is to emphasize your strengths, not reveal your weaknesses. If you have been honest in assessing your skills and have targeted a job that you feel confident about, you need only tell the truth—leaving out all irrelevant information.

☑ SOME BASIC TRICKS FROM A MASTER

While most interviewers will know less about interviewing than you (because you have read this book), some will be masters of the craft. Books have also been written to help professional interviewers and one of my all-time favorites is entitled *The Evaluation Interview*. Written by Richard Fear (I just love the irony of his name), it is a must read for interviewers wanting to increase their ability to manipulate an unsuspecting job seeker. Following are some of Fear's suggested techniques for eliciting negative information. Learn to recognize them so they cannot be used to eliminate you from consideration:

Quick Reference

FACIAL EXPRESSIONS

Just as you use your posture—leaning forward, smiling, good eye contact—to express interest, the interviewer may also attempt to guide your answers with facial clues. For instance, lifting the eyebrows a little and smiling slightly conveys that the listener is receptive and expectant—and that is all it takes to convince some people to divulge negative facts about themselves to their new "friend." This half-smile and raised eyebrows routine also takes the edge off a delicate or personal question. Don't be misled: You must still answer these sensitive questions with the careful wording you have rehearsed, no matter how concerned and nonjudgmental the interviewer appears.

THE CALCULATED PAUSE

Experienced journalists have long elicited information from hard-boiled criminals, slick-tongued politicians, and interview-savvy celebrities by

Quick Reference

using the calculated pause. The technique works even better on job applicants. Most of us are not comfortable with silence, and will rush to fill the void with verbal noise. Therefore, when the interviewer says nothing but maintains eye contact, most job seekers either feel pressured into giving more details to their answer or starting another topic altogether.

The best way to handle silence is by remaining quiet and appearing pleasant. This creates a nonhostile stand-off and, in the interest of time, the interviewer eventually asks the next question. It is not as bad as it seems—most pauses are measured in seconds, and it is rare for more than two to pass without the interviewer realizing you have not fallen for this ploy.

If you are compelled to say something, at least turn the tables. "I think that answers the question, unless there is something else you wish to know," forces the interviewer to become the respondent.

Quick Tip

Here, according to Richard Fear, are the most common words or phrases an experienced interviewer might use to encourage you to give them negative information:

- *To what extent did you …?*
- *How do you feel about/like …?*
- *Is it possible that …?*
- *How did you happen to…?*
- *Has there been any opportunity to…?*
- *To what do you attribute …?*
- *might …*
- *perhaps …*
- *somewhat …*
- *a little bit …*

DIRECT AND INDIRECT QUESTIONS

While you are not all that likely to run into many well-trained interviewers, they are out there. Experienced interviewers will often use indirect language to encourage you to tell them more than you might if you were asked the same question more directly. Following are examples of different versions of the same question asked in a direct and then in an indirect way.

Direct Question	Indirect Version
1. Why did you leave that job?	1. How did you happen to leave that job?
2. Why do you think you had trouble with your boss?	2. To what do you attribute the minor difficulties you experienced with your supervisor?
3. How much money did you save that summer?	3. Was there an opportunity to save any money that summer?
4. Why did you decide to take a cut in pay in order to get transferred to that other job?	4. What prompted your decision to take a cut in pay in order to get transferred to that other job?
5. Do you lack self-confidence?	5. Is self-confidence perhaps a trait that you might improve to some extent?
6. Are you overly sensitive?	6. Is it possible that you may be somewhat oversensitive to criticism?

Quick Reference

TIPS ON ANSWERING INDIRECT QUESTIONS

During the course of an interview, keep your ears tuned for phrases such as "To what extent did you …?", "How did you feel about/like …?", and "Is it possible that …?" Fear calls these phrases "wonderful" and "remarkably effective" because they turn leading questions into open-ended ones. But don't be lulled into missing their sting: "To what extent were you successful on that job?" still carries the meaning of its harsher counterpart, "Were you successful on that job?" Keep your answer directed toward satisfying that unspoken question, and your value will jump in the interviewer's estimation.

ANSWERING THE TWO-STEP INTERVIEW QUESTION

Just as a dance partner leads you through a series of premeditated steps to complete a specific dance, so are the interviewer's questions designed to guide you into an overall pattern. The best way to do this is to introduce a general subject, then hone in on the "why" of your answer. It works like this: The interviewer leads off a round of questions with a query such as "What subject did you decide to major in?" He or she then comes back with "Why?"

Interviewers use the two-step method to probe for clues to your judgment, motivation, and other factors of your personality. So, do not think you are completely off the hook with a smooth answer like "History, because I believe it ultimately holds the solutions to problems in the future." When you are in the hands of a master interviewer, he or she is likely to ask you why that aspect seems important to you, or why that compelled you to spend four years devoted to it instead of just taking a course or two.

The best way to perform the two-step is to be prepared before you ever enter the interviewer's office. The more you understand yourself, the more gracefully the two of you will dance.

SORTING LAUNDRY LIST QUESTIONS

Beware of questions that offer a variety of options from which to choose (the so-called laundry list). The interviewer is not always trying to help you think in a stressful situation. In fact, it is just the opposite.

When interviewers throw out a question with a series of possibilities from which to select, they are often trying to confirm details they picked up from a previous comment you made. Richard Fear's example: Assume that you, the applicant, have dropped some hints that seem to indicate a dislike for detail. The interviewer can often follow up on such clues by including a reference to detail in the laundry list question at the end of the discussion of work history.

Quick Case Study

▲ Here is an example of how an experienced interviewer might present a laundry list question: "What are some of the things that a job has to have to give you satisfaction? Some people want to manage whereas others are more interested in an opportunity to come up with new ideas; some like to work regular hours whereas others do not mind spending additional hours on the job; some like to work with details while others do not; some are quite happy working at a desk while others prefer to move around a good bit—what's important to you?"

▲ If you respond, "Well, I certainly do not want anything that involves a lot of detail." Bingo! The interviewer has gotten further confirmation of your reaction to detail. In fact, as Fear points out, the very fact that you selected this item for discussion reflects the importance you attach to it.

Do not be afraid to take a minute to consider your answer to a laundry list question, and do not feel pressured into selecting one of the interviewer's choices over one that would better suit your case.

DOUBLE-EDGED QUESTIONS

Another tricky technique that is used to probe a job seeker's weaknesses is the double-edged question. It is called this because you are asked to choose between a rock and a hard place: You won't choose the first option unless you have a high degree of skill or personality in that area; the second is phrased so that it is easy to choose it, even though it is the more undesirable one. Ouch!

Here is an example: "What about your spelling ability—do you have that ability to the extent that you would like, or is that something you could improve a little bit?" (Notice the liberal use of softening words thrown in for good measure.) If you select the first option, it implies you feel no need for improvement—and you had better be prepared to back that up with perfect spelling! The second choice invites you to confess you are not up to speed in this area.

Your best answer to a double-edged question is to stick to the pattern for revealing any negative aspects. Frame it in the context of your strengths. Here is one example of a response that won't hurt you. "Because I'm a perfectionist, my spelling ability probably will not ever be what I hope for, but I am an above-average speller. And I am very careful to check any words that I am not sure of so that no spelling errors remain."

"Job interviews are built on the gaming theory."

Quick Fact

MORE GAMES INTERVIEWERS PLAY

Veteran personnel manager Dean P. Peskin identifies more interviewer tricks in his book, *Human Behavior and Employment Interviewing*. According to this expert, job interviews are built on the gaming theory, which assumes that each of the players understands the other and that each reacts in a logical way. They then engage in a series of moves with the objective of winning. Here are some of the trickier games he suggests an interviewer should be willing to play:

FORCED CHOICE

Most of us recognize the forced choice trap in the notorious question, "Do you still beat your spouse?" Fewer of us catch this same dilemma when it is presented in the interview. However, if the interviewer asks, "What type of leadership experience have you had?", you cannot answer without affirming or denying the assumption on which the question is presumably based. So, because the real question is "Do you have leadership experience?" frame your answer in that direction. Be honest if you do not have whatever trait the interviewer mentions.

YOU THE JURY

In this game, the interviewer drops you squarely in the middle of an honesty-versus-conformity quandary to see if your integrity wins. In Peskin's illustration, the interviewer tells you (in a conversational way and in a pseudoconfidential tone) about an unnamed individual who, although in management, always locked his desk at five sharp. The story ends with a smile of ridicule and the question, "Can you imagine such a thing?"

Quick Fact

Here's the dilemma: If you conform to the interviewer's stance and say that no, you cannot imagine that happening, you sacrifice honesty. The interviewer knows perfectly well that you know the job requires a balance between leaving on time and putting in extra hours. However, if you decide to challenge the query, you are also challenging the principle, and that may not sit well with the organization.

My advice—in these days of heightened attention on honesty, ethics, and need for self-thinkers, it is better to give your opinion in a polite, non-threatening manner than to do your impersonation of a sheep and go along with the company line.

HOW WE DO IT

The "how-we-do-it" game is so subtle in its purpose, few applicants ever recognize they have been backed into a corner until it is too late. Yes, a majority of interviewers will deliver information and insights about the job—you can hardly discuss your qualifications without this input. However, some interviewers go a step further and suggest technical skills to build—even though your present skill level is adequate for the job— and social and personal traits you should cultivate.

If you recognize this game in advance, you have the ability to respond without damaging yourself. This game forces you to continually reinforce your present level of skills and development to uphold your acceptability, as Peskin notes. On the other hand, you must indicate that you are willing to seek out developmental opportunities that will make you a better employee more adaptable to new job circumstances, skill demands, procedures, and people. The trick: You cannot emphasize your need to learn at the expense of your already stellar qualifications.

TRAP-PLAY

This game is played quickly and may be over before you know it. Shortly after the interview begins, the interviewer makes a personal comment or statement that he or she does not actually believe, just to see your reaction. So, if someone mentions that your tie is too old-fashioned or that your blouse is a bit "loud," your best response is to reply neutrally, without a trace of commitment or emotion. Do not, however, grovel by agreeing with the interviewer.

Quick Tip

Good news—you are unlikely to run into the interviewer-oriented technique if you are applying for a non-management, entry level, or middle-level management position. The technique is, however, often used in interviews for sales positions of all levels. If you handle yourself well in this stressful interview, you stand a better chance of finding the job itself rewarding.

INTERVIEWER-ORIENTED TECHNIQUE (A.K.A. STRESS TEST)

Peskin lists the interviewer-oriented game as an often used technique that relies on the deliberate heightening of anxiety. In it, the interviewer wants to pull you so far off track that you may not be sure of your name, let alone your qualifications.

You will often recognize this game the second you walk into the office. In Peskin's words, the interviewer's posture will be challenging and accusatory in the extreme. You typically will be received with a stern, cool, and distant personality—a crisp, "How do you do?" that does not invite an answer. The interviewer may treat your resume with contempt and appear to be annoyed with your presence altogether. This person may try to deflate you by stating that after reviewing your credentials, he or she cannot determine exactly what you are qualified for and would appreciate clarification.

The pressure usually never lets up throughout the ordeal, because the entire point behind this aggression is to see how well you can stand the heat in the kitchen—and for how long. Expect to experience anxiety, frustration, and psychological fatigue during your trial by fire.

To score well in this situation, do not give the interviewer what he or she is digging for: anger; hurt feelings; a retreating, meek personality; defensiveness; panic; tears. Continue to present your strengths with calmness, confidence, and dignity.

Quick Case Study

▲ Although the psyche-you-out techniques presented in this section are often devious, they are predictable. There was no book or course that could have prepared Theresa DeWitt Turner for her first job interview out of college. She was met by a 6-foot 2-inch robot named Sico who insisted on shaking hands and telling blue techy jokes. ("I had a hot date with a computer last night. She was really cute, only she had floppy disks.") Turner had the presence of mind to go with the flow. She ended up with a job that involved promoting Sico, and managed to get her "interviewer" a spot in the *Rocky IV* movie.

Quick
Reference

CONQUER INTERVIEW FEAR THROUGH PRACTICE

This section will give you some ideas on how to overcome your anxiety about handling an interview. Practice, of course, is one way to improve your performance and several experts will give other suggestions. Practice and perseverance will help stop the fear and procrastination that can shoot you down.

Quick Case Study

▲ Does this sound familiar? You have an interview scheduled for 9 A.M. on Thursday with the leading organization in your field. On Monday, you stop by the library, gather some research, and jot down a few questions. Then you slide the information into a folder until Tuesday evening, when you decide you're too tired to deal with it. After all, you still have 24 hours to prepare—and the closer to the interview you practice, the "fresher" your answers will be. On Wednesday, you silently practice answering a few of the trickier questions, playing out a very impressive scenario in your mind. It's time to ace the interview!

▲ However, during the actual appointment, the answers you had rehearsed don't come out quite right. You stutter a few times, start every sentence with "Well, umm," and never come close to matching the glorified performance in your head.

Quick Tip

Interviewing is not like riding a bicycle. Instead, you must learn and relearn it in order to maintain your balance. As Robert Half, founder of Robert Half International, points out, "Interviewers have had to develop new approaches to questioning in order to evaluate the true potential of each candidate effectively and choose the best one." So, this is not your father's interview—nor is it the same process you went through several years ago. It's more like learning to ride a bike from scratch, so plan to take your spills in the privacy of your own living room rather than in front of an audience.

Quick Tip

It's a myth that good work speaks for itself. According to George Dudley, many people step into interviews thinking, "If I simply describe faithfully what my contributions will be, the organization—wishing to grow and being a rational organism—will evaluate me, see what I'm capable of doing, and hire me." But someone else comes in willing to put a little bit of flair into their presentation and bingo! They get hired instead of you.

APPROPRIATE SELF-PROMOTION PAYS OFF

Research supports the value of self-promotion. In one study, Behavioral Sciences Research Press took a group of administrators and management personnel and measured their reluctance to promote their accomplishments. For five years, the firm tracked how many dollars in salary increases and how many promotions each participant received. It found that the people who made the most money and were promoted most frequently were not necessarily those who could be considered the most technically competent or deserving. Instead, those who got ahead were the ones who were assertive in making their achievements most visible.

The firm then repeated the study with engineers and systems analysts. The group again found the same conclusion. "Today, being good at your job isn't good enough. You have to be good at what you do and be good at letting others know it," says George Dudley, author of *Earning What You're Worth?* "It's not just something general, like low self-esteem. I see people with very high self-esteem that have problems with this."

Unfortunately, many people back away from self-promotion because they believe it falls into the "tasteless and unprofessional" category, which is a characteristic we want to avoid at all costs. The Behavioral Science Institute estimates that 80 percent of capable workers are silent because they think all self-promotion is inherently wrong. But Dudley defines self-promotion as using all opportunities to make the best possible presentation of your background, skills, and abilities to suit the situation. "Notice I didn't say take credit for things you haven't done, can't do, won't do, or drop names of people you don't know," he points out. "The difference between an ethical and unethical self-promotion is whether or not you are deserving of the recognition and approval you are seeking."

BREAKING THE SILENCE HABIT

There are two types of self-promotion downfalls that particularly apply to job interview situations. In psychological terms, they're known as inhibited contact initiation syndrome (in the layperson's terms, fear of calling people and setting up appointments) and close reluctance (fear of taking the appointment beyond a social chit-chat to talk about your qualifications and ask for the job). The trick is to forestall either habit with something more concrete than a mental pep talk.

If you are reluctant to make contact (and failing to prepare in advance is one sign of this problem), try sensory injection. It works like this:

1. **Select a fragrance cue.** It can be something you already identify with being loved, cared for, nurtured, contented, or relaxed. Salesman Dave Richardson carries a vial of lake water to remind him of fishing. Another executive who learned to relax as part of his rifle marksmanship hobby carries a spent brass ammunition cartridge. If you have no such associations, choose something you've never smelled before.

2. **Calibrate the desired state, relaxation.** What relaxes you the most? Music? Deep breathing? Prayer? Reading? This is very individualistic, so choose whatever works best for you and proceed to do it.

3. **Connect the fragrance cue.** Engage in your relaxing activity to the point where you are distracted from your worry or fear. Once you

**Quick
Reference**

have achieved that state, dab a drop of your fragrance cue onto a piece of cotton and sniff it three times for about one second each time. Then put the cotton aside and continue relaxing for a few more minutes.

4. **Fortify.** Practice this sequence at least once a day for five days, until you develop a strong association with the physical sensations of relaxation.

5. **Aromashots:** Carry your fragrance cue on a cotton ball in a small pillbox. Then, just before entering a potentially stressful situation, sniff your cotton ball three times for about one second each. Congratulations—you've just sent your body a signal to relax that's stronger than the one urging panic.

For those who suddenly develop a frog in their throats when the time comes to promote themselves, Dudley recommends wrapping a rubber-band around your wrist. Then when you find yourself in the chit-chat rut, reach down and snap your wrist sharply with the rubber band. "You are doing the best thing you can do to a habit: interrupting it in sequence," Dudley says. (In Pavlovian terms, for those of you who remember Psychology 101, the action is called extinguishing.)

Now wait a minute, you're saying. How can I carry out this advice during an interview? After all, it's not practical to stop in the middle of a sentence, roll up your sleeve, and proceed to sting your wrist. This behavior will earn you a one-way trip to the exit sign after the interviewer jots down "emotionally disturbed" on your resume. The answer is, of course, you don't actually inflict pain on yourself in the interviewer's office—you do it beforehand, during your practice sessions.

"You only have to do it the first few times," Dudley assures. "I personally only had to do it for two days and then the band became symbolic. It reminds you just by being there." And remember, you don't snap that rubberband to punish yourself; you do it to interject a distraction that severs the connection between the interview and your negative behavior.

TACKLING THAT INNER VOICE OF DOOM

In addition to convincing themselves that it isn't nice to "brag," some people also are good at downgrading their abilities and accomplishments until there's nothing resembling a scrap of positive energy left. You fall into this category if the little voice inside your head urges, "I'm not really smart. I got ahead by luck. I'm just a salesman/secretary/middle manager," etc.

Unfortunately, Paul Curro of Paul Curro and Associates out of Omaha, Nebraska, points out, the way we see ourselves and our experiences is filtered through these negative beliefs. So, we unconsciously say to ourselves:

- "Here's the kind of person I am."
- "Here's how I will perform."
- "These are the only jobs I can do."
- "Here's what certain people think of me."

One tool Curro labels "powerful" for combating this negative attitude is sentence completion. Use the following sentence roots to identify what is causing your suppressed, limiting self-beliefs—then work to change them!

Finish These Sentences to Identify Your Emotional Blocks:

- If I were to take responsibility for my feelings, for my own life, for my unhappiness, ... (e.g., I'd have to face up to my real fears. I'd have to think about what I really wanted in life.)
- As I learn to be more honest about what I think and feel ...
- If I persist in blaming other people (or God) ...
- If I insist on seeing myself as a victim ...
- If I were willing to know what I'm choosing or doing when I act ...
- If I were to take full responsibility for my job search, calling on "new" people, I would have to ...
- I lack the most confidence in myself when I am doing (what?) or when I'm in front of (whom?).
- It's not easy for me to admit ...

✎ One of the thoughts I tend to push out of my mind is …

✎ The scary thing about being self-accepting is …

Quick Tip

From America Online's Career Center, hosted by Jim Gonyea.

Q: I'm beginning to find that my interview "jitters" may be getting in the way of my attaining positions. Are there resources outside of a university environment to go to for help? I was thinking of joining Toastmasters to get used to public speaking. Any ideas?

A: The "jitters" are often caused by the fact that most people do not know how to handle the interview. If you could improve this, you would be less anxious. Let's start by having you read Sweaty Palms—The Neglected Art of Being Interviewed *by H. Anthony Medley.*

THE PROPER WAY TO PRACTICE

Now that you've identified what's destroying your presentation at the roots, it's time to solve the problem through practice, practice, practice … And there's no getting around it—you must practice giving your answers aloud. Written replies may read well and mental compositions may be flawless, but interviews themselves are inherently verbal in nature.

Start the practice conversation in a room by yourself to work out the kinks in relative privacy, and to get comfortable hearing your voice. Get familiar, too, with a posture that allows you to look relaxed but interested and gestures that support your presentation but do not distract.

Next, invite an objective friend to play the role of the interviewer and critique your answers. Of course, most friends will automatically tell you that you're doing fine— that's the nature of friendship. Sometimes it's because they have limited experience and don't see any flaws, but most of the time it's because they value your relationship too much to put it on the line over a practice interview.

An interviewer won't be so kind, so before you walk into an interview, turn to outside sources to critique your answers. These include professional societies and clubs (most cities have groups of unemployed executives who meet for support to work on such exercises), campus career offices, and military transition offices.

Quick Reference

Finally, videotape yourself during a mock interview. This allows you to concentrate strictly on the sound of your answers and then compare that audio with a picture. Do the two match? Which is weaker? Look hard to see if you've controlled the problems others pointed out in earlier practice rounds. Look for annoying habits that others may have over-looked, too. For instance, do you glance at your watch every few minutes? If so, you may want to remove the watch right before you meet with the interviewer.

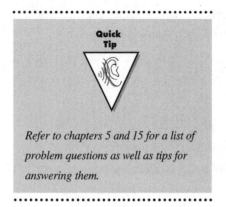

Quick Tip

Refer to chapters 5 and 15 for a list of problem questions as well as tips for answering them.

WHAT TO PRACTICE

Always put yourself in the role of a customer and it will be easy to see which attitude to adopt and practice. How do you want a receptionist to greet you when you call a company? How quickly do you want a customer representative to respond to your questions? How cheerfully do you want the nurse's aide to help you fill out insurance forms? And while you are giving your answers in this frame of mind, don't leave out the power words that all business people want to hear: profit, savings, quality, and teamwork.

17

PRE-EMPLOYMENT
TESTING

**Quick
Tip**

*You are going to see
more and more testing in
the future as employers
try to avoid hiring peo-
ple that eventually do not
work out. While pre-
employment tests have
been around for years,
they are getting better
now at predicting which
job candidates are most
likely to work out.
Private companies are
also providing pre-
employment screening
for employers, for a fee,
so be prepared to take
one or more.*

TYPES OF TESTS

The use of pre-employment tests actually spans more than
40 years, but they are being used more now than in the past.
Experts are urging more and more employers to include
personality testing as part of the screening process. And
because personal conversations can never guarantee that
what you see is what you get, employers are eager to
explore any possibility that claims to tell the future
for them. This chapter briefly describes some of the types
of tests you may be asked to take during the interview
process.

HONESTY AND INTEGRITY TESTS

A variety of tests are designed to find out if you are honest. They ask if you have ever stolen anything, if you stole from a previous employer, if you lied on an application, ever took illicit drugs, and other questions. Some of the questions are not so obvious, although they are often easy enough to figure out. These types of tests are of great interest to certain kinds of employers because dishonest employees are very expensive.

According to the Association of Personnel Test Publishers in Washington, DC:

✎   Monetary losses due to employee theft and related acts of dishonesty are estimated at between $40 and $50 billion a year. For example, one researcher reports an increase in internal bank fraud and embezzlement from approximately $165 million in 1981 to approximately $534 million in 1987. Arthur Young Inc. documented a 5 percent increase in the retail industry's shrinkage rates from 1982 to 1987, representing roughly $1.8 billion in losses due to the increase alone.

✎   The average percentage of employees who steal ranges from 20 percent to 40 percent, depending on the industry.

Even a small amount of theft can make a big difference to a company that has an operating profit of 2 percent, such as the grocery business. Honesty tests have been fairly effective in screening out people who are most likely to steal. London House Systems claims that a retail drugstore chain saved an estimated $1.25 million in shrinkage costs through the use of their honesty tests.

WHAT THE TESTS LOOK FOR

Tests of honesty and integrity attempt to screen out common counterproductive behaviors on the job. Following is a list of negative behaviors published by the Association of Personnel Test Publishers that these tests attempt to isolate.

HONESTY TESTS LOOK FOR THESE NEGATIVE BEHAVIORS:

- Theft of cash, merchandise, and property
- Damaging merchandise to buy it on discount
- Unauthorized work break extensions
- "Time" theft
- Repeatedly coming to work late
- Coming to work with a hangover or intoxicated
- Selling illicit drugs at work
- Breaking rules
- Damage and waste
- Preventable accidents
- Misuse of discount privileges
- Getting paid for more hours than worked
- Turnover for cause
- Unauthorized use of company information
- Using sick leave when not sick
- On-the-job drug abuse
- Intentionally doing slow or sloppy work
- Gross misconduct
- Vandalism
- Physical assault

REPRESENTATIVE PERSONALITY TESTS

There are dozens of personality tests out there, most of them variations of each other, and detailing them all here would be impossible. Instead, take a glance at the tests in publisher London House's library, and use this as a guide for other types of tests you may encounter.

Quick Reference

THE PERSONAL AUDIT

The paper-and-pencil Personal Audit test measures nine personality traits to assess your adjustment capabilities:

> seriousness/impulsiveness, firmness/indecision, tranquility/irritability, frankness/evasion, stability/instability, tolerance/intolerance, steadiness/emotionality, persistence/fluctuation, and contentment/worry.

Employers use this test to evaluate candidates for a variety of professional occupations and clerical positions. There is no time limit for this particular test, but most job candidates finish in 30 to 40 minutes.

☑ SAMPLE QUESTIONS

1. Indicate the degree of your liking for each of the following activities:
a) acting as master of ceremonies at a night club, b) introducing strangers at a
party, c) playing a part in a movie, d) attending a masquerade party, e) performing on the radio.

2. Of these statements, draw a circle around "T" for the ones you believe to be
usually true; draw a circle around "D" for those whose truth you doubt; and
draw a circle around "F" for the ones you believe to be usually false:

Individuals who are very good looking usually have less sense than people with
ordinary looks. (Several more of these types of questions would follow.)

3. Draw a circle around the word that seems to you to go most naturally with
the word in capitals: TRAVEL boat ship train car.

SURVEY OF INTERPERSONAL VALUES

The Survey of Interpersonal Values measures six critical values involving a person's
relationships with others: support (being treated with understanding and consideration), conformity (doing what is socially correct and accepted), recognition (being
looked up to and admired; being considered important), independence (having the
right to make one's own decisions and having one's own way), benevolence (doing
things for other people), and leadership (being in charge of other people, having
authority or power).

This paper-and-pencil test takes approximately 15 minutes, and is used to screen for a
variety of occupations and job levels.

☑ SAMPLE QUESTION

In each set, mark one statement as representing what is most important to you, and
one statement as representing what is least important to you. You will leave one
statement unmarked:

To be the one who is in charge

To conform strictly to the rules

To have others show me that they like me

Quick Fact

According to London House Assessment Systems, by using Interpersonal Values testing one fast-food chain reduced its turnover rate by 50 percent in its troubled units and saved an estimated $2 million in annual turnover costs. Also, a trucking firm reduced its insurance losses by 80 percent, which meant an estimated annual savings of $242,000.

Quick Reference

SURVEY OF PERSONAL VALUES

The Survey of Personal Values is a 15-minute test that indicates how a person is likely to approach a job or training program. It measures six values that influence how you cope with problems and choices of every-day living:

- Practical mindedness—To always get one's money's worth, to take good care of one's property, to do things that will pay off

- Achievement—To work on difficult problems, to strive to accomplish something significant, to do an outstanding job

- Variety—To do things that are new and different, to go to strange places

- Decisiveness—To have firm convictions, to make decisions quickly, to come directly to the point

- Orderliness—To have well-organized work habits, to keep things in their place, to follow a systematic approach

- Goal orientation—To have a definite goal, to stick to a problem until it is solved, to know precisely where one is headed

Employers commonly use this test when interviewing applicants for the position of cashier, collection clerk, reservation clerk, communications representative, gas station attendant, manager, merchandise handler, meter reader, telephone service representative, and insurance supervisor, to name a few.

☑ SAMPLE QUESTION

In each set, mark one statement as representing what is most important to you, and one statement as representing what is least important to you. You will leave one statement unmarked:

To work on something difficult

To have well-defined goals or objectives

To keep my things neat and orderly

Quick Reference

THURSTONE TEMPERAMENT SCHEDULE

The Thurstone Temperament Schedule evaluates six personality traits: active (works and moves rapidly), impulsive (carefree disposition, makes decisions quickly), dominant (leadership ability, capable of taking initiative and responsibility), stable (cheerful, even disposition), sociable (enjoys company of others), and reflective (thinks meditatively, enjoys theoretical problems). This test is particularly effective in evaluating potential office workers, retail store sales employees and, surprisingly enough, third- and fourth-grade teachers.

☑ SAMPLE QUESTION

Answer yes or no:

Are you more restless and fidgety than most people?

Do you ordinarily work quickly and energetically?

In conversation, do you often gesture with hands and head?

Do you drive a car rather fast?

Quick Reference

EMO QUESTIONNAIRE

The EMO Questionnaire helps identify adjustment problems that may hinder individuals' work efficiency or ability to get along with others. It's most often used for stressful occupations such as transit bus operator, police officer, and high-pressure sales forces.

☑ SAMPLE QUESTION

Record your feelings about each experience by putting a check mark in the appropriate box.

During the past month, there was at least one time when:

I was pleased	Yes ☐	No ☐
I was troubled/little	Yes ☐	No ☐
I was troubled/much	Yes ☐	No ☐
I felt relaxed and easy	Yes ☐	No ☐
I felt dizzy or faint	Yes ☐	No ☐
I had stomach trouble	Yes ☐	No ☐

Quick Reference

CREE QUESTIONNAIRE

The Cree Questionnaire measures your overall creative potential and the extent to which your behavior resembles that of creative individuals. The test measures the following levels: social (submissive vs. dominant, conforming vs. independent), work practices (structured vs. unstructured, relaxed vs. pressured), internal (low vs. high energy level, slow vs. fast reaction time, low vs. high ideation rate) and interest (low vs. high theoretical, low vs. high artistic, low vs. high mechanical) levels. The Cree Questionnaire generally takes 20 minutes to complete.

☑ SAMPLE QUESTION

Answer yes, no, or undecided:

Do you like to work with theoretical ideas?

Do you find it difficult to address an audience?

Do you enjoy presenting a new project before a group?

Quick Reference

TESTS FOR JOB-RELATED SKILLS AND OTHER FACTORS

Of course, personality and integrity aren't the only things employers will test. You should be on alert for a battery of quizzes and hands-on demonstrations designed to determine specific skills that are related to the job including: office skills, computer skills, cash-handling ability, mechanical skills, recall, mental quickness, reasoning, adaptability, general learning ability, repetitive, language fluency … again, the list is almost endless. However, it is possible to increase your skills in these areas ahead of time even though you cannot possibly guess the exact questions. It's best to concentrate on remembering details, improving your vocabulary, or strengthening your weaker areas overall.

SOURCES OF ADDITIONAL INFORMATION

Here are some additional sources of more specific information related to the use of pre-employment testing:

- National Academy of Sciences, *Fairness in Employment Testing*, National Academy Press

- Department of Justice, Uniform Guidelines on Employee Selection Procedures (provides technical regulations on assessing applicants)

- *Model Guidelines for Pre-employment Integrity Testing Programs*, Association of Personnel Test Publishers

SALARY NEGOTIATIONS— HOW TO MAKE A FEW THOUSAND DOLLARS IN A MINUTE

Introduction

In case you have forgotton, the topic of salary negotiations is part of the title of this book. While the subject only gets a few chapters, this can be one of the more important things you can learn in this book. Knowing how to use just a few good negotiating techniques in the right way and at the right time can be worth what it would cost you to buy a thousand or so of these books.

I am not kidding. Getting a bigger pay rate as you begin a job or career can compound over the years into a sizeable amount. Yet few people know much about basic salary negotiation techniques.

Here's a qoute from management speaker Suzanne Greene to support my observation: "We spend years in school. We spend a large sum of money getting that education. We spend hours writing resumes and cover letters and interviewing. But when we finally get to the last detail—money, perks and benefits—we usually negotiate this in less than five minutes."

Actually, most salary negotiations take far less than five minutes because the applicant is not prepared to do it. Even worse, many employers use discussions of salary as a preliminary tool to screen people out of consideration. So if you don't know what to do, discussing salary at the wrong time can get you quickly eliminated from consideration. This section will give you techniques, sources of information, and details that will help you do a superior job in knowing what you are worth and in doing your best to get it.

Chapters in This Section:

Chapter 18: Salary Negotiations—the One Who Speaks First Loses

This chapter reviews and adds to salary negotiations information that I provided back in Section 1. It also includes a section with tips from a variety of other salary negotiations experts.

Chapter 19: Researching What Others Earn in Similar Positions—Plus Average Earnings for Hundreds of Jobs

It just might be true that the last is not least. In this case, the very last chapter (gasp!) of this book provides some neat information: Just how much does you neighbor make?

Okay, it's not that specific, but there is a list of 250 jobs and their average pay rates— and these jobs cover about 85 percent of the workforce. There's also a variety of additional information, including specific reference materials for getting information on pay in various jobs and industries, including how to get local information.

18

SALARY NEGOTIATIONS—THE ONE WHO SPEAKS FIRST LOSES

Quick Tip

Chapter 5 gave you some tips on answering pay-related questions. Because of its importance, I'd like to review that information and add a variety of additional tips and details. Pay attention! This one chapter could be worth thousands of dollars to you over the years to come ...

THE ART OF NEGOTIATION

Most people don't negotiate their salaries partly because few know how to negotiate effectively. Each of us, at one time or another, has failed at this process. Most job seekers accept the first offer thrown their way because they're afraid that negotiating will kill any chances to get the job. I personally never attempted to negotiate a salary package during the early years of my career because nodding politely and saying, "That's fine" was the path of least resistance. But in today's economy that passive acceptance can cost us more than we can afford to lose.

THE KEY QUESTION: "WHAT SORT OF PAY DO YOU EXPECT TO RECEIVE?"

This was one of the problem questions examined in chapter 5. While that material took only a few pages, it was the essence of how to handle salary negotiations. This chapter reviews that process in more detail and provides additional tips from a variety of sources.

Negotiation experts cite four strategic mistakes that novice negotiators often make. While these mistakes refer to negotiations in general, they are often at the root of salary negotiation problems as well.

1. **Lack of persistence.** Herb Cohen, author of *You Can Negotiate Anything*, told *USAir* magazine, "People present something to the other side, and if the other side doesn't 'buy' it right away, they shrug and move on to something else. If that's a quality you have, I suggest you change it. Learn to hang in there. You must be tenacious."

2. **Impatience.** As Michael Schatzki warns, "The impatient negotiator has two strikes against him. He's not willing to let the process work itself out, and he's not willing to be deadlocked for a while and see what happens. And time often is the key to successfully concluding a negotiation."

3. **Going in too low.** All too often one side in the negotiation process accepts in advance a settlement that is lower than the other side had in mind. Once a low position is revealed, an experienced negotiator is unlikely to go higher.

4. **Lack of research.** Few people are prepared with facts to back up their position in negotiations. They go on "feel" to establish a value. Lack of preparation can be a very expensive mistake.

Quick Alert

INITIAL DISCUSSIONS ABOUT PAY CAN OFTEN GET YOU SCREENED OUT

Early in the traditional screening process many employers want to know how much you expect to be paid. Before the actual interview, they may seek this information on applications and in want ads. And some employers ask you how much you expect to earn very early in the interview process.

Just why is this so important to them? The reason is that many employers don't want to waste their time with people who have salary expectations far above what the employer is willing to pay. Put simply, they want the information so that they can screen you out.

Quick Reference

Farr's Salary Negotiation Rule #1

Employers look for ways to eliminate as many people as possible during the early phases of a traditional interview process. There may be many applicants for an opening, particularly if the job was advertised or is reasonably attractive in some way. Employers will try to find out if you want more money than they are willing to pay. If so, they figure that, if hired, you may soon leave for a better paying job. That is the reason for my first rule regarding salary negotiations:

FARR'S SALARY NEGOTIATION RULE 1

Never talk money until after they decide they want you. It is not to your advantage to discuss salary early in the interviewing process. Your best position is to use techniques that are likely to satisfy a curious employer without giving a specific dollar amount.

Some Preliminary Things You Can Say to Delay

Here are a few ways you could respond to an initial interview inquiry about your pay expectations:

- "What salary range do you pay for positions with similar requirements?"
- "I'm very interested in the position and my salary would be negotiable."
- "Tell me what you have in mind for the salary range."
- "I am interested in the job and would consider any reasonable offer you might make."

Quick Tip

"Employers are anxious to know how your joining the organization will impact their bottom line, and they'll try to get to the subject as soon as possible," says Doug Matthews, managing director of Right Associates' Cincinnati office, an executive outplacement firm. Salary issues are the main reasons candidates are knocked out of the running during the screening process, according to outplacement industry surveys. In fact, responding appropriately to salary questions can get you past screening interviewers, who rarely have authority to negotiate salaries, and in front of decision-makers with whom the real negotiations take place.

So, always defer the question as many times as you have to until you are sure it's the real thing and not just part of a screening process. Then, when the timing is right, maneuver the interviewer into naming the starting point. Just remember the most important rule: The one who speaks first loses.

With a bit of luck, stall tactics such as these will get the employer to tell you the salary range or at least delay further discussion until later, when it matters. If that doesn't work and the employer still insists on knowing your salary expectations, there are still some things you can do. Which leads me to the second rule of negotiation.

Farr's Salary Negotiation Rule #2

It is not wise to approach an interview without being prepared for discussions of pay. While it may take a bit of research, it is essential that you know what an employer is likely to pay.

FARR'S SALARY NEGOTIATION RULE 2

> *Know in advance the probable salary range for similar jobs in similar organizations.*

The trick here is to think in terms of a wide *range* in salary, rather than a particular number. It is absolutely essential that you know how much others in a similar position are being paid. Larger organizations tend to pay more than smaller ones and various areas of the country differ greatly in pay scales. Find out the general range that jobs of this sort are likely to pay in your area. That information is relatively easy to obtain; all it may take is asking those who work in similar jobs or a trip to the library.

Thinking in terms of salary ranges makes sense. Back in chapter 11, you did an activi-

Quick Tip

The current edition of the Occupational Outlook Handbook *indicates that the average annual salary for all secretaries is $26,700. But it also points out that pay varies considerably based on skill, experience, and level of responsibility. Pay ranged from $20,000 to $36,000 for experienced secretaries—a very wide range. Beginning secretaries often earn less, with the federal government paying $16,400 a year for inexperienced secretaries. And, of course, some parts of the country pay less than other areas. Getting a realistic sense of what a given employer is likely to pay for a specific job is most important—and you need to know this information before you go in to an interview.*

ty where you were asked to figure out your preferred level of compensation. You were asked to define the minimum you were willing to accept, and then define an acceptable or probable range. If you don't remember what you decided back there, this might be a good time to review that information. Knowing what you really want in salary (as well as what you are willing to accept) must be decided in advance.

Farr's Salary Negotiation Rule #3

Let's assume that you have done your homework and you know a range that you are likely to be offered for a given job in your area. And let's also assume that you run into an interviewer who insists on knowing how much you expect to be paid. If this happens, I suggest negotiation rule #3:

FARR'S SALARY NEGOTIATION RULE 3

> *Always bracket your stated salary range to begin within the employer's probable salary range and end a bit above what you expect to settle for.*

Quick Alert

WHAT CAN HAPPEN IF YOU ARE NOT PREPARED

Even if you have a good idea of how much a job might pay, it is easy for you to get trapped into making a very costly mistake.

For example, suppose that the employer is expecting to pay someone

**Quick
Tip**

*Chapter 19 provides tips on research-
ing pay rates for various jobs. It also
includes a list of 250 jobs and the
salary ranges you can expect for
each. These jobs cover about 85 percent of the workforce, and the list will
give you a good place to start
researching what salary to expect for
various jobs.*

about $25,000 a year. Your research indicates
that most jobs of this type pay between
$22,000 and $29,000 a year. Let's also
assume that you have run into an interviewer
who insists on your revealing your pay expectations in the first interview.

IF YOU GO HIGH:

You want to be a clever negotiator, so you say
you were hoping for $30,000. You figure that
doing so will make them think you are not an
easy target and will encourage them to make
a higher offer later. Wrong: In many cases,
saying this will probably get you eliminated
from consideration.

IF YOU GO LOW:

If you say you would take $22,000 one of
two things could happen.

1. You could get hired at $22,000 a year, probably making that response the
   most expensive two seconds in your entire life or;

2. The employer may keep looking for someone else, because you must only be
   worth $22,000 and they desire someone who is "worth more."

Once again, questions about pay during the early phases of the interviewing process
are designed to help the employer either eliminate you from consideration or save
money at your expense. You could get lucky and name the salary they had in mind,
but the stakes are too high for me to recommend that approach. Your best bet is to be
informed!

**Quick
Reference**

SOME EXAMPLES OF BRACKETING

In the example above, you figured that the probable range for the salary
would be from $22,000 to $29,000. That is a wide range but you could
cover it by saying:

"I was looking for a salary in the mid- to upper twenties."

This response avoids mentioning a specific salary, and it covers a *very*
wide range.

Quick Reference

Think about it: If you were an employer and someone responded this way, how might you react? Most employers will take a moment to consider the response and, after doing so, will often conclude that your range is in the same one that they are considering. The particular number the firm has in mind just happens to be $25,000 and your response "brackets" that figure. The impasse is over and you can both get on with the interview. You win and they don't lose.

You can use the same strategy for any salary bracket you may be considering. For example, if you want $28,000 a year and their range is $25,000 to $33,000, you could say "A salary in the mid-twenties to low thirties." The same bracketing techniques can be used with any salary figure. Below are a few examples to give you an idea of how this might work for your particular situation.

SOME EXAMPLES OF BRACKETING

They are thinking:	You Say:
About $15,000 a year	Mid- to upper teens
$27,500 to $32,000, depending on experience	Mid-twenties to low thirties
Mid-thirties	Mid- to upper thirties
$38,000 to $42,000	High thirties to mid-forties
$150,000 to $400,000	Low to mid-six figures

THE BRACKETING TECHNIQUE CAN RESULT IN HIGHER PAY

OK, that last example was a stretch, but you can see how the bracketing principle can work. Using this technique will help you avoid having to name a specific figure that could get you screened out, or that might result in a low offer later. While it won't work in each and every situation, bracketing can often delay your discussion of salary until it counts—after the company decides it wants to hire you.

Farr's Salary Negotiation Rule #4

Avoiding early discussion of pay has another very important benefit. Talking in terms of brackets that extend a bit above what the employer was likely to consider often results in one of two positive outcomes:

1. If you are offered the job, you are likely to get offered more than they (or you) may have originally been willing to consider.

2. It gives you the option of negotiating your salary when it matters most—after they want you.

Which brings me to rule #4:

FARR'S SALARY NEGOTIATION RULE 4

> *Never say "no" to a job offer either before it is made or within 24 hours afterwards.*

Quick Fact

Too often, people lose the ability to negotiate salary because they mishandle the offer or its discussion. Going back to the original example, let's assume that an initial interview does discuss salary. You had decided in advance that you really wanted to earn about $25,000 a year. Using the bracketing technique correctly, you say you would accept offers in the range from the mid- to upper twenties. In response, the employer then tells you that it wanted to pay about $23,000. Because that is below what you had hoped for, you display some subtle signs of disappointment. An employer just might notice that reaction and decide to keep looking for someone who would be delighted with the $25,000 it was actually willing to pay. This is sad, because if you had just had a bit more patience, you might have made a good fit. Perhaps that lost job would have turned out to be just the sort you had been looking for—a very nice job in all respects except the salary.

Had you handled things differently and not acted disappointed, you might have continued a pleasant chat, and the (now lost) employer would have gotten to know you as the wonderful person you are. She or he just might have been able to come up with a few thousand more, having discovered you were worth it.

To avoid all this, you might consider countering a lower-than-hoped-for offer by saying something like this: *"That is somewhat lower than I had hoped but this position does sound very interesting. If I were to consider this, what sorts of things could I do to quickly become more valuable to this organization?"*

Or, you might say that you would be happy to get more specific later, after you have both gotten to know each other better.

So, I hope you now see why you should *not* negotiate your pay too early in an interview. Only later, when they want you, are wages an appropriate topic. Remember that a discussion of salary is not necessarily a job offer. More often, it is an attempt to screen you out.

SOME ADDITIONAL NEGOTIATION TIPS FROM EXPERTS

Quick Reference

Now that I've reviewed the basics of what you need to know about the salary negotiation process, here are a variety of additional tips from me and others.

> **"**Be assured that the interviewer will make every effort to discover your acceptable salary.**"**

SNEAKY WAYS THE SALARY ISSUE CROPS UP

There are a host of ways an employer will strive to discover your acceptable salary, and thus force you to speak first. Classified ads are notorious for demanding that respondents list their salary requirements. While I don't think highly of responding to want ads via mail, sometimes your efforts are rewarded. If you feel that a particular ad is a good bet, indicate that your salary requirements are open to negotiation. Some cover letters go so far as to state that the subject shouldn't prove to be a barrier to a mutually satisfactory relationship—a phrase I think appropriate if there is any hint you may be overqualified for the job.

Next, an employer may try to trick you on the standard job application. Almost all of these forms have blanks that not only ask what salary you are expecting, but what dollar figures you previously made. Doug Matthews of Right Associates says, "In many cases, your most recent earnings may not be relevant to the value of the new position. Scope of responsibility, the organization's culture and size, risk, location, industry segment, and competition can vary greatly." Plan to fill in the blank concerning current expectations with the word *negotiable*, and enter "confidential pending employment" in the spaces for your previous salaries.

Be assured that the interviewer will attempt to wrangle this information from you early in the screening process. The question often is phrased in a casual tone and comes in many forms. Among the more common:

"What is your current compensation?"

"What are your salary requirements?"

"How much do you need to live on?"

"We're offering $X amount for this position. Is this acceptable to you?"

This last question is a clever trick. While it does reveal the employer's position to some extent, your answer also paints you into a corner from which there can be no retreat.

Quick Case Study

Here is what happened to one unfortunate gentleman who, wishing to remain agreeable and work out the specifics later, indicated that the amount his interviewer quoted was fine. When he attempted to up the ante at hiring time, the employer balked, claiming that if that salary had been acceptable at the beginning of the week, it was certainly good enough now.

**Quick
Reference**

TECHNIQUES TO DELAY DISCUSSION OF PAY UNTIL LATER, WHEN IT MATTERS

Never, ever, ever mention a dollar figure until you are sure you're talking to the decision-maker and not a go-between. Only the person you will work for directly has the power to say "yea" or "nay" to your requests and make counteroffers. The pressured candidate's natural response to any direct question is to volunteer information (in this case a dollar figure). Instead, practice your version of these answers:

✔ **"What is your current compensation?"** Tom Jackson, author of *Interview Express*, offers this reply: "In my last job, I was paid below the market price for my skills. I was willing to accept this for awhile because it gave me the opportunity to learn and develop. Now I am very clear about the value I can offer to an employer and I want my salary to be competitive."

If you feel this type of answer does not reflect your situation, smile and politely reply, "I didn't realize we were ready to discuss salary so soon. I'd feel more comfortable tabling this subject until we are both sure we have a fit."

You might try another effective tactic that Bernard Haldane Associates recommends in its book, *Job and Career Building*: offer a future-oriented salary figure. The conversation would run something like this: "The job you have described, if carried out in a superior manner, should be worth about $30,000 in three or four years." Most employers don't hesitate to agree because you are talking about a time in the future to work up to that figure. After you reach an agreement, say, "Since we agree that the job will be worth $30,000 in three or four years, I'm content to leave the starting salary up to you. What do you think would be a reasonable figure?"

Quick
Reference

According to the same book, demonstrating your high performance and income expectations raises the interviewer's sights and motivates him or her to offer a reasonable starting figure.

✔ **"What are your salary requirements?"** Matthews recommends replying: "Compensation is an important issue. However, my goal is to explore positions that allow me to maximize my strengths and solve significant challenges within an organization. I'm looking for a strong fit between my skills and specific company needs. When that happens, I'm certain the compensation issue will fall into place. Could you give me an idea of the range you've established for this position?"

> **❝***Job seekers who press for more money based on personal needs often create a bad impression.***❞**

If the interviewer provides a range, remain quiet for a few seconds, then say that the upper end of the range is in your ballpark and that you would like to learn more about the position's responsibilities. Notice that you did not agree to anything, and avoided the "Is this OK?" bait discussed earlier.

Should the interviewer push for salary requirements, Matthews advises parrying, "I understand the need to discuss specific compensation requirements. However, it might be more effective for me to know how your organization values this position. I'm certain you have ranges for various levels within the organization that are fair, based on experience, responsibility, and contribution. I'd be pleased to work within those ranges. If this is a new position, I'd like to discuss your needs further. Then I might be able to provide a proposal that would help us arrive at an appropriate compensation figure."

Yes, that is a mouthful. If you believe that type of answer is too complex for your needs, simply say, "I hesitate to disclose compensation figures because this position contains elements that may differ from my recent position. We may be comparing apples and oranges. Let's table this subject until we're both more comfortable with making an employment offer."

✔ **"How much do you need to live on?"** This appears to be such an innocent and caring question on the surface. Don't be fooled: a literal answer is not in your best interest, as it takes the focus away from how much you are worth and concentrates instead on whether you could do better with your finances. Unfortunately, some employers will use any information you provide to your disadvantage.

Job seekers who press for more money based on their personal needs or wants rather than their value to an employer will often create a bad impression. The employer might think "Why should I believe that you are responsible and stable if you have financial problems of your own making?" or "My dream of traveling Europe is just as important as your desire to buy a fishing boat." The most sensitive employers may try to help you find ways to reduce your living expenses by suggesting cheaper restaurants, lower-rent apartments, loan consolidation services, etc. Remember, this is a virtual stranger you are dealing with, and it's completely inappropriate to ask this person to sympathize with your personal value judgments. Instead, base a vague answer on your ability to do the job. Haldane's example: "I can be quite flexible if I have to be. Money isn't my highest priority. But I feel I have quite a lot to offer to an organization like yours. I'd like my salary to be based on my value to you. I'm sure you have a fair income structure for this kind of job—how much do you have in mind?"

WHAT TO SAY WHEN IT'S TIME TO GET SERIOUS

Serious negotiation often begins only after you've been invited to several interviews. Some employers come right out and say, "We'd like to offer you the position provided we can come to a salary agreement." Again, let the employer open up the bidding.

Quick Case Study

▲ Salary negotiations often begin on the telephone, so keep a script handy and your wits about you to avoid mistakes such as this one: A job seeker's husband broke his leg one evening playing basketball, and the emergency room physician didn't have enough experience to set the difficult break that night. So, the next morning, she rushed her husband to a specialist and got in line behind those with appointments. Exasperated with this unexpected delay, she used the pay phone to check her answering machine for messages. There was only one, but it was "The Call" she had been waiting the entire week to receive. In her excitement she immediately called to accept the job and agreed to start right away. The problem came when the employer said, "I did tell you this job paid $17,000, didn't I?" With the whole waiting room listening in, she negotiated a higher rate and all ended well—but it could have ended badly.

▲ Sabeth suggests to her clients seeking business communication advice that they begin the salary conversation by asking, "What's the best you can do?" This approach assumes the employer will treat you honestly, and most people live up to the standards you set for them. However, don't make the grave mistake of assuming the figure quoted is non-negotiable. It simply gives you a framework for what the employer believes is your top value. It's up to you to convince the company to rethink that position.

Quick Fact

ONCE A REAL OFFER IS MADE

It can be a mistake to accept a reasonable offer right away. Even if it is acceptable, it is often wise to discuss the offer with others before saying yes. Here is one way to delay until you can give the offer some thought:

"Thank you for the offer. The position is very much what I wanted in many ways and I am delighted at your interest. This is an important decision for me and I would like some time to consider your offer."

Even if their offer is an insult, do not break their office furniture and stamp out. Be nice (any job offer is good for your ego when you get to turn it down). At worst, you can call them tomorrow and say:

"I am flattered by your job offer, but feel that it would not be fair of me to accept. The salary is lower than I would like and that is the one reason I cannot accept it. Perhaps you could reconsider your offer or keep me in mind for future openings that might allow me to be worth more to you?"

Quick Fact

Even as you say no, leave the door open to keep negotiating. If the employer wants you, they may be willing to meet your terms. It happens more than you might imagine.

Do *not* use the above example as a technique to get a higher wage. Understand that once you say "no" to their offer, the deal *is* off. You must be willing to lose that job forever.

Quick Alert

DON'T SAY "NO" TOO SOON

Never, never turn down a job offer in an interview! Let's say that you get an offer at half the salary you expected. Avoid the temptation to turn the offer down there and then. Instead say:

"Thank you for your offer. I am flattered that you think I can do the job. Because this decision is so important to me, I would like to consider your offer and get back with you within two days."

Leave, and see if you change your mind. If not, call back and say, in effect:

"I've given your offer considerable thought and feel that I just can't take it at the salary you've offered. Is there any way that I could be paid more, in the range of _____?"

If the employer cannot meet your salary needs, say thank you again, and let him or her know you are interested in future openings within your salary range. Then, stay in touch. You never know …

SAYING "YES"

As with saying "no" too quickly, take time to think about accepting a job, too. If you do want it, do not jeopardize obtaining it with unreasonable demands. Ask for 24 hours to consider your decision and, when calling back, consider negotiating for something reasonable. A bit more money, every other Tuesday afternoon off, or some other benefit would be nice if you can get it easily. If there is a problem with your request, make it very clear that you want the job anyway.

THEY OFFER, YOU WANT IT—NOW IT'S TIME TO NEGOTIATE!

The employer you've spent the past two weeks wooing has opened the bidding with a lukewarm figure—one that would certainly pay your bills and yet is somewhat below what you feel you are worth. But exactly how should you ask for more? And since you aren't a professional athlete with a savvy manager to wheel and deal the details, isn't the time limit on this opportunity short?

Quick Tip

Always heed the advice Tom Jackson dishes out in Interview Express: *Negotiations should never be angry or emotional, no matter how much pressure there is on either side. Assert your value so that the employer will view you as a highly worthwhile addition rather than as someone who is overpriced.*

EVERYTHING HAS ITS PRICE

At this stage of the game you're in tune with industry standards and local pay ranges, and have correctly "encouraged" the interviewer to name the opening dollar figure. But there's one final ingredient you must have squared away before you make a counteroffer: How much cash and fringe benefits will it take to make you accept the position?

Michael Schatzki, owner of the New Jersey-based Negotiation Dynamics, recommends that you know your worst case or Least Acceptable Settlement (LAS) and your best possible result or Maximum Supportable Position (MSP)—numbers you can arrive at through your research on the industry and a serious study of your personal financial position. Plan to start the bidding at your MSP, but should the offer fail to rise above your LAS, continue job hunting.

Quick Case Study

....

▲ Imagine Tim Flanagan's shock when, at his third interview with a high-tech Boston company, officials there proposed a salary that was less than half of what he was expecting.

▲ "I was speechless," Flanagan told *USAir* magazine. It took the executive recruiter who arranged the introduction to restart Flanagan's heart and teach him Interview Basics 101: The company expects job candidates to bargain.

▲ Flanagan eventually talked the firm into going up in salary while he came down in his expectations. And even that personal concession had its trade-off—he convinced the company to throw in an extra week of vacation, a company car, and a cash bonus contingent on his performance. The company didn't walk away from the table feeling downtrodden or resentful either—it got a gentleman whose skills merited a promotion to chief of public relations in only three years. Therein lies the first key to negotiation: You must make sure your requests set up a win-win situation for both parties.

Quick Reminder

Never assume the salary range is fixed, even if the interviewer insists that's the case. Bernard Haldane Associates cites a wonderful example in its *Job and Career Building* book. A client with a Ph.D. from Harvard University was told that the salary range for the type of position he was being offered was fixed. The officials even handed him a booklet that explained the range. He studied the booklet politely. He then said he thought this to be a very sound compensation policy, but had they ever had a person of his background (and a Ph.D. from Harvard) in that position? Well, the spokesperson stalled, no. The savvy applicant suggested that he didn't really fit into any of the preprinted categories and that he would like to discuss establishing a new category or expanding an existing one. After two more meetings, the company created a special income category and the man received a much higher offer when they returned to the bargaining table.

Quick Reference

STEP-BY-STEP NEGOTIATION INSTRUCTIONS

As *Job and Career Building* points out, the first number the interviewer mentions is rarely the highest possible salary offer, but in the spirit of the

**Quick
Reference**

negotiating game, you really can't blurt that out to the person on the other side of the table. So when that initial salary figure is mentioned, your first reaction must be silence. According to authors Richard Germann and Peter Arnold, your silence signals two things: a) you are carefully considering the offer, and b) you are not satisfied with it. Words at this moment weaken your position, because they require the interviewer to defend his or her offer. In fact, Haldane Associates has discovered that in more than 50 percent of all situations where silence is used, the interviewers cough up a higher figure without further discussion!

However, when a better offer isn't immediately forthcoming, one of two things will happen: The interviewer will either explain the offer or ask for your reaction. In the first instance, the *Job and Career Building* authors recommend you listen politely but continue your thoughtful silence as long as necessary. In the latter case, indicate that you are enthusiastic about the job, but the offer is on the modest side. Then suggest continuing the discussion at another meeting—the following day, if possible.

Unfortunately many job candidates interpret this tactic as "playing hard to get." Haldane Associates scoffs at this label, and so should you. In fact, this consulting firm has interviewed a number of employers who have stated that employees who handle themselves well during their salary negotiations were treated with greater respect and given more opportunities to advance within the organization.

CALLING IT QUITS

Several clues tip you off to the fact that the employer has extended its best possible salary package. If the same figure is repeated after a day or two break, chances are good it won't change. Perhaps the employer may begin tossing in additional benefits without changing the figure, again signaling the price is firm.

Whether or not you are satisfied with the salary eventually settled upon, don't forget Haldane Associates' most valuable advice: Always ask for a commitment to review your salary in six months, based on your demonstrated value.

Then begin hashing out these areas:

- Stock options
- Vacation time
- Performance bonuses
- Flexible time (work four 10-hour days and take Fridays off; work 10 A.M. to 6:00 P.M. to avoid rush hours; or time-share)
- Parking privileges
- Company car
- Geographic location, if there is more than one office

Quick Fact

According to the International Association of Corporate and Professional Recruiters Inc., financial incentives, equity opportunity, and geographic location rank as the top three motivating factors respectively in evaluating a job offer in the '90s. Time flexibility, health insurance policies, and maternal/paternal leave policies ranked fourth through sixth.

Germann and Arnold list the following considerations that many people ignore in the rush to accept or reject a job offer:

- Is the job description (duties, responsibilities, authority) clear?
- What is the employer's attitude toward advancement?
- Who will you be working with?

If you don't have a straight answer yet for these questions, don't make a move you could regret. Instead, keep plugging away until the picture comes into clear focus. And before you shake hands to seal the deal, ask for 24 hours to think it over. Such careful thought and responsible consideration can only be viewed as professional, and will earn the respect of a potential employer.

19

RESEARCHING WHAT OTHERS EARN IN SIMILAR POSITIONS— PLUS AVERAGE EARNINGS FOR HUNDREDS OF JOBS

Quick Tip

This chapter is divided into two sections. The first provides tips for researching pay for various positions including specific references. The second section provides a table that gives you the approximate earnings for the most popular jobs in the workforce. While the listed jobs include those you are most likely to seek, pay ranges do differ widely for a variety of reasons, so do use the information with caution.

You have already learned a variety of good techniques for negotiating your pay, but their effective use assumes that you know in advance the prevailing pay scale for the jobs you want. While you often won't know precisely how much a particular employer might pay, some quick research will often give you a good idea. This chapter reviews several of the researching techniques presented earlier and presents a few additional ones.

THE TOP EXCUSE FOR AVOIDING RESEARCH

When asked to relate the number one mistake job candidates make during the negotiation process, most employers say it is a failure to prepare. So, for those job seekers who take the time and effort to investigate salary ranges and benefits rather than simply "winging it," the rewards are worth every second of research. This chapter gives you a handle on where to locate such information quickly and painlessly.

The reasons why individuals fail to prepare for salary negotiations—"I didn't realize the subject would come up so quickly and didn't have time to prepare," "I could tell the interviewer wasn't going to budge, and I didn't want to blow the opportunity,"—can often be boiled down to one excuse: Most of us are uncomfortable putting a dollar value on our skills.

"The reason many of us are hesitant to take our foot off the brake, get off our butts and let people know who we are and what we do well is because we feel it is tasteless and unprofessional to do so," says behavioral scientist George Dudley. "We reached that conclusion because the people who have done it in the past are so oily. 'If I have to be like them to do that,' the logic runs, 'then I don't want to do it.'"

Michael Schatzki, of Negotiation Dynamics, has an even more colorful way of describing job seekers' lack of enthusiasm for salary negotiations. "They see it as high stakes, table-pounding, your worst nightmare of a used-car salesman, and it all seems negative," he comments.

In the business world, modesty will get you nowhere. There is nothing shameful about asking for the amount of money you are worth. In fact, in today's environment, knowing yourself and your capabilities is a valuable commodity in itself.

SOURCES OF INFORMATION ON SALARY AND WAGES

Like other parts of the job search process, the key to salary negotiations is preparation. It is very important for you to do your research before you begin negotiations. In order to determine the salary you are willing to accept, investigate the salary range someone with your skills and experience can expect to receive. Here are some of the best sources of information.

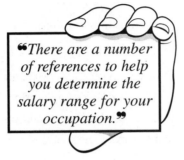

> **"***There are a number of references to help you determine the salary range for your occupation.***"**

REFERENCE BOOKS

Your local library or bookstore should have a number of references to help you determine the salary range for the occupation you are considering. A list of such references follows. Those marked with an asterisk are most likely to be available through a library or bookstore. Others are more specialized and may only be available through larger libraries. Ask your librarian for assistance as most libraries provide a variety of references that may not be listed here.

✎ *The *Occupational Outlook Handbook* and *America's Top 300 Jobs*. Both books contain the same information and are updated every two years based on information from the U.S. Department of Labor. I mentioned these books earlier as an important source of information on jobs. Both include starting and average pay rates for most larger jobs. For example, the current editions indicate that earnings for engineering technicians range from $18,900 to $22,600 for entry-level positions to $28,800 for those with more experience and the ability to work with little supervision. Those in supervisory and senior-level jobs earn more than $40,000 a year. These references also indicate that federal government pay begins at $14,600 to $18,300, depending on training and experience, but that the average pay for all engineering t echnicians working for the federal government is $37,337. This higher average rate is due, apparently, to the higher pay received by the more experienced and supervisory employees.

Use detailed information such as this to know what pay to expect for various jobs at differing levels of experience.

Career Guide to America's Top Industries. This book includes information on about 60 major industries. Written mainly for job seekers, it provides a description of each industry, employment projections, working conditions, typical occupations, training and advancement, outlook for industry growth, and earnings information.

For example, earnings information in the drug manufacturing industry indicates that workers there have higher than average earnings, averaging $831 a week ($43,000 a year) compared to $454 a week ($23,672 a year) for all industries. Production workers earn an average of $540 a week ($28,157 a year) compared to $346 ($18,041 a year) for all industries. As you can see, there can be substantial earnings differences among industries, even for the same types of work. It is important to know about these differences in advance so that you are not unpleasantly surprised. On the other hand, you can also benefit from your industry research by looking for jobs in industries that tend to pay better.

Career Connection for College Education and the *Career Connection for Technical Education.* Both books are by Fred Rowe and each allows you to look up jobs related to major courses of study. Information on the average earnings for each of these jobs is included, and this provides a useful starting point for those considering additional education—as well as information that can prove valuable in salary negotiations.

America's Federal Jobs. This book provides information on all major divisions of the federal government including the types of

**Quick
Reference**

positions available, college training sought, and pay ranges for each job, plus many additional details.

✎ *State and Metropolitan Area Data Book.* This is a specialized book published by the U.S. Department of Commerce. It compiles statistical data from many public and private agencies, and includes unemployment rates, rate of employment growth, and population growth for every state. Also presented is a vast amount of data on employment and income for metropolitan areas across the country.

✎ *White Collar Pay: Private Goods-Producing Industries.* Produced by the U.S. Department of Labor's Bureau of Labor Statistics, this is a good source of salary information for white collar jobs in manufacturing.

✎ *AMS Office, Professional and Data Processing Salaries Report.* (Administrative Management Society, Washington D.C.). Provided are salary distributions for 40 different occupations, many of which are professional. Subdivisions include company size, type of business, region of the country, and 41 different metropolitan areas.

✎ *American Salaries and Wages Survey* (Gale Research, Detroit). This title gives detailed information on salaries and wages for thousands of jobs. Data is subdivided geographically. It also gives cost-of-living data for selected areas, which is very helpful in determining what the salary differences really mean. Finally, it provides information on numbers employed in each occupation, along with projected changes.

✎ **American Almanac of Jobs and Salaries* (Avon Books, NY). This title provides information on wages for specific occupations and job groups, many of which are professional and white collar. It also presents trends in employment and wages.

PROFESSIONAL ASSOCIATIONS

There are associations for virtually every occupation or industry you can imagine—and some that you can't imagine. Most of the larger ones conduct salary surveys on an annual basis, and this information is available to members and, sometimes, in their publications. If you can get back issues of an association's journals or newsletters, they can provide excellent information on trends, including pay rates. Consider joining to get access to this information, as well as access to local members with whom you can network.

GETTING LOCAL INFORMATION

▼▼

Local pay rates can differ substantially from national averages; starting wages are often substantially under those for experienced workers; some industries pay better than others; and smaller organizations often pay less than larger ones. For these reasons, it is important for you to find out prevailing pay rates for jobs similar to those you seek. Following are some additional sources of this information.

Professional associations: Once again, joining one or more professional associations related to your field often will allow you to obtain salary information collected for their members. More importantly, it also gives you sources of local contacts. You can ask these people for help in determining local pay rates—and they can often help you with job leads as well.

Your network: Talk to colleagues in your professional network. Although people frequently don't want to tell you what they personally are making, usually they are willing to talk about salary ranges. Ask colleagues, based on their experience, what salary range you might expect for the position.

Job search centers: These centers (which can be found in schools; libraries; community centers; or as part of federal, state, or local government programs) frequently keep salary information on hand.

Your past experience: If you are applying for a job in a field in which you have experience, you probably have a good idea of what someone with your skills and abilities should be paid. Think about your past salary. Unless the job you are applying for requires a dramatically different amount of responsibility than your former position, your previous salary is definitely a starting point for negotiations.

▲▲

Does Education Pay Off?

▲ Americans today invest more time than ever and go to considerable expense to acquire an education. Is the return worth the investment? Yes, when you look at statistics published by the Labor Department in 1992 and shown in the table below.

EDUCATION LEVEL	AVG. MONTHLY EARNINGS	PERCENT PREMIUM OVER HIGH SCHOOL GRADUATES
High school graduate	921	—
Some college but no degree	1,088	18
Postsecondary vocational school	1,088	18
Associate degree	1,458	58
Bachelor's degree	1,829	99
Master's degree	2,378	158
Doctorate	3,637	295
Professional	4,003	335

Quick Tip

When you're stuck for local sources to determine salary ranges, try calling the following agencies:

• Chamber of Commerce, especially the economic development division, which may have statistics on what individual companies are paying.

• Area business organizations such as Women in Communications or Society for Retired Executives.

• Area government assistance programs such as the Small Business Association.

The trend continues today. Researchers Martha Farnsworth Riche and Kelvin Pollard analyzed census data and discovered that the average income for U.S. women increased by 30 percent from 1980 to 1990. A poll by executive search firm Paul Ray Berndtson and Cornell University's Center for Advanced Human Resource Studies in April 1994 found that senior executives with Ivy League School degrees earned $32,581 more per year and had significantly more promotions than managers who graduated from other universities. The survey, which questioned 3,500 executives, found a school's reputation helped salary and career advancement well after graduation.

PAY RATES FOR THE TOP 250 JOBS

The information that follows provides median weekly earnings for about 250 occupations as reported by the U.S. Department of Labor in 1994. The occupations cover more than 85 percent of the workforce and the information is a useful starting point for salary negotiations. It is important, however, to understand the limitations of these figures. For one thing, remember that the median means that one half of all workers in these occupations earned more and one half earned less. Workers with less experience, for example, will tend to earn less than the median. Those with more experience earn significantly more than the listed rate. The pay rates are also based on national surveys, and your local rates can differ significantly. Even so, this table should provide you with a good starting point for your research—and ample ammunition for salary negotiations.

The occupations are arranged into groupings of related jobs. This allows you to quickly locate jobs that are most closely related to your interests and to identify other jobs—requiring similar skills—that may pay somewhat more. You should look through the entire list for jobs for which you may be qualified but may have previously overlooked.

Most of the jobs listed here are described in considerable detail in the *Occupational Outlook Handbook* and *America's Top 300 Jobs*. I have mentioned these books on several occasions, including earlier in this chapter, and again I encourage you to refer to them for more detailed information on the job as well as the pay and other details.

OCCUPATIONAL GROUPINGS OR SPECIFIC JOB	MEDIAN WEEKLY EARNINGS
Managerial and Professional Specialty	**$ 675**
Executive, administrative, and managerial	664
Administrators and officials, public administration	724
Administrators, public services	733
Financial managers	776
Personnel and labor relations managers	723
Purchasing managers	773
Managers, marketing, advertising, and public relations	851
Administrators, education and related fields	778
Managers, medicine and health	692
Managers, food serving and lodging establishments	407
Managers, properties and real estate	511
Management-related occupations	597
Accountants and auditors	612
Underwriters	595

Other financial officers	670
Management analysts	775
Personnel, training and labor relations specialists	598
Buyers, wholesale and retail trade except farm products	495
Construction inspectors	588
Inspectors and compliance officers, except construction	671

Professional Specialty **682**

Engineers, architects, and surveyors	902
Architects	694
Engineers	911
Aerospace engineers	1008
Chemical engineers	996
Civil engineers	867
Electrical and electronic engineers	941
Industrial engineers	861
Mechanical engineers	895
Mathematical and computer scientists	816
Computer systems analysts and scientists	821
Operations and systems researchers and analysts	793
Natural scientists	722
Chemists, except biochemists	745
Biological and life scientists	626
Medical scientists	631
Health diagnosing occupations	994
Physicians	1019
Health assessment and treating occupations	687
Registered nurses	687
Pharmacists	913
Dietitians	495
Therapists	633
Respirator therapists	572
Physical therapists	716
Speech therapists	683
Teachers, college and university	795
Teachers, except college and university	585
Teachers, prekindergarten and kindergarten	353

Teachers, elementary school	596
Teachers, secondary school	625
Teachers, special education	596
Counselors, educational and vocational	621
Librarians archivists and curators	577
Librarians	567
Social scientists and urban planners	670
Economists	793
Psychologists	583
Social, recreation and religious workers	492
Social workers	511
Recreation workers	259
Clergy	499
Lawyers and judges	1170
Lawyers	1164
Writers, artists, entertainers, and athletes	574
Technical writers	720
Designers	570
Actors and directors	601
Painters, sculptors, craft artists, and artist printmakers	497
Photographers	450
Editors and reporters	574
Public relations specialists	613

Technical, Sales and Administrative Support **419**

Technicians and related support	528
Health technologists and technicians	458
Clinical laboratory technologists and technicians	533
Health record technologists and technicians	336
Radiological technicians	585
Licensed practical nurses	435
Engineering and related technologists and technicians	550
Electrical and electronic technicians	591
Drafting occupations	528
Surveying and mapping technicians	470
Science technicians	501

Biological technicians   446
Chemical technicians   577
Technicians, except health,
  engineering, and science   658
Airplane pilots and
  navigators   1086
Computer programmers   747
Legal assistants   536

Sales Occupations   **457**
Supervisors and proprietors   495
Sales representatives, finance
  and business services   604
Insurance sales   565
Real estate sales   610
Securities and financial
  services sales   783
Advertising and related sales   590
Sales occupations, other
  business services   577
Sales representatives
  commodities, except retail   625
Sales workers, retail and
  personal services   281
Sales workers, motor vehicles
  and boats   496
Sales workers, apparel   262
Sales workers furniture and
  home furnishings   381
Sales workers, radio, television,
  hi-fi, and appliances   448
Sales workers, hardware
  and building supplies   361
Sales workers, parts   347
Sales workers, other
  commodities   268
Sales counter clerks   288
Cashiers   226
Street and door-to-door
  workers   449

**Administrative Support,
including Clerical**   **392**
Supervisors   585
General office   548
Financial records processing   623
Distribution, scheduling, and
  adjusting clerks   597
Computer equipment operators   435

Computer operators   437
Secretaries, stenographers,
  and typists   385
Secretaries   386
Stenographers   448
Typists   366
Information clerks   329
Interviewers   359
Hotel clerks   263
Transportation ticket and
  reservation agents   417
Receptionists   316
Records processing, except
  financial   376
Order clerks   478
Personnel clerks, except
  payroll and timekeeping   373
File clerks   310
Records clerks   383
Financial records processing   380
Bookkeepers, accounting,
  and auditing clerks   375
Payroll and timekeeping
  clerks   411
Billing clerks   361
Billing, posting, and
  calculating machine
  operators   397
Duplicating, mail and other
  office machine operators   324
Communications equipment
  operators   385
Telephone operators   386
Mail and message distributing   585
Postal clerks, except mail
  carriers   612
Mail carriers, postal service   633
Mail clerks, except postal
  service   306
Messengers   365
Material (recording, scheduling,
  and distributing clerks)   392
Dispatchers   423
Production coordinators   513
Traffic, shipping, and
  receiving clerks   362
Stock and inventory clerks   386
Meter readers   471

Weighers, measurers,
checkers, and samplers 364
Expediters 354
Adjusters and investigators 412
Insurance adjusters,
examiners, and investigators 482
Investigators and adjusters,
except insurance 400
Eligibility clerks social welfare 416
Bill and account collectors 381
Miscellaneous administrative
support occupations 360
General office clerks 350
Bank tellers 292
Data-entry keyers 344
Teachers' aides 270

Service Occupations **293**

Private Household 187
Child care workers 152
Cleaners and servants 205
Protective Services 511
Supervisors 706
Police and detectives 750
Firefighting and fire prevention 614
Firefighting 619
Police and detectives 578
Police and detectives,
public service 632
Sheriffs, bailiffs, and other
law enforcement officers 524
Correctional institution officers 498
Guards 338
Guards and police, except
public service 344

Service occupations, except
private household and
protective services 271
Food preparation and
service occupations 243
Supervisors 314
Bartenders 289
Waiters and waitresses 230
Cooks, except
short order 251
Food counter, fountain,
and related occupations 199
Kitchen workers, food

preparation 235
Waiters' and waitresses'
assistants 213
Miscellaneous food
preparation occupations 218
Health service occupations 289
Dental assistants 325
Health aides, except
nursing 306
Nursing aides orderlies,
and attendants 281
Cleaning and building
service occupations 291
Supervisors 374
Maids and housemen 245
Janitors and cleaners 303
Personal service
occupations 279
Supervisors 342
Hairdressers and
cosmetologists 273
Attendants, amusement
and recreation
facilities 291
Public transportation
attendants 733
Early childhood
teacher's assistants 240

Precision Production,
Craft and Repair **501**

Mechanics and repairers 510
supervisors 667
Mechanics and repairers
except supervisors 504
Vehicle and mobile equipment
mechanics and repairers 475
Automobile mechanics 422
Bus, truck, and stationary
engine mechanics 479
Aircraft engine mechanics 628
Small engine repairers 389
Automobile body and
related repairers 407
Heavy equipment mechanics 539
Industrial machinery repairers 510
Electrical and electronic
equipment repairers 603

Electronic repairers, communications and industrial	517
Data processing equipment repairers	587
Telephone installers and repairers	664
Miscellaneous electrical and electronic repairers	603
Heating, air conditioning, and refrigeration mechanics	494
Miscellaneous mechanics and repairers	496
Office machine repairers	470
Millwrights	627
Construction Trades	495
Supervisors	634
Construction trades, except supervisors	477
Brickmasons and stonemasons	479
Carpenters	439
Drywall installers	399
Electricians	549
Electrical power installers and repairers	697
Painters, construction and maintenance	398
Plumbers, pipefitters, steamfitters, and apprentices	520
Concrete and terrazzo finishers	419
Insulation workers	477
Roofers	338
Extractive occupations	643
precision production occupations	490
Supervisors	573
Precision metalworking occupations	527
Tool and die makers	632
Machinists	512
Sheet-metal workers	519
Precision woodworking occupations	340
Precision textile, apparel, and furnishings machine workers	298

Precision workers, assorted materials	348
Electrical and electronic equipment assemblers	331
Precision food production occupations	348
Butchers and meat cutters	354
Bakers	344
Precision inspectors, testers, and related workers	517
Inspectors, testers, and graders	517
Plant and system operators	600
Water and sewage treatment plant operators	505
Power plant operators	682
Stationary engineers	581

Operators, Fabricators, and Laborers — **365**

Machine Operators, Assemblers, and Inspectors	348
Machine operators and tenders except precision	333
Metalworking and plastic working machine operators	410
Punching and stamping press machine operators	382
Grinding, abrading, buffing, and polishing machine operators	382
Metal and plastic processing machine operators	369
Molding and casting machine operators	361
Woodworking machine operators	333
Sawing machine operators	331
Printing machine operators	418
Printing press operators	427
Textile, apparel, and furnishings machine operators	247
Textile sewing machine operators	226
Pressing machine operators	248
Laundering and dry cleaning machine operators	251
Machine operators, assorted materials	366

Packaging and filling machine operators 290

Mixing and blending machine operators 407

Separating, filtering, and clarifying machine operators 622

Painting and paint spraying machine operators 383

Furnace, kiln, and oven operators, except food 497

Slicing and cutting machine operators 330

Photographic process machine operators 298

Fabricators, assemblers, and hand working occupations 376

Welders and cutters 453

Assemblers 342

Production inspectors, testers, samplers, and weighers 367

Production inspectors, checkers, and examiners 390

Production testers 448

Graders and sorters, except agricultural 282

Transportation and Material Moving Occupations **447**

Motor vehicle operators 437

Supervisors 584

Truck drivers 445

Drivers, sales workers 479

Bus drivers 403

Taxicab drivers and chauffeurs 311

Transportation occupations, except motor vehicles 715

Rail transportation 722

Water transportation 675

Material moving equipment operators 440

Operating engineers 503

Crane and tower operators 544

Excavating and loading machine operators 437

Grader, dozer, and scraper operators 423

Industrial truck and tractor equipment operators 390

Handlers, Equipment Cleaners, Helpers, and Laborers **312**

Helpers, construction and extractive occupations 293

Helpers, construction trades 290

Construction laborers 379

Freight stock and material handlers 307

Stock handlers and baggers 271

Machine feeders and offbearers 313

Garage and service station related occupations 246

Vehicle washers and equipment cleaners 268

Hand packers and packages 278

Laborers, except construction 321

Farming, Forestry, and Fishing **269**

Other agricultural and related occupations 263

Farm occupations, except managerial 248

Farm workers 246

Related agricultural occupations 277

Supervisors, related agricultural 401

Groundskeepers and gardeners, except farm 273

Animal caretakers, except farm 271

Forestry and logging occupations 356

Timber cutting and logging 359

More Good Books from JIST Works, Inc.

The Very Quick Job Search
2nd Edition
Get a Good Job in Less Time

By J. Michael Farr

This is the down-to-earth, focused-purely-on-getting-the-job alternative to *What Color Is Your Parachute?* The first edition of *The Very Quick Job Search* has been hailed as the best self-directed job search book available. It contains results-oriented methods proven to cut job search time in HALF. Updated, expanded, and redesigned, this revised edition of a JIST best-seller includes more resumes than the first edition, updated job search techniques, and information on electronic job search. Comprehensive and easy-to-read, *The Very Quick Job Search, 2nd Edition*, covers all major career planning and job search topics.

7 1/2 x 9 1/2, Paper, 320 pp.
ISBN 1-56370-181-2
$12.95   Order Code J1812

Other Information

- Updated information on the 250 most popular jobs
- New labor market research
- First edition has sold more than 50,000 copies

Look for these and other fine books from JIST Works, Inc. at your full service bookstore or call us for additional information

More Good Books from JIST Works, Inc.

The Quick Resume & Cover Letter Book
Write and Use an Effective Resume in Only One Day

By J. Michael Farr

7 1/2 x 9 1/2, Paper, 307 pp.

ISBN 1-56370-141-3

$9.95   Order Code RCLQG

First title in JIST's new *Quick Guides* series, by a best-selling author whose job search books have sold more than one million copies! Contains an "Instant Resume Worksheet" that enables job seekers to put together a basic, acceptable resume in less than one day. Provides helpful advice on creating job objectives, identifying skills, dealing with special situations, and getting a job. No matter what your employment history, read this book to discover how your resume can emphasize your strengths and diminish your weaknesses.

Other Information

- Contains more than 60 sample resumes and cover letters
- Logical structure makes information easy to locate
- Includes crucial career planning and job search sections
- Gives tips on using computers to develop superior resumes
- Advice on writing cover letters, thank-you notes, and other correspondence

Look for these and other fine books from JIST Works, Inc. at your full service bookstore or call us for additional information

More Good Books from JIST Works, Inc.

Gallery of Best Resumes
A Collection of Quality Resumes by Professional Resume Writers

by David F. Noble

A showcase collection of quality resumes for those seeking a job or changing careers. Contains outstanding examples of different types of resumes for a variety of occupations grouped by category, such as Accounting/Finance, Administrative Assistant/Secretary, Graduating/Graduated Student, Management, etc. Includes helpful tips and techniques consistently used in the best resumes. A set of sample resumes printed on high-quality paper stock is bound right into the book.

Other Information

- Contains more than 200 resumes and 25 companion cover letters written by members of the Professional Association of Resume Writers
- 101 best resume tips
- 30 tips for polishing cover letters

8 1/2 x 11, Paper, 368 pp.
ISBN 1-56370-144-8
$16.95 Order Code GBR

Look for these and other fine books from JIST Works, Inc. at your full service bookstore or call us for additional information

More Good Books from JIST Works, Inc.

The Resume Solution
2nd Edition
How to Write (and Use) a Resume That Gets Results
By David Swanson

8 1/2 x 11, Paper, 188 pp.
ISBN 1-56370-180-4
$9.95   Order Code J1804

The first edition of this book, published in 1990, quickly became a JIST best-seller. This revised second edition includes even more resume samples than the first, as well as resumes grouped by occupational categories, such as Administrative, Management, Sales, etc. This easy-to-use book provides a step-by-step approach to resume writing, clearly defines common problems, and provides tips for design and resume printing. *The Resume Solution* tells the TRUTH about how resumes are read and used. You will be able to write a superior resume that stands out from the competition after reading this book.

Other Information
- Proven JIST best-seller
- Many sample resumes, grouped by occupational category
- Numerous examples and worksheets in each resume section
- Includes strategies for more effective job seeking and successful interviews.

Look for these and other fine books from JIST Works, Inc. at your full service ⌐
or call us for additional information

More Good Books from JIST Works, Inc.

Occupational Outlook Handbook

The OOH is the most widely used career exploration resource published by the U.S. Department of Labor. It provides detailed information on current and emerging jobs in the 1990s. The OOH describes 250 different jobs—the jobs held by 85 percent of the American workforce. Each description covers the nature of work; future employment outlook; earnings; related occupations; training, other qualifications, and advancement; employment opportunities; and sources of additional information. This is the current edition through June 1996.

Other Information

- The latest trends and salary projections from the U.S. Department of Labor
- Includes completely revised content
- THE standard career reference book
- Best known career reference for professionals and schools

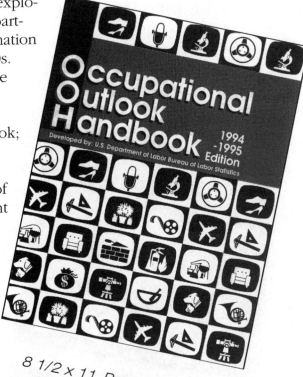

8 1/2 x 11, Paper, 512 pp.
ISBN 1-56370-160-X
$15.95   Order Code OOH4

Look for these and other fine books from JIST Works, Inc. at your full service bookstore or call us for additional information

More Good Books from JIST Works, Inc.

The Complete Guide for Occupational Exploration

Based on a commonsense and easy-to-use system developed by the U.S. Department of labor, this book organizes virtually all jobs in the U.S. labor market into groups of related jobs. The result is a valuable tool for career and educational planning, career exploration, career changing, and job seeking. The data is cross-referenced to the new *Dictionary of Occupational Titles* which contains 12, 741 job titles. The descriptions are organized into 12 major interest clusters, 66 work groups and 350 more specific subgroups of related jobs. The appendices cross-reference these jobs by interest, training, school subjects, and a variety of other useful ways.

Other Information

- Based on most recent data from the *Dictionary of Occupational Titles*
- First major revision of the GOE in 10 years
- Cross-references to other standard occupational information systems

8 1/2 x 11, 936 pp.
ISBN 1-56370-052-2
Paper, $37.95   Order Code CGOE
ISBN 1-56370-100-6
Hardcover, $47.95   Order Code CGOEH

Look for these and other fine books from JIST Works, Inc. at your full service bookstore or call us for additional information

More Good Books from JIST Works, Inc.

America's Top Job Books

Packed with solid and reliable information, the books in our *Top Jobs* series sell themselves. Based on the latest information from the U.S. Department of Labor and other government sources, each of the nine volumes has detailed information about occupations including projected growth, skills and education required, working conditions, salary, related occupations, labor market trends, and more. No career library or resource center should be without this series. All books are 8 1/2 x 11, paper.

America's Top 300 Jobs
ISBN 1-56370-163-4
$17.95, 512 pp.
Order Code T300

America's Federal Jobs
ISBN 0-942784-81-2
$14.95, 272 pp.
Order Code AFJ

**America's
Top Military Careers**
ISBN 1-56370-124-3
$19.95, 476 pp.
Order Code ATMC

**America's 50 Fastest
Growing Jobs**
ISBN 1-56370-091-3
$12.95, 272 pp.
Order Code AFF

**America's Top Medical and
Human Services Jobs**
ISBN 1-563700-118-9
$11.95, 208 pp.
Order Code ATM

**America's Top Technical
and Trade Jobs**
ISBN 1-56370-116-2
$11.95, 230 pp.
Order Code ATT

**America's
Top Office, Management,
and Sales Jobs**
ISBN 1-56370-117-0
$11.95, 248 pp.
Order Code ATO

**America's Top Jobs for
College Graduates**
ISBN 1-56370-140-5
$14.95, 288 pp.
Order Code ATCG

**Career Guide to America's
Top Industries**
ISBN 1-56370-111-1
$11.95, 228 pp.
Order Code CGTI

*Look for these and other fine books from JIST Works, Inc. at your full service bookstore
or call us for additional information*

More Good Books from JIST Works, Inc.

The Career Connection Books

By Fred A. Rowe, Ed.D.

These books are two easy-to-use reference tools to help students and adults explore post-secondary career and education or training options. The descriptions in these two references include information on: types of degrees available, educational requirements, typical courses, prerequisite courses, and average starting salaries. *The Career Connection for College Education* provides information on more than 100 college majors and the careers to which they can lead. *The Career Connection for Technical Education* provides information on more than 60 technical majors and the careers to which they can lead.

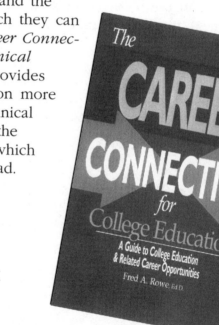

The Career Connection for Technical Education
6 x 9, Paper, 192 pp.
ISBN 1-56370-143-X
$14.95   Order Code CCTE

The Career Connection for College Education
6 x 9, Paper, 288 pp.
ISBN 1-56370-142-1
$16.95   Order Code CCCE

Look for these and other fine books from JIST Works, Inc. at your full service bookstore or call us for additional information